*OF*
*CE*

# THE DUALITY OF
# HUMAN EXISTENCE

*ISOLATION AND COMMUNION IN WESTERN MAN*

---

*DAVID BAKAN*

*University of Chicago*

BEACON PRESS    BOSTON

*To*
*my wife, Mildred,*
*and our children,*
*Joseph, Deborah, Abigail, Jonathan, and Daniel*

# CONTENTS

CONTENTS

# ACKNOWLEDGEMENTS

A number of people have read the manuscript either in part or in its entirety and have offered important criticisms and suggestions. My chief critic has been my wife, Mildred Bakan, who, in addition to being spiritually involved in the whole of the essay, carefully went over each of its several versions making numerous suggestions for improvement. Of particular value have been the suggestions made by Charles A. Curran, Daniel G. Freedman, Richard M. Jones, Salvatore R. Maddi, Paul W. Pruyser, and Judah Stampfer. Others who have given valuable aid and comfort are Bruce Cushna, Barry Dworkin, Thomas J. Erwin, Lawrence J. Freedman, Donald W. Fiske, Hannah H. Gray, Stanley Gevirtz, Meyer W. Isenberg, Sidney M. Jourard, Emile Karafiol, Lester K. Little, Norman Miller, Susanne H. Rudolph, Zalman Schacter, John M. Shlien, Gerald Sider, Charles R. Stinnette, Jr., Russel L. Tracy, Robert B. and June L. Tapp, Walter A. Weisskopf, Paul Wohlford, Marc Yudkoff, and my students at the University of Chicago who commented on some of these ideas which I have expressed in my classes.

I am indebted to the Social Science Divisional Research Fund and the College of the University of Chicago for secretarial and editorial assistance. I would like to thank Sue Cullen, Lynne Tilford, and Cheryl Weinberg for their help with the manuscript.

For permission to quote, I am indebted to: *The American Journal of Psychotherapy,* Appleton-Century-Crofts, Basic Books, Beacon Press, *Cancer Research, Commentary, Daedalus,* E. P. Dutton and Co., Inc., Grune and Stratton, Inc.,

## Acknowledgements

Willam Hodge and Co., Ltd., to Sigmund Freud Copyrights, Ltd., Mr. James Strachey, and The Hogarth Press, Ltd., to quote from Volumes XI, XIII, XIV, XVIII, XIX, and XXIII of the Standard Edition of *The Complete Psychological Works of Sigmund Freud*, Holt, Rinehart and Winston, Inc., Houghton Mifflin Co., *The Journal of the American Medical Association, The Journal of Nervous and Mental Diseases*, Alfred A. Knopf, Inc., Liveright Publishing Corp., Macmillan Company, Methuen and Co., Ltd., Odyssey Press, *Psychosomatic Medicine*, G. P. Putnam's Sons, Ronald Press Company, Charles Scribner's Sons, W. B. Saunders Company, Washington Square Press, Inc.

D.B.

*So God created man in his own image, in the image of God created he him; male and female created he them.*

GENESIS 1:27

*And the Lord God called unto Adam, and said unto him, Where art thou? And he said, I heard thy voice in the garden, and I was afraid, because I was naked; and I hid myself.*

GENESIS 3:9-10

# CHAPTER I

# A PERSPECTIVE ON SCIENCE, PSYCHOLOGY, AND RELIGION

In a certain sense, this essay deals with the roots of religion. However, that "certain sense," which I shall try to specify, is extremely important for the appreciation of the considerations which I attempt to set forth. The book deals with a core dynamic, largely psychological, but not exclusively so. The nature of this dynamic is such that the roots of being human and the roots of what is more conspicuously religious are basically one.

In the contemporary intellectual world, any writer who uses the term "religion" and who seeks the attention of those who are not concerned with religion *as such*, addresses a hostile audience. The contemporary intellectual world is, so to speak, fresh from the war between science and religion; and attitudes are heavily conditioned by accretions, many of them arising from the institutionalization rather than from the more intrinsic characteristics of both science and religion. This is not an attempt to "reconcile" science and religion in the usual sense. Rather, it is an attempt to tie in with the basic thrusts in human existence which have led to the formation of both science and religion. It is the purpose of this book to bring to bear evidences and considerations which are generally acceptable in the contemporary intellectual world to the problem of *ultimate concern*.

## ULTIMATE CONCERN

Paul Tillich has made a very significant advance in our thinking by giving emphasis to the term "ultimate concern" as a designation of our quest for meaning at its depth. *"Our ultimate concern,"* he has written, *"is that which determines our being or not-being. . . .* Man is ultimately concerned about that which determines his ultimate destiny beyond all preliminary necessities and accidents."[1] For Tillich, ultimate concern is the region of *theological* investigation. He distinguishes between preliminary concerns, such as artistic creation, scientific and historical theory, healing, social reconstruction, and politics, on the one hand, and ultimate concern, on the other. He asserts, "The first formal principle of theology [is] guarding the boundary line between ultimate concern and preliminary considerations."[2] Although my respect for Tillich and his contributions is very great, I feel that thus drawing and guarding a boundary interferes with our pursuit of the very understanding which we are all interested in obtaining. Unfortunately, on the other side of the boundary there are those who guard it against the theological. On the one hand, such a boundary keeps the theological relatively impoverished; on the other hand, it prevents us from endowing our other concerns with context. The subject of this essay is, indeed, ultimate concern. The book does not, however, respect the boundary. (Nor has Tillich himself respected it.) This essay deals with social organization, science, ideology, myth, sexuality, death, disease, and man's psychological life. These are relevant to man's ultimate concern, to being and not-being.

## IDOLATRY IN RELIGION AND SCIENCE[3]

According to Tillich, "Idolatry is the elevation of a preliminary concern to ultimacy."[4] There are idolatrous tendencies

[1] Paul Tillich, *Systematic Theology* (Chicago: University of Chicago Press, 1951), I, 14.

[2] *Ibid.*, p. 12.

[3] Some of the material in this section has been published previously in David Bakan, "Idolatry in Religion and Science," *Christian Scholar*, XLIV (1961), 223-30.

[4] *Op. cit.*, p. 13.

not only in connection with the preliminary concerns, but also in the religious concerns. In order to clarify this, let us consider some of the relationships between religion and science.

There exists a view of the relationship between science and religion in which science is envisaged as preempting the role of religion. This view has it that in primitive times man needed answers to questions about his nature, creation, existence, and destiny, and that his need for answers was greater than his need for well-founded beliefs. Presumably, his urgency led him to create myths, and these myths are the foundation of religion. In the enlightened present, in which there has been a considerable amount of scientific advance, science has produced "better" answers to these very same questions, and we no longer have need for the myths.

There can be little question but that there is *some* validity associated with this point of view. For example, our knowledge of the physical nature of the universe differs critically at a number of points from that which is classical in our religious history. There have been courageous efforts on the part of some theologians to come to grips with the contributions of contemporary intellectuality. A good example is the point of view expressed by Rudolph Bultmann. Bultmann, a Protestant theologian, is perfectly willing to reject the *mythical* content of the Bible, including not only the view of the universe "as a three-storied structure, with the earth in the centre, the heaven above, and the underworld beneath,"[5] but he is also willing to speak of "the incredibility of a mythical event like the resuscitation of a corpse."[6] However, his rejection of the mythical does not entail a complete rejection of religion. Quite the contrary. The task of the theologian is to extract and reformulate the kerygma, the message and deeper human meaning, which was earlier embodied in the myth. We can here speak of idolatry in religion. The function of the myth is

[5]Rudolph Bultmann, *Kerygma and Myth*, trans. Reginald H. Fuller (London: Billing and Sons, 1960), p. 1.
[6]*Ibid.*, p. 39.

to be indicative of a kerygma which is beyond the myth itself. When the myth is worshipped instead of that of which the myth is the carrier and indicator, we have idolatry. Bultmann's distinction between myth and kerygma is similar to the distinction in psychoanalytic thought between the *manifest* and the *latent*. In the same way that Freud sought to interpret the myths of mankind as indicative of something deeply human, so does a contemporary theologian like Bultmann.

Paradoxical as it may seem, even the worship of God may turn out to be idolatrous in a certain sense. For God has meaning in no other way but with respect to man's ultimate concern. To conceive of God as separate from man and his ultimate concern is already indicative of man's alienation, and is thus sinful. In an essay entitled "What Sense Is There to Speak of God?" Bultmann has argued that to speak *of* God, to "regard God as an object of thought toward which I can take a position" is either sinful or senseless. According to Bultmann,

... every "talking *about*" presupposes a standpoint apart from that which is being talked *about*. But there can be no standpoint apart from God, and for that reason God does not permit himself to be spoken of in general propositions, universal truths which are true without reference to the concrete existential situation of the one who is talking.[7]

Bultmann's theological thought appears to be an invitation to advance our understanding of the nature of ultimate concern by turning to psychology, in which the problem of the relationship between the person and the thought of the person is taken as problematical and to be probed. The temptation would be to "reduce" religious thought to the psychological processes, being relatively cavalier with respect to that which the thought is *of*. This temptation has been yielded to by a number of thinkers under the general rubric of "psychology *of* religion." This essay takes the position that ultimate concern is not to be reduced to the psychological processes; but one

[7]Rudolph Bultmann, "What Sense Is There To Speak of God?" *Christian Scholar,* XLIII (1960), 213-22.

should probe the nature of these processes in order to enhance our appreciation of the nature of what concerns man ultimately. Psychology has too often been thought of as being a way of reconciling the conflict between religion and science by identifying concerns which are conspicuously close to ultimate concern in terms of psychodynamics. Psychology is a possible meeting ground for science and religion, in that both presumably deal with man's mind, or heart, or spirit, in one sense or another. But one has to be very wary of either psychological reductions or apologies for religion. The validity of religious insight is *sui generis*. It need not hang on the coat-tails of psychology. At the same time, the psychological processes constitute an important aspect of that insight.

The fundamental impulse in both science and religion is the singular impulse of man to appreciate the nature of his existence in time, in space, in history, and in his peculiarly self-conscious corporeality. All that falls under the heading of either science or religion issues from this singular impulse. The self-definitional activity of man, in substance and in concept, is his most abiding characteristic beyond any specific definition of him; and both the scientific and the religious enterprises are expressions of this self-definitional activity. *This impulse presupposes that the manifest is but the barest hint of reality, that beyond the manifest there exist the major portions of reality, and that the function of the impulse is to reach out toward the unmanifest.*

From this singular and most restless impulse in man have come both science and religion; within science many sciences, within religion many religions, within science many scientific concepts, and within religion many religious concepts. The splintering of the expression of the impulse is necessary to its expression; yet, at the same time, there are associated dangers if the splintered parts are not again brought together.

The impulse moves toward the fulfillment of an objective, but its essence is the motion toward fulfillment and not the objective itself. Sometimes, in man's impatience to realize the fulfillment, he may seek to satisfy himself more immediately. When man tarries too long, when man seeks to be completely fulfilled on the way toward the objective, when, in effect, he allows the impulse to be bribed by some fulfillment which he takes to be exhaustive, he commits the sin of idolatry.

Later in this essay I attempt to be somewhat more analytic of the nature of idolatry with the help of two notions, agency and communion, which are the central notions in this essay. But at the moment, I would only observe that the injunction against idolatry is one of the essential features of the whole of the Judeo-Christian tradition. I believe that the notion of idolatry is indicative of the condition which is the root of all psychological difficulties. It is precisely the point of juncture of sickness and sin which have sometimes been identified with each other in the history of Western thought. That sickness of the spirit which is supposed to have ensued from the practice of primitive idolatry is not too far removed from the sickness of the spirit in the modern world with which we need to be concerned.

As with primitive idolatry, neither contemporary science nor contemporary religion is lacking in ardor. I would generalize Tillich's definition of idolatry by defining it as *the worship of the means toward the fulfillment of the impulse as the fulfillment of the impulse itself.* In the particular context of the specifically religious, myth, ritual, formal worship, and so on, are not idolatrous until they themselves become the objects of worship rather than the means. Idolatry is the loss of the sense of the existence of the unmanifest, the loss of the sense of search, the loss of the continuous freshness of the encounter with the unmanifest. Idolatry is to yield to the bribe of the manifest.

One of the most important characteristics of the God of the Judeo-Christian tradition is precisely his ultimate unknowableness. Never could mankind have any sense of closure in connection with such a God, and yet His knowability is ever in the realm of possibility. This God is to be continuously worked toward. He is as continuous, frustrating, and fulfilling as life itself. The commandment against idolatry is a commandment to the effect that contact with God must always be in the nature of a search. One must always be filled with the sense of that which is not yet realized. One must always yearn toward fulfillment, but fulfillment must be maintained as an ideal. Fulfillment is always away, and seeming fulfillment mythical. When the mythical is taken as reality, then one is idolatrous.

Let us consider science. The scientific impulse and the religious impulse are not nearly as separate as some modern thought might lead one to believe. To point to the religiosity of people like Newton, Kepler, Fechner, and others cannot be taken as a priori evidence for the view that the impulses are the same. But the dynamics of the relationship become a bit clearer in a figure like that of Jonathan Edwards, the Puritan minister. To study the nature of God was his obligation. The God whom he had in his thoughts was a God of a self-distancing nature, who predestined the universe. How did this predestination of God work itself out? For Jonathan Edwards, Newton almost literally opened up the sky. God had predestined the world by fashioning the world-machine as Newton had conceived it. He had made the law of inertia and given the universe a shove, and then the universe carried on and would thus carry on through eternity. To study the physics of Newton was then to study the nature of God. In Edwards' thought, God's omnipresence was translated into the equation of God and space. In the mind of a man like Edwards the acceptance of Newtonian mechanics, later to become the chief competitor of the religious outlook, is the answer to the problem of how to know God. It is the *means* for the knowledge of God.

The mechanical conception of the nature of the universe has for several centuries been one of the major pawns in the struggle between religion and science. It has sometimes been offered as a major contender for a concept of the nature of the universe to replace that which is held by the exponents of the Judeo-Christian tradition. In the minds of many intellectuals who have grown up in the last century, the question has seemed to be that of making a *choice* between the one and the other because of apparent incompatibility between them. *The degree of strain between religion and science is the direct function of the degree of idolatry in both religion and science.*

The Bible is indeed one of the finest expressions and means of fulfillment of the religious impulse. Yet to make it the *end* of worship and devotion is idolatrous. It is only when the Bible is worshipped idolatrously that it can be seriously threatened by the Darwinian theory of evolution, the discovery of the Law of Moses in Hammurabi, or the "higher criticism" of the Bible which ascribes a later date than is commonly believed and an origin less than that of divine revelation in the literal sense.

Similarly, the mechanical conception of the nature of the universe was a magnificent intellectual achievement in the way of coming to an understanding of the operation of the heavenly bodies and matter in motion on the earth itself. Yet, especially in the nineteenth century, the conception became the object of idolatrous worship. It became in time, not something to examine or even to believe in, but an item of *faith* which it was considered unscientific (a word which was used almost synonymously with blasphemous) to challenge. In some scientific circles to challenge the proposition that the universe was exhaustively explainable in terms of matter and motion could only be labelled "heretical." Yet this worship of the mechanical conception was as idolatrous as any religious activity could be.

Insofar as the scientific enterprise is concerned, the disease of idolatry has been dubbed the disease of methodolatry, the worship of method. In terms of the conception of idolatry in this essay, it is certainly the case that certain ways have been of value and will continue to be of value in exploring the nature of man and the world and their relationships. However, when there is a worship of these methods themselves rather than that to which they are directed, then indeed does science become idolatrous.

In both science and religion the assumption is made that the fundamental reality is that which is beyond the manifest. No matter how far our explorations go, and no matter how much we manage to uncover, there is always the infinite world of the unmanifest. If, at any stage of development, we begin to worship the manifest or the means whereby we have made some part manifest, then can it be said that we are being idolatrous.

If it were possible to root out idolatrous tendencies in both science and religion, then the singularity of the impulse expressed in both would emerge clearly. It is not that religion, as some have maintained, supplies mythical answers until science can provide more valid ones. Rather, it is that both religion and science are attempts on the part of mankind to search out the nature of himself and the world in which he lives. But it is *search* rather than answer which is significant. Indeed, as soon as either the scientist or the theologian allows himself to fix upon an answer as if it were the ultimate fulfillment of his impulse, he stops being either scientist or theologian and becomes an idolater.

PSYCHOLOGY AND ULTIMATE CONCERN

One of the latest developments in the history of Western man is the emergence of a self-conscious science of psychology. For several centuries, the term "science" was understood as a certain kind of investigation of the nature of the physical world, of things which appeared to be, to use Tillich's term, in the region of "preliminary concern." As I shall attempt to demonstrate, not even these were preliminary. In the thought of Newton, Kepler, and Fechner, for example, there was a great deal of preoccupation with ultimate concern, and their very scientific investigations were probing efforts emerging from their concern with what is ultimate. The secular quality of science is a later development. It arose from the combination of science with industry; and it may be associated with the idolatrous tendencies in man. With the emergence of psychology, especially psychology relevant to the psychotherapy situation, the possibility of a scientific approach to the spiritual problems of mankind has begun to loom as a significant possibility. When a person has become sick and incapacitated, and it is evident that his sickness and incapacitation are related to the deepest problems of his "being and not-being," the distinction between preliminary concern and ultimate concern must fall away. That which the psychotherapist is so dramatically confronted with forces the concern with ultimate concern. The psychotherapist is daily witness to the despair associated with the paradox of finitude, the problems of good and evil, truth and illusion, self and relations to that which is not-self, the interrelationship between that which is revealed and not revealed, and the like.

The root phenomenon in man which is of central interest to both theologian and psychologist is that he combines, on various levels, an intrinsic self-reference and other-reference simultaneously. In its clearest and perhaps its most developed form, this combination is manifest in human thought. Human thought is characteristically both of its own nature and referential of something other than itself. It is because of this that the religiously concerned fear the psychologist; but this is fear of the idolatrous tendency within the psychologist, who would, it seems, reduce ultimate to preliminary concern. For example, when a psychologist analyzes a religious experience in terms of propositions that refer *only* to its psychodynamics, that is, in terms of the intrinsic self-reference only, excluding the other characteristic of human thought, then he is engaging in a kind of reductionism which not only violates the considerations of the theologian but also violates the nature of man. However, when full cognizance is given to this root phenomenon in man, the theological and psychological enterprises converge.

This essay leans very heavily on the thought of Freud. The major reason for this is that Freud's thought appears to me to be the least idolatrous, as contrasted with other psychological approaches. This may appear very paradoxical. For Freud, especially in his explicit pronouncements on religion, was most guilty of what I have called idolatry. My sense of Freud is that he was actually coming closest to the matter of ultimate concern when he was *not* writing of religion explicitly; and this is the way in which I use the Freudian insights. As I have suggested, the absence of idolatry is in the sense of the existence and significance of that which is not manifest. In this sense, the notion of the *unconscious* guards against idolatry. For most often in Freud's thought, the word "unconscious" is literally "un-conscious," that of which one is not aware, that which is not directly manifest in consciousness. In psychoanalysis, this basic concept names and attributes great significance to a major region of the unmanifest and seeks to make it manifest—aware that it is inexhaustible and can never be made fully manifest. Thus, in psychoanalytic thought, that root phenomenon to which I have referred is taken as the core notion of the approach. Conceptually, the ego-id distinction, the I-it distinction, combined with the full appreciation that what is "it" to the ego is still part of the psyche nonetheless, expresses exactly what I have referred to as the combination of self- and other-reference. I might point out parenthetically, however, that this is not a foolproof protection against idolatrous tendencies even in psychoanalytic thought. For as soon as the notion of the unconscious is taken not as that which is un-conscious, but as something manifest by itself, as sometimes happens in psychoanalytic thought, then even psychoanalysis is idolatrous. The intellectual task which psychoanalysis sets itself is that of making what is thus unconscious conscious. To the degree that it tends to fix upon that which it has made conscious, it is idolatrous. But to the extent that it stresses the existence of that which is still un-conscious, it avoids being idolatrous. To put this another way, psychoanalysis may be idolatrous when it considers *"the* unconscious," but anti-idolatrous when it considers "the *un-*conscious."

Many scholars who read the work of Freud tend to make a distinction between what they regard as his genuine contributions to our understanding of the human psyche and some of what seem to be his more bizarre ideas; the latter exemplified in such notions as the inheritance of guilt over many generations through the genetic materials and the death instinct. But I believe that, in spite of all of the difficulties associated with notions such as these, they serve an important function of at least pointing toward critical features in the unmanifest, as yet unclear and vague. In the same way that the material of the manifest dream points toward significant regions, yet certainly does not delineate their nature clearly, so, I believe, can we understand some of the bizarre notions in Freud's writings. To take them at their face value, so to speak, would be erroneous. But to dismiss them as containing no meaning whatsoever, as one might naively dismiss a bizarre dream, is also erroneous. For just as a bizarre dream is indicative of material of which we are not conscious, however distorted, so may bizarre notions be.

There are two dangers which we need to guard against in our effort to increase our understanding. The first is the danger of irrationalism. Behind any avowedly irrational position is indeed the sense of the unmanifest and an avoidance of fixing upon the manifest. The second is the danger of ultrarational-ism, which does tend to fix upon the manifest. Irrationalism and ultrarationalism are both dangerous in that they prevent continuous progress in making the unmanifest manifest. The intellectual work of mankind must be located in the boundary region. The movement into the regions of the unmanifest has to be from the base of the manifest. Leaving this base com-pletely, as the irrationalist does, provides no lever for making the unmanifest manifest. Similarly, clinging to the base, as the ultrarationalist does, makes it impossible to understand afresh what has not been understood already.

The writer of a book usually has at least one of two claims to make to his reader: what he has to say is new, or if not new, it is at least firm. In this case, the material which is presented for consideration is not new. To it are added interpretations, and these interpretations are not firm. This book is rather in the nature of a quest. One of the major ways by which any exposition is made clear and firm is by carefully drawing boundaries and conscientiously staying within them. Yet it is in the nature of what we are dealing with not to be on one or another side of a boundary, but at it. In a certain sense, the reader of this book takes a risk, a risk like going into a wilderness with a guide who himself is not clear about the terrain, and on to a region in which anything like ultimate clarity is intrinsically impossible. This metaphor is, however, not quite accurate; for it presumes that one has a choice about entering the terrain, and everyone who is alive in the real world is already on that terrain. Our choice is only the way in which we "go it" alone or together; and in this I am already alluding to the two basic notions of this exposition, agency and communion.

Every book that has ever been written proceeds on at least two levels. The first is that of the ideas which are presented. The second level pertains to the developmental process and the direction of the developmental process of the person who is in any sense "educated" by the ideas. There is always a "moral" to an exposition, no matter how implicit it is or how unaware of it both the writer and the reader may be. Every textbook on physics asserts the orderliness and comprehensibility of the physical world. Every textbook on mathematics provides the reader with a vision of how profoundly orderly thought can be, and constitutes an injunction to order our thought. Every textbook on history is an assertion of the continuity of human existence over and beyond the life of any single individual. Every biography asserts the significance of a single life. Every analytic description of the nature of a social problem speaks in some way of the possibility of its rectification by human decision. In this book, the effort is made to be at least a shade more explicit with respect to the moral than is usual in an exposition which presumes to talk of what is the case, backed by empirical findings. The villain is unmitigated agency. The moral imperative is to try to mitigate agency with communion. The moral imperative to which I subscribe was magnificently expressed by Hillel many years ago: "If I am not for myself, who will be for me? But if I am only for myself, what am I?" The first part speaks of agency; the second, of communion; both together, of the integration of the two.

Much of what is said in this essay is conditioned by a sense that we are collectively at a major turning point in history. For several hundred years, the agency feature of mankind has been dominant in the prevailing life strategies. As a result, we have succeeded in dramatically converting the face of the world so that the classical problems of frustration of physical want have to a very large degree, at least in principle, been solved. Our so-called affluent society is evidence of the success of the agentic strategy. But at the moment, we are in danger of becoming like Don Quixote, equipped to cope with life problems in one way while the nature of the world has been so changed that this approach is rapidly becoming archaic. There is a rising sense of emptiness, meaninglessness, and absurdity. There is the condition in which comforts make us uneasy; where creative energies choke us for not finding something worth the effort; where love becomes dry, formal, and ritualized; where there is anxiety that knows of no reasonable reason; where there is a sense that there is something which mastery itself cannot master. There is a sense in which leisure has forced its own necessity, the necessity for concern with ultimate concern.

I have adopted the terms "agency" and "communion" to characterize two fundamental modalities in the existence of living forms, agency for the existence of an organism as an individual, and communion for the participation of the individual in some larger organism of which the individual is a part. Agency manifests itself in self-protection, self-assertion, and self-expansion; communion manifests itself in the sense of being at one with other organisms. Agency manifests itself in the formation of separations; communion in the lack of separations. Agency manifests itself in isolation, alienation, and aloneness; communion in contact, openness, and union. Agency manifests itself in the urge to master; communion in noncontractual cooperation. Agency manifests itself in the repression of thought, feeling, and impulse; communion in the lack and removal of repression. One of the fundamental points which I attempt to make is that the very split of agency from communion, which is a separation, arises from the agency feature itself; and that it represses the communion from which it has separated itself. The meaning of these two terms requires a lengthier exposition than any simple dictionary definition, and the remainder of this book is an attempt to provide this exposition.

As will become evident in the course of this essay, I conceive of agency and communion at a rather high level of abstraction, as manifested in various ways and in various contexts. I have sought to avoid the idolatry associated with abstractions by continuously referring back to varieties of expressions of important human experience and to systematic studies of them. And I have sought to overcome the idolatry of concreteness by returning to the abstract. Thus, this is a discourse which goes in circles. And I hope thereby to somehow push back the fringe of the unmanifest. In the last analysis, of course, the validation of the various considerations which are set forth must be in human experience — in our *individual* experience and in our *collective* experience.

# CHAPTER II

# PROTESTANTISM, SCIENCE, AND AGENCY

In this chapter, I consider Protestantism, largely as it was conceived of by Max Weber, to be an expression of the agentic in man. I consider the image of the Protestant drawn in his *The Protestant Ethic and the Spirit of Capitalism.*[1] Weber, as is well known, conceived of the Protestant personality as having been integral to the formation of modern capitalism. Within Weber's thesis, there is not only an interpretation of history, but also some observations which can help us understand the nature of the agentic. I believe that I can clarify some of the features of Weber's hypothesis by pointing out that the intrinsic unity of Protestantism and capitalism lies in the fact that they both involve exaggeration of agency and repression of communion. In the last part of the chapter, I come back to the question of science and religion and show how Newton and Darwin, two of the greatest figures in the history of science, articulated with Protestant thought.

## WEBER'S PROTESTANT

Weber's famous essay *The Protestant Ethic and the Spirit of Capitalism* commends itself to our attention for two reasons. First, it is an attempt to relate the psychological characteristics of man to major historical movements. The psycholo-

[1]Max Weber, *The Protestant Ethic and the Spirit of Capitalism,* trans. Talcott Parsons (New York: Charles Scribner's Sons, 1958).

gies available to Weber were not adequate to his task, and he essentially developed an ad hoc psychology in order to understand the relationship between the psychological characteristics of the participants and the growth of capitalism. Second, Weber outlined with great perspicacity the way in which the agentic feature of man's psyche rose to dominance in the world of the last few centuries. In seeking for a touchstone for the appreciation of man's psychological condition, Weber was drawn to consider the religious concern of the participants, recognizing its significance in the total life of man. Weber helps us to understand how, although the exaggeration of agency is related to man's ultimate concern, it also played its role in the secularization of all of life, thus being associated with the repression of the very concern out of which it arose. In criticism of Weber's thesis of the relationship between Protestantism and capitalism, it has been observed that capitalists are often secularists. But Weber's religious psychohistorical analysis itself illuminates this contemporary secularism.

The psychology which Weber implicitly developed is one which takes account of the complexity of human motivation and the relationships between motives and actions. He eschewed a simple cause-effect model, and especially the overrationalized hedonistic version of the cause-effect model. Indeed, his major assertions are of the *paradoxes* of human motivation and action. Thus, Weber pointed out how the concern with salvation among Calvinists is associated not with neglect but with devotion to secular affairs; asceticism is associated not with eschewing wealth but with its increase; predestination by God is associated not with the surrender of initiative but with its heightening; and the alienation of man from man is associated with superiority in social organization. Weber succeeded in drawing attention to the agentic and helped to define it: control over others, a high degree of deliberate channeling of activity, accumulation of material goods, high initiative, profound alienation of men from each other, are some of the features which emerge as having characterized the Protestant and the spirit of capitalism.

It is important to try to understand the methodological strategy which is associated with Weber's thesis. The critical feature of this strategy is *Verstehen,* which entails consideration of historical materials to produce an "ideal-type." Weber sought

... an historical individual, i.e. a complex of elements associated in historical reality which we unite into a conceptual whole from the standpoint of their cultural significance.

Such an historical concept ... must be gradually put together out of the individual parts which are taken from historical reality to make it up.[2]

It is possible to construct other "ideal-types" so that, as Weber says,

Other standpoints would, for this as for every historical phenomenon, yield other characteristics as the essential ones. The result is that it is by no means necessary to understand by the spirit of capitalism only what it will come to mean to *us* for the purposes of our analysis [pp. 47-48].

The significance of the particular ideal-type inheres in its ability to enhance our understanding of the culture investigated. In my view, Weber managed to depict the type of the agentic personality which has been dominant in our culture. And even though there may be few "pure" cases, it is this composite personality which has played the dominant role in the fortunes of the culture.

A major decision which Weber made in connection with his research strategy was the selection of what was and what was not relevant, and this decision was guided by his sense of the historical personage whom he was attempting to analyze.

... it is indeed sufficient to establish the causal irrelevance of the given circumstance if the latter appears not to have been the co-cause of that which alone interests us, i.e., the concretely essential components of the action in question.

... the attribution of effects to causes take place through a pro-

2*Ibid.,* p. 47.

Protestantism, Science, and Agency

cess of thought which includes a series of *abstractions.* The first and decisive one occurs when we *conceive* of one or a few of the actual causal components as modified in a certain direction and then ask ourselves whether under the conditions which have been thus changed, the same effect... or some other effect "would be expected."[3]

His object was to create a psychologically tenable personality in a way which bore on the major cultural events. Causality is not the classical notion of causality as abstracted from the physical sciences, but rather a notion of causality which is closer to dynamic psychology, allowing for paradox and the creative meeting of the "cause" by the human personality. An item is a cause if it can be understood as being psychologically involved in the determination of an action. Thus, psychologically, fear may be the cause of flight in some instances, for example; but fear may also, in a particular psychodynamic constellation, be the cause of outstanding bravery. I cannot but think that Weber's psychology would have been hindered rather than helped by the kind of thought concerning the scientific method which prevails in some contemporary psychology, in which the paradoxical character of human psychodynamics receives little attention and elucidation.

At the same time, one needs to be aware of the limitations associated with Weber's method. At root, it is not so different from "stereotypic" thinking which is intimately related to prejudice. Its deepest defect is that it overlooks the reality of individual differences. However, if we are aware of this limitation, the method still has considerable value.

Weber's task was, then, the isolation of the relevant characteristics and the construction of the psychodynamics of the historical individual. Within Protestantism, he identified predestination and the preoccupation with personal salvation, the idea of the calling, and the ascetic ideal. In the personality, he

[3]Max Weber, *On the Methodology of the Social Sciences,* trans. and ed. Edward A. Shils and Henry A. Finch (Glencoe, Ill.: The Free Press, 1949), p. 171.

identified directed activity, social and personal organization, the pursuit of vocation with little thought to its extrinsic consequences, saving and profit-making, uniformity, regularity, personal reliability, self-control, the eschewing of sociability (*Gemütlichkeit*), the eschewing of magic and mystery, the pursuit of physical science, suspicion of emotion and feeling, great loneliness, and impersonality and distrust in interpersonal relations.

That there may be capitalism without the notion of the calling, or the notion of the calling without the presence of capitalism, did not seem an objection to Weber. Indeed, it would seem that their presence without each other in other times and places was an aid in the abstraction process for identifying them. It was rather the psychodynamics of their congruence with which he was principally concerned. Weber did not believe that there was anything "natural" about capitalism. He specifically wrote that "a man does not 'by nature' wish to earn more and more money...."[4] Fanfani, one of the major critics of Weber, has argued that capitalism is natural: "... we would point out that man has an inborn instinct for gain.... *in nuce*, the capitalist spirit has always been and always will be."[5] The kind of labor which Weber had his historical individual engaging in "can only be the product of a long and arduous process of education."[6]

The Protestant ethic is allied to the spirit of capitalism in that both entail the vaulting exaggeration of the agentic feature of the psyche and the repression of the communion component. Later in this essay, I deal with the matter of sex differences and point out that, although the agency and the communion features are present in both males and females, agency is greater in males and communion greater in females.

[4]Weber, *The Protestant Ethic* ... , p. 60.
[5]Amintore Fanfani, "Catholicism, Protestantism, and Capitalism," in Robert W. Green (ed.), *Protestantism and Capitalism: The Weber Thesis and Its Critics* (Boston: D. C. Heath and Company, 1959), pp. 91-92.
[6]Weber, *The Protestant Ethic* ... , p. 62.

It is interesting to note that, in Weber's discussion of the attitude toward work which he was depicting for his historical individual, the contrary attitude toward work

. . . is to-day very often exemplified by women workers, especially unmarried ones. An almost universal complaint of employers of girls, for instance German girls, is that they are almost entirely unable and unwilling to give up methods of work inherited or once learned in favour of more efficient ones, to adapt themselves to new methods, to learn and to concentrate their intelligence, or even to use it at all.[7]

Although he did except Pietistic girls, nonetheless the historical individual whom Weber depicted was characteristically male.

The historical individual was, for Weber, a personage in whom three elements of Protestantism were originally of pronounced significance: predestination, asceticism, and calling. The notion of predestination raises the fundamental question of whether one is or is not in grace. Even though the doubt itself is there, and it is sinful to doubt, there arises a deep anxiety to experience signs of grace. In subtle, unconscious ways, the individual moves in directions whereby he has demonstrations made to him that he is in grace, and this is principally in the increase of wealth. Salvation, although sometimes entailing stewardship, is essentially an individual matter, since some persons are in grace and others are not.

Each person is on his own with respect to grace. The major business of life is a private affair between each person and God. This is associated with a considerable alienation of each individual from other persons, including the members of his family. His relationships with other people are not *gemütlich,* and in place of sociability he substitutes formal social organization, especially relationships which entail money.

The ultimate agent in the universe is God. If the indi-

---

[7]*Ibid.,* p. 62. Walter A. Weisskopf (*The Psychology of Economics* [London: Routledge & Kegan Paul, 1955]) has cogently explicated the significance of male and female symbolism in the economic thought of Ricardo, Malthus, Engels, and Marx. Unfortunately this book came to my attention too late to have informed the thinking expressed in this chapter.

vidual is anything at all, he is the instrument of God's will. At the same time, he must eschew any effort to have any magical relationships to God. This paradoxically leaves man himself as agent, and there emerges a vaulting development of the will in man. Since God has predestined the world, everything in the world is orderly, and man's behavior must then be made methodical and orderly. He eschews magic and becomes interested in science. The latter, which we have already discussed and to which we shall return, is a way by which he can come to understand God through God's work. The interest in science integrates itself with the agency of man by providing him with the means of controlling the world and increasing his wealth. The asceticism of this historical individual does not entail any mortification of the flesh. It is the asceticism of discipline and labor and entails their use to relieve anxiety, which we can identify as repression. It involves abstention from personal social relationships, which we can identify as the repression of communion. It involves the methodical regulation of behavior, which we can identify as the effort to repress the impulse life. The principle feature of the notion of the calling is that it entails the regulation of one's life largely by vocation, and thus a separation of work from the use of the products of labor.

Later, I attempt to demonstrate that one of the important manifestations of the agency feature of the human psyche is in the *separations* which take place within the psyche. Although Weber did not make this point explicitly, it nonetheless plays an important part in all of the psychodynamics which he pointed to: There is the separation of man from God, the separation of man from his associates, including members of his family. Work entails separation of production from use, separation from the household, and separation of the desire for wealth from the possession of wealth. Wealth is separated from gratification, greed from the making of money, man from tradition, and pleasure from human functioning.

## PREDESTINATION AND SCIENCE

From Weber's essay, we are able to see how Protestantism, which is a religious movement, and capitalism, which is
conspicuously secular, are deeply and intrinsically related;
and how the very splitting of the religious and the secular is
associated with an intrinsic characteristic of religion. We need
to consider how science, as a special instance, is related to
this tendency to compartmentalization, conspicuous in Protestantism, yet lodged in the agentic feature of human personality.

Calvin had envisaged a God who was infinitely distant
from this world, a God who had created the world for His
Majesty. This distant God, while still the ultimate judge, had
in effect set man the task of life on this earth. The physical
nature of the world was God's arbitrary imposition. Person-
ally, yet sinfully, man longed for God's presence, but he
struggled to root out the presence of God in this world. As he
did so, he repressed the communion feature within himself.

In order to see the development of the kind of secular
science we currently possess, we turn to a brief consideration
of the place of two major figures in the history of science,
Newton and Darwin. I believe that the line of development
begins with Calvin's reassertion of the notion of predestination. The function performed by Newton and Darwin was the
elaboration of the way in which God's predestination had
worked itself out.

Weber pointed out that there was a "decided propensity
of Protestant asceticism for empiricism, rationalized on a
mathematical basis." He explained this relationship as follows:

For the attitude of Protestant asceticism the decisive point was
... that just as the Christian is known by the fruits of his belief,
the knowledge of God and His designs can only be attained through a
knowledge of His works. The favourite science of all Puritan, Baptist,
or Pietist Christianity was thus physics, and next to it all those other
natural sciences which used a similar method, especially mathemat-

ics. It was hoped from the empirical knowledge of the divine laws of nature to ascend to a grasp of the essence of the world, which on account of the fragmentary nature of the divine revelation, a Calvinistic idea, could never be attained by the method of metaphysical speculation. The empiricism of the seventeenth century was the means for asceticism to seek God in nature. It seemed to lead to God, philosophical speculation away from him.[8]

This relationship between Protestantism and the development of science has been elaborated upon by Robert Merton, who shows the close historical parallels of the growth of science with Puritanism in England and Calvinistic Pietism in Germany. "In every instance, the association of Protestantism with scientific and technologic interests and achievements is pronounced."[9] And, "Perhaps the most directly effective element of the Protestant ethic for the sanction of natural science was that which held that the study of nature enables a fuller appreciation of His works and thus leads us to admire the Power, Wisdom, and Goodness of God manifested in His creation" (p. 10).

Although God, in Newton's thought, was not completely transcendent, a consequence of Newton's picture of the heavens was that it preempted the world of the myth of heaven, earth, and hell, the "three-storied structure" which Bultmann writes of, and thus contributed to a secular view of the universe. The *Principia* articulated with the Calvinistic notion of predestination. The Calvinistic conception of God, whose principle function was *creation* by predestination, had left the question of how God's predestination worked itself out. Newton's world-machine was in this sense a fulfillment of the Calvinistic theology. God had created the world all together in great harmony, every part of it made by taking account of all of the other parts, all of the planets together, and the eye of man and the animals built with cognizance of the laws of the refraction of light which God had also created. God had made

[8]*Ibid.*, p. 249.
[9]Robert K. Merton, "Puritanism, Pietism and Science," *Sociological Review*, XXVII (Jan., 1936), 29.

the world, and endowed it with laws whereby it continued to function. One law is particularly important. This is the law of inertia: "Every body continues in its state of rest or uniform motion in a right line unless compelled to change that state by forces impressed upon it." This law makes it possible for the world-machine to go on indefinitely without any further intervention by God. Newton's system was one which had as its avowed purpose giving glory to God. The magnificence of the system which he developed was a glorification of God's greatness; but at the same time it made possible one of the major features of contemporary thought, its secularism.

The effect of Newton, to be distinguished from Newton's own thought—for he had God intervening occasionally—was to make God essentially a thing of the past. God's effect was in the physical world and in the laws with which it had been endowed. Worship became the adoration of the world and its understanding. It was sufficient to study the nature of the world to express one's religiosity. Devotion to the mundane, that is, to God's creation, could easily become exhaustive of the religious concern.

Reflecting on the possibility that there are close relations between what people themselves are and the kind of a God that they project, Newton's thought worked to endow God with privacy. One of the characteristics of Protestantism was deference to man's privacy, partly in rejection of the Confessional, and partly for other reasons. God, according to the thought which followed Newton, was very private. Interpsychic contact with God had become impossible or sinful in Calvinism, because of the essential mystery and distance of God's contemporary thought, and this was supported by Newtonianism. The interpersonal silence on things intimate became associated with a silent God whose nature was to be inferred only from his works. Revelation was replaced by secular discovery and inference.

The Newtonian vision of science articulated with the growth of technology by giving a special place to physics, and especially to mechanics. In the older Christian tradition, the physical world was essentially to be despised. Newton facilitated the transfer of reverence previously reserved to the spiritual realm to the physical world by showing it to be an expression of God, and perhaps the way in which God had critically revealed himself to mankind. It also gave "prestige," if one may use such a term in this connection, to the fabrication of machines, since this was now in imitation of God. If man was made in the image of God, and if God was a machine-maker, man imitated God in the role of machine-maker.

The Newtonian scheme, by fixing so strongly the character of God's predestination of the world, tended to counteract the classical moral atmosphere of the Judeo-Christian tradition as obedience to the commandments of God. The use of the word "law" to characterize the regularities of the physical universe is extremely interesting, since it has an original meaning of regulation by obedience to authority. In the Newtonian system, the universe did indeed operate in accordance with the divinely established law, but not in the sense of commandment and obedience. It facilitated the liberal political and ethical thought which attempted to find the foundation for ethical practice in laws to be found in the nature of man. The obligation of mankind was to discover the nature of the universe as it was and attempt to fabricate on the basis of these findings. In the fields of politics and ethics, one was moved to investigate the character of man, to find the laws of his operation, and to build upon them. It was out of this climate that John Locke, John Stuart Mill, Jeremy Bentham, and others arose, and this climate still prevails in substantially the same form among many contemporary thinkers including psychologists.

Thus although for Newton himself space, time, and mass did not exhaustively explain the universe, nonetheless the intercessions of God were only occasional. God as an intervener in the daily affairs of mankind was practically driven out by the forms of thought that followed Newton. Once man had given God a place as arch-artisan, creator of the world-machine which was so well provided for that it needed only occasional further attention, man's affairs became largely his own. I am reminded in this connection of Freud's discussion of the taboo on rulers. He cited Frazer's discussion of the way in which a king is "hedged in by ceremonious etiquette, a network of prohibitions and observances, of which the intention is not to contribute to his dignity, much less to his comfort, but to restrain him from conduct which, by disturbing the harmony of nature, might involve himself, his people, and the universe in one common catastrophe."[10] What Newton in effect brought about was a fettering of the Divine by uncovering its "secrets" and giving them to mankind. This left a psychological void, in the sense that there was no God who looked on from moment to moment on the affairs of mankind and who provided for them. This vacuum of "management" is central to man's development since the Reformation, since it allowed and demanded that man exert his agency as a fulfillment of the total plan which God had presumably established for the conduct of the world.

A consequence of the Newtonian scheme was the reinforcement of the notion that God was known by his works. The post-Reformation personality was one in which the doctrine of works was extremely important. This whole style of thinking was reflected in the attitude of man to himself and to others, associated with what David C. McClelland has identified as the need for achievement in our society.[11] In the United States, this is identifiable with a harsh "democratic" doctrine in which we evaluate in terms of outcome, success, cash value, and the like; and in a morality, as Benjamin Franklin once commented, in which one is not interested in the good or evil

[10]Sigmund Freud, *Totem and Taboo*, from *The Basic Writings of Sigmund Freud*, p. 841 trans. and ed. Dr. A. A. Brill. Copyright 1938 by Random House, Inc. Reprinted by permission.

[11]David C. McClelland, *et al.*, *The Achievement Motive* (New York: Appleton-Century-Crofts, 1953); David C. McClelland, *The Achieving Society* (Princeton, N.J.: D. Van Nostrand Company, 1961).

of motives of actions but only in whether the action of the person is good or evil.

Let us indulge ourselves in myth and whimsy for a moment. In the story of the fall of Adam, the sin of mankind is depicted as plucking the fruit from a forbidden tree. In Augustine's *Confessions*, he tells of the sin of his youth, which was stealing pears from a pear tree.[12] The myth of Newton is that he was sitting in the garden, and the apple *fell* from the tree; and it was at this moment that he received the insight concerning the nature of gravity. This is a marked shift in myth. The fruit is not plucked from the tree as a result of the agency of man, but falls because of the law of gravity. The separation of the fruit from the tree is not man's sin, but the result of an inexorable law which God himself had created. With the kind of knowledge that the law of gravity provides, mankind was in a position to exert his agency with less sin or guilt.

Charles Darwin appeared on the intellectual scene in the middle of the nineteenth century, approximately a century and a half after Newton. This appearance is again momentous in the developing intellectual current. The interval between Newton and Darwin contained vast social change. Great revolutions in Europe and America had come about. Industrialization, urbanization, trade, communication, and transportation, had proceeded at a fast pace. The thought of the liberal philosophers had advanced, and much of it had been put into practice.

The Newtonian vision, with all of its beautiful, pristine perfection in connection with the physical world, was, however, deficient in explaining the biological world. In the interval between Newton and Darwin, man's observations of botanical and zoological creations had multiplied greatly as a result of his travels over the face of the earth. Whereas the heavenly bodies appeared to be governed by simple laws, and their behavior was characteristically quite regular and quite

[12]Augustine, *Confessions*, trans. Edward B. Pusey (New York: Washington Square Press, 1962), pp. 24ff.

predictable with the aid of the laws of mechanics, the variety and the complexity of animals and plants to which mankind was newly witness were not easily grasped by such simple principles. The richness of plants and animals was, in some important ways, threatening to the point of view associated with urban-industrial-mercantile activity which thrived on Newtonianism. The seeming purposefulness of plant and animal life was strongly suggestive of a continuing and abiding spiritual presence. Even in modern times, the various manifestations of purpose constitute one of the major threats to a strictly "scientific" approach to biology. The Biblical story of creation was more cognizant of plant and animal life on the face of the earth than was the Newtonian scheme. For all of its power, Newtonianism was lacking in explanatory value for the existence of life; and there was nothing comparable to Newtonianism for the explanation of biological phenomena.

The interpretation of nature which had been given by the romantic movement stood as a major alternative to Newtonianism. As a matter of fact, it may well be understood as a re-action to the onslaught of Calvinism and its associated urbanism and industrialism. The romantics held out a vision of the primitive world as beautiful and serene before it fell victim to machine-associated man. Robert Burns' little poem addressed to a mouse in a field who has been disturbed by his man-plow, or Wordsworth's contemplation of daffodils, or the celebration of the free emotional life in the form of poems on love, and so on, may be cited. The romantics conceived of nature as the locus of peace, personal freedom, love, and serenity; and their view of nature stood in criticism of the cramping of personality associated with the new society of city and industry.

The Protestant spirit needed to come to grips with these factors and especially needed an alternative view of nature. The Darwinian theory of evolution filled this need. Darwin's theory had significance of a social nature, beyond explaining how the plants and animals came to be. The theory of evolution was an attempt to describe the evolutionary process by principles which were fundamentally simple and which could be thought of as being beyond any intervention on a day-to-day basis by God. Indeed, at the very beginning of *The Origin of Species*, Darwin quoted the following from Whewell: "But with regard to the material world, we can at least go so far as this — we can perceive that events are brought about not by insulated interpositions of Divine power, exerted in each particular case, but by the establishment of general laws."[13]

This was Darwin's motto in his work, to find out how things could operate without "Divine power, exerted in each particular case." This impulse in Darwin may be interpreted as associated with the fundamentally Calvinistic attempt to regard all things in terms of the doctrine of predestination. There was a need to fix the character of God's predestination in connection with the plant and animal world, to remove the immediate agency of God. Consider the following passage from Darwin: "Can we wonder . . . that Nature's productions should be far 'truer' in character than Man's productions; that they should be infinitely better adapted to the most complex conditions of life, and should plainly bear the stamp of far higher workmanship?" (p. 66). Here, like Newton before him, he gave glory to God by admiring his workmanship. In the same way that Newton saw the wonderful adaptation of the eye to the laws of refraction, Darwin saw magnificence and proof of God's glory in all the complexities of plant and animal life. In the same way that Newton had, in effect, pushed God out of the physical realm, so did Darwin in the biological realm. As God had created the laws of motion which governed the movement of the heavenly bodies, so had he created the law of natural selection, in accordance with which the evolution of plants and animals took place.

[13]Charles R. Darwin, *The Origin of Species by Means of Natural Selection: Or, the Preservation of Favored Races in the Struggle For Life* (New York: Modern Library, 1936), p. 2.

The relationship of Darwin to Protestantism also entails another feature of the Calvinistic view, the doctrine of the natural depravity of man. Here I must touch on the problem of evil in the history and religiosity of man, to which I later give greater attention.

The strong moral emphasis in the Judeo-Chistian tradition has often been pointed out. In particular, the moral tradition has directed itself largely to sins of *sex, aggression,* and *avarice,* the three sins of mankind that Freud enumerated in *The Future of an Illusion.*[14] According to Western religion and tradition, sin consists in disobedience to God, disobedience which makes man subject to punishment. When an individual commits sins of sex, aggression, or avarice, he experiences intense guilt. In part, the function of religion is, on the one hand, to keep the individual from committing these sins and, on the other, to help him manage his guilt. It is with respect to this part of the religious tradition that Freud directed his attention. It is significant that Freud's thought, dealing as it does with the problem of evil in mankind, comes after Darwin. Implicit in Darwinism is the notion that the sins of sex, aggression, and avarice are meaningful and essential to survival; and survival was, in the Darwinian framework, an ultimate. That survival should be an ultimate is related to the Calvinist tendency to evaluate in terms of works. Darwin's whole scheme of survival is based precisely on characteristics which had previously been regarded as sins — sex, aggression, and avarice. Somehow, in Darwin's thought, sin turned out to be associated with the very survival of the species, a notion too powerful to be shaken off. Here was the Calvinistic idea of the natural depravity of man scientifically vindicated, "discovered" as an aspect of nature. Darwinism followed upon a long struggle of Protestantism to come to terms with the problem of evil. It provided a scientific vindication of a good deal of the

[14]Sigmund Freud, *The Future of an Illusion,* trans. W. D. Robson-Scott (Garden City, N.Y.: Doubleday & Company, 1957), p. 15.

thought which preceded it, which sought somehow to rationalize the self-interest which was involved in the Protestant development.

One of the most important social consequences of the Reformation was the qualification of the injunctions with respect to what had previously been regarded as sinful. Whereas, for example, sexuality had been denied to the priests under Catholicism, marriage became possible for Protestant ministers. Although the Reformation resulted in no license for overt aggression except in the economic sphere, it often articulated with rebellion against authority and restraint. Avarice had been a critical sin in the world before the Reformation; certainly, with the developments that came after the Reformation, the taking of interest and the accumulation of wealth became virtues rather than vices.

There are intimate connections between the Darwinian mode of thought and the thought of the English philosophers. Weber's thesis takes the service of self-interest as the product rather than the telos of the Protestant ethic. Yet, in the course of history, this distinction tended to fade. It was part of the effort of English philosophy to find a rationalization of the self-interestedness of the Protestant personality. One writer has said that what English philosophy sought to find were ways in "which 'self-interest' coincides with the interests of others or with general interest."[15] In Hobbes, we find the effort to define good and evil in terms of the appetites and desires of man. Hobbes wrote:

But whatsoever is the object of any man's appetite or desire, that is it which he for his part calleth *good*; and the object of his hate and aversion, *evil*; and of his contempt, *vile* and *inconsiderable*. For these words of good, evil, and contemptible, are ever used with relation to the person that useth them: there being nothing simply and absolutely so; nor any common rule of good and evil to be taken from the nature of the objects themselves....[16]

[15]Zevedei Barbu, *Problems of Historical Psychology* (New York: Grove Press, 1961), p. 202.

[16]Edwin A. Burtt (ed.), *The English Philosophers from Bacon to Mill* (New York: Random House, 1939), pp. 149-50.

Bentham wrote:

> Now, pleasure is in *itself* a good—nay even, setting aside immunity from pain, the only good; pain is in itself an evil—and, indeed, without exception, the only evil; or else the words good and evil have no meaning [p. 815].

Locke attempted to resolve political power into the essential characteristics to be found in man in a more or less original state, a state some would find to be fundamentally self-seeking. He wrote:

> To understand political power aright, and derive it from its original, we must consider what state all men are naturally in, and that is a state of perfect freedom to order their actions and dispose of their possessions and persons as they think fit, within the bounds of the law of nature, without asking leave, or depending upon the will of any other man [p. 404].

It was because of the tensions between Locke's ideas and the contemporary ideas of morality and religion that he found himself forced to write his famous *Essay Concerning Human Understanding,* to buttress the seeming immorality of his ideas with the new morality based on the essential nature of man. Adam Smith made the distinguishing feature of man his self-seeking and avaricious nature. This self-seeking quality is what underlies all of his activity. In discussing the matter of the division of labor, for example, Smith wrote:

> This division of labour, from which so many advantages are derived, is not originally the effect of any human wisdom, which foresees and intends that general opulence to which it gives occasion. It is the necessary, though very slow and gradual, consequence of a certain propensity in human nature which has in view no such extensive utility; the propensity to truck, barter, and exchange one thing for another.[17]

This automatic achievement of a larger good as a result of actualizing what is presumably man's essential nature on the individual level is exactly the pattern of thought adopted by Darwin for the whole pattern of evolution. According to Adam

[17]Adam Smith, *An Inquiry into the Nature and Causes of the Wealth of Nations,* ed. Edwin Cannan (New York: Modern Library, 1937), p. 13.

Smith, further, this bartering propensity is based on man's self-love.

... man has almost constant occasion for the help of his brethren, and it is in vain for him to expect it from their benevolence only. He will be more likely to prevail if he can interest their self-love in his favour, and shew them that it is for their own advantage to do for him what he requires of them. Whoever offers to another a bargain of any kind, proposes to do this. Give me that which I want, and you shall have this which you want, is the meaning of every such offer; and it is in this manner that we obtain from one another the far greater part of those good offices which we stand in need of. It is not from the benevolence of the butcher, the brewer, or the baker, that we expect our dinner, but from their regard to their own interest. We address ourselves, not to their humanity but to their self-love, and never talk to them of our own necessities, but of their advantages [p. 14].

Darwin wrote in a similar vein:

... the instinct of each species is good for itself, but has never, as far as we can judge, been produced for the exclusive good of others.... Although there is no evidence that any animal performs an action for the exclusive good of another species, yet each tries to take advantage of the instincts of others, as each takes advantage of the weaker bodily structure of other species.[18]

Darwin emerged out of this tradition, and with this as his background, found that he could attribute such characteristics to the whole of evolution. Darwinism undercut the romantic tradition. The romantics had used the idyllic image of nature as a moral criticism, holding up an image of nature before it was touched by man's devices and craft. Darwinism converted the romantic image of nature from one of peace and contentment to one in which sex, aggression, and avarice were paramount.

Darwin's thought helped resolve another difficulty in Protestant thought. In Protestantism there is a paradox in the seeming contradiction between the doctrine of election and the doctrine of the natural depravity of man. This is resolved

[18]*Op. cit.*, p. 186.

by interpreting the paradox of the doctrine of predestination in its Darwinian form; not by any airy, wispy theology, but by science. In characterizing the principle of natural selection, Darwin indicated that he liked very well the Spencerian formula of the "survival of the fittest," which we can easily translate into the "survival of the elect." He wrote:

> I have called this principle, by which each slight variation, if useful, is preserved, by the term Natural Selection, in order to mark its relation to man's power of selection. But the expression often used by Mr. Herbert Spencer of the Survival of the Fittest is more accurate, and is sometimes equally convenient.[19]

We can now see the articulation of the Darwinian mode of thought with Protestantism. God had predestined the world, by making it and leaving it. The classical modality of morality, obedience and punishment, had essentially been dissolved, with a God so transcendent as to be unimportant in the day-to-day activities of mankind. The doctrine of depravity was given confirmation in the significance of the sins of sex, aggression, and avarice. Their relation to election was in terms of survival, so that it was the "fittest," the "favored," as Darwin's subtitle indicates, that is, the elect, who survived. And this, after all, was most important since the doctrine of works makes consequences important and intentions unimportant.

Darwin's thought had its place in the exaggeration of the agentic feature in the century following. This is most clearly seen in the role that Darwinian thought played in the struggle between scientific and religious thought and in the way in which Darwinism was used as a rationalization for ruthless business practices. But if, on the one hand, Darwin had, in effect, carried forth and validated certain basic principles in Protestantism, on the other hand, his thought also worked against the thoroughgoing secularization associated with Protestantism. For, by rendering an account of biology compatible with the Protestant orientation, he moved the scientific

[19]*Ibid.*, p. 52.

thought of men from the physical to the biological, thus opening a way to a modern consideration of man. Our transition has been from the physical, to the organic, to man.

Darwin opened the way for the reintroduction of time as a significant item of human concern in the scientific context. In the same way that, in the Judeo-Christian tradition, time is the major framework within which to think of man's problems, so is it in the evolutionary thought which was given new status by Darwin's investigations and theorizing. Using the terms to which Tillich has drawn our attention, Darwin's thought moved us from thinking of time from chronos, clock time, to kairos, essentially the historical. In the Newtonian scheme of things, the significant moment of time was the time of creation. But beyond that there is only chronos, the view of time as a variable, the view of time as measured on a clock in which any temporal interval is the equivalent of any other temporal interval, the time which is associated with the movement of the planets in which there is a regular return to the same point in the cycle. But in Darwin, we return to time as historical, and time as related to the forward movements of events, to stages, metamorphosis, and organic growth. Through Darwin we move our thoughts to the question of purpose which, in consequence of Newton, had been dispatched once and for all in creation. It is true that Darwin's theory of evolution was a mechanical one. However, by drawing attention to time as kairos, he opened the question again, providing a takeoff point, a fulcrum, for vitalistic thought such as is perhaps best expressed by Henri L. Bergson in his *Creative Evolution*,[20] and for the reintroduction of the *wish* as a critical component of the psychological life, as in the writings of Freud. It is also true that Darwin forced a profound reevaluation of the Biblical story of creation insofar as the details were concerned; but nonetheless it fitted in with the fundamental way of thinking of time as expressed in the Bible.

[20]Henri L. Bergson, *Creative Evolution*, trans. Arthur Mitchell (New York: Henry Holt, 1911).

By presenting us with a paradox, the most critical paradox that man must live with, of the possibility that all that is characteristically associated with evil is, in some way, intimately intertwined with good, the notion that the sins of mankind, sex, aggression, and avarice, are related to the survival of mankind, Darwin's thought provided the invitation to look clearly at the nature of the demonic, as Freud did. Freud once pointed out that there were three major blows to man's narcissism, the Copernican, which took man from the center of the universe, the Darwinian, which tied man to the world of animals, and the psychoanalytic, which showed man to be under the dominion of something other than his grand and narcissistic consciousness. In this, Freud tied himself in with Darwin. The deeper relationship between Freud and Darwin is that the aggrandizement of the primitive which is implicit in Darwin's thought made it possible for man, in all of his narcissism, to have a good look at what he thought was so ignoble in himself and to discover the possibility of aggrandizing the condition of man by facing that which, at first sight, appears to be ignoble. The next chapter deals with this mechanism in human thought in greater detail. The dread of the demonic, the dread of the primitive, the dread of the dark forces of the mind of man, were overcome by Darwin precisely because they appeared, in his thinking, to be in some way related to the things which we value most positively, life and progress. He smashed the idyllic myth of the romantics and overcame our reluctance to think of nature rationally, replacing the lyrical and the innocent with thought and investigation.

# CHAPTER III

## THE PROJECTION OF
## AGENCY ON THE
## FIGURE OF SATAN

One of the valuable ways of apprehending the nature of the
human mind is through the analysis of the myths and mythical
personages that it creates. This chapter deals with the image of
Satan, an image which has prevailed throughout much of
Judeo-Christian history. The image of Satan contains that
which is regarded as evil and sinful. It was important in the
late Middle Ages and persisted through the Reformation. The
strong modern tendencies toward secularism and the elimination of the mythical within Protestantism have tended to make
the figure of Satan pale compared to what it has been at other
times.

   An image which has played such an important role over
many centuries must contain clues to the nature of the human
mind which has created and been preoccupied with it. The
psychologist Henry A. Murray, in an interesting analysis of
the meaning of Satan, has written the following:

   The ground for this undertaking of mine, as well as for the hope
   that other psychologists will invade the abundant field of religious
   images and imagents, and grapple with one or another of its many
   mysteries, is a conclusion, or value judgment, I have come to, on the
   periphery of science, which might be termed a credo. It is the belief
   that the evidence set forth by anthropologists and psychoanalysts,
   particularly by Frazer and by Freud, in favor of the proposition that
   religions are products of human imaginations revised by rationality,
   is so massive and persuasive that it adds up to a veritable discovery,

potentially the most consequential discovery since Darwin's theory of evolution.[1]

Murray earlier developed the Thematic Apperception Test, a series of pictures about which subjects are instructed to make up stories. The stories they tell are used to assess their personality characteristics in ways similar to Freud's use of dreams, on the assumption that these are of man himself and not really "other" to him. David C. McClelland has made good use of the technique of analyzing mythical figures in order to establish and point up designable psychological constellations. Thus, he has used Hermes as representative of the achievement motive and Harlequin as representative of attitudes toward death in women.[2] In order to understand myth, the psychologist must oscillate between the posture of the believer, in order to appreciate the significance of the myth, and the posture of the rational investigator, whose conception of reality is, as in Bultmann, consistent with the scientific view of the universe.

My thesis with respect to the Satan figure may be put rather simply: Satan is a projection in which the agentic in the human psyche is personified. The characteristics attributed to Satan are universal in man, and through the appreciation of these characteristics we can come to a better understanding of the agentic aspect of man himself.

A major condition for the *projection* of the image of Satan is the agentic reaching its limit of effectiveness and coming to despair. The projection of the figure of Satan as being "other" than the person who entertains the image stems from the individual's effort to cope with his despair by ejecting the agentic from himself. It is for this reason that the figure of Satan, when it has appeared in human history, characteris-

[1] Henry A. Murray, "The Personality and Career of Satan," *Journal of Social Issues*, XVIII, No. 4 (1962), 39.

[2] *The Achieving Society*, chap. 8, "The Spirit of Hermes," pp. 301-35; David C. McClelland, "The Harlequin Complex," in Robert W. White (ed.), *The Study of Lives: Essays on Personality in Honor of Henry A. Murray* (New York: Atherton Press, 1963), pp. 94-119.

tically has associated with it an exaggerated phenomenological "objectivity" and "reality." However, we need to recognize that what is associated with this severe separation of the self from the Satanic image which it creates is the agency feature. This is one of the major paradoxes associated with all of the thought in connection with the image of Satan: that the repugnance toward the Satanic entails the very agentic function which is involved in the creation of the image. As long as the Satanic image is not real, not projected, it exists simply as the agentic in man's psyche. Historically, man attempted to manage the agentic feature in himself that had brought him to despair by projecting this feature in the image of Satan. Today, when image-making in the same sense is considerably inhibited, we must come to grips with the despairing agentic by viewing the psyche directly.

The mechanism involved in projecting an image of Satan is only partially effective because in this projection the very feature of the psyche which is involved in the despair in the first place is exercised. The sense of separation of the self from Satan is illusory. In the contemporary world, we can only move in the direction of trying to understand the mechanism. Understanding, in the sense of opening up to view that which is hidden, is associated with the communion feature of the human psyche. The psychological problem of the Satanic image is agency unmitigated by communion. Thus, in our very seeking to come to grips with it by understanding, we try to mitigate agency through communion.

It is worth dwelling for a moment on the general context of Murray's paper. He presented it at a meeting of the American Psychological Association in 1962. The paper came in the wake of such marks of esteem as come to a distinguished man when others wish to honor him while he is still alive. He has pursued a brilliant career in which he has, at times singlehandedly, held out for the richness of human being while others have been nibbling away at it. Murray begins his paper with an expression of the awareness of the aversion of his psychological colleagues to myth, especially the myth of the Devil. "By what deplorable slip of judgment did the Program Committee of Division 8 let the Devil—that shadow of a bygone superstitious age—crash the gates of this emporium of genuine scientific commerce?" (p. 36). But he ends the paper with a section entitled "Is the spirit of Satan operating in our midst?" (p. 51) and talks of psychology:

And here is where our psychology comes in with the bulk of its theories, its prevailing views of human personality, its images of man, obviously in league with the objectives of the nihilist Satanic spirit. Man is a computer, an animal, or an infant. His destiny is completely determined by genes, instincts, accidents, early conditionings and reinforcements, cultural and social forces. Love is a secondary drive based on hunger and oral sensations or a reaction formation to an innate underlying hate. In the majority of our personological formulations there are no provisions for creativity, no admitted margins of freedom for voluntary decisions, no fitting recognitions of the power of ideals, no bases for selfless actions, no ground at all for any hope that the human race can save itself from the fatality that now confronts it. If we psychologists were all the time, consciously or unconsciously, intending out of malice to reduce the concept of human nature to its lowest common denominators, and were gloating over our successes in so doing, then we might have to admit that to this extent the Satanic spirit was alive within us [p. 53].

What we see in Murray is an awareness of the agentic feature active in contemporary psychology and the effort to come to grips with it by playfully "projecting" the Satanic image *and* trying to understand it psychologically.

In an earlier treatment, I dealt with the significance of the Devil metaphor in Freud's thought and, in particular, of the way in which this had a role in his transition from neurophysiologist to psychoanalyst.[3] The existing biographical materials, including Freud's own writings on the meaning of the Devil, indicate deep despair prior to and early in his development of psychoanalysis. Freud's great preoccupation with his own death throughout his life is also important, and this will

---

[3]David Bakan, *Sigmund Freud and the Jewish Mystical Tradition* (Princeton, N.J.: D. Van Nostrand Company, 1958).

be discussed in somewhat greater detail later in this essay. I used Roheim's suggestion that one could understand the Devil psychologically as the suspension of the superego in explaining Freud.[4] In the case of Freud's development of the psychoanalytic notions, his concern with the image of the Devil may be interpreted as having made it possible for him to overcome in his thought the various literalistic scientific strictures in order that he might creatively come upon a deeper understanding of the nature of the human psyche. If we assume that the agentic feature of the psyche is involved in the formation of both the ego and the superego, the latter partly the incorporation of the agency of others, particularly of the father, then we can understand how, in the despair which is associated with unmitigated agency, the interpretation of the Devil as the suspension of the superego makes sense.

Let us consider the two postures with respect to the apprehension of the image of the Devil. One posture makes the Devil "real" and the personification of evil to be eschewed. The other is that the Devil is the fantastic creation of the human psyche. O. Hobart Mowrer, a psychologist who is currently deeply involved in an effort to bring together certain features of religion with psychology,[5] has chastised me because, on the one hand, I have collected various evidences which suggest the significance of the metaphor of the Devil in the thought of Freud, and yet, on the other hand, I still think of Freud as "an inspired scientific genius," as he puts it. I think that the difference between Mowrer's approach and mine is the difference with respect to these postures. I believe that Mowrer still, in a certain sense, thinks of the Devil as a real personage. He has essentially taken Freud to be the Devil of modern times and appears to feel that I have proven it! The problem of these two postures is an extremely general one in

[4]Geza Roheim, *Psychoanalysis and Anthropology* (New York: International Universities Press, 1950), p. 469.

[5]O. Hobart Mowrer, *The Crisis in Psychiatry and Religion* (Princeton, N.J.: D. Van Nostrand Company, 1961); "The 'New' Psychological Liberty," *The Christian Scholar*, XLIV (1961), 206-22.

the contemporary world, and hardly limited to the esoteric problem of the significance of an image in the development of psychoanalysis. It is the problem of whether we are to deal with what we take to be immoral or evil in the human being simply as the object of condemnation and rejection, or we are to examine and understand it; and of whether, if we are to act, we undertake to act on the basis of our understanding, instead of simply adding to our own sense of moral virtue. The very effort of separating ourselves from evil stems from the same source in the psyche as does the image of the Devil.

A valuable "countermyth," if such a notion can be entertained, is the myth in the Jewish mystical tradition that, at the time of creation, the holy vessel was shattered and the holy sparks dispersed. Hope lies in the possibility of the ingathering of these holy sparks. Implicit in this countermyth is the notion that holiness may be anywhere, in both what appears good or evil; and it tends to overcome the sharp distinction between them. With this "faith," one can move anywhere. One need not be completely aversive to anything; for if one is, one may well be aversive to something which contains the holy sparks. There is, however, a danger in this countermyth, that it should appear to be a license for wantonness and irresponsibility in action. This it is not. It is in no sense a license for "acting out." It is rather an injunction to examine and investigate what appears to be evil, with the recognition that examining evil is not evil itself, but the way to discover its nature.

Freud was evidently sympathetic to this countermyth, for he essentially repeated it in *Beyond the Pleasure Principle*, in the first sentence of the passage quoted below. Furthermore, he appeared to be aware of the dynamic whereby both separations and reunions take place. He wrote:

> Shall we follow the hint given us by the poet-philosopher, and venture upon the hypothesis that living substance at the time of its coming to life was torn apart into small particles, which have ever since endeavoured to reunite through the sexual instincts? that these instincts, in which the chemical affinity of inanimate matter per-

sisted, gradually succeeded, as they developed through the kingdom of the protista, in overcoming the difficulties put in the way of that endeavour by an environment charged with dangerous stimuli — stimuli which compelled them to form a protective cortical layer? that these splintered fragments of living substance in this way attained a multicellular condition and finally transferred the instinct for reuniting, in the most highly concentrated form, to the germ-cells? — But here, I think, the moment has come for breaking off.[6]

But Freud did not quite break off at this point. He continued with a paragraph of misgivings, in which he referred to himself as *"advocatus diaboli."* I believe that the misgivings he cited were based on the difficulty which has already been mentioned. The Satanic figure demands its own reality. Yet the penetration of its nature requires that we come to appreciate its fantastic quality. If the figure is real, our morality prevents us from associating ourselves with it. Yet to regard it as fantastic makes it difficult to appreciate its phenomenological reality. Freud was aware that, by somehow suspending belief and commitment in order to enter into this realm, "it is possible to throw oneself into a line of thought." This is entertaining without necessarily believing; or, what is in some sense the same, entering into participation in a dangerous line of thought with the full sense that in so doing one is still in "grace"; or, what is still in some sense the same, entering upon a realm aware that the holy sparks are everywhere. Let us see how Freud expressed his misgivings in the paragraph which immediately succeeds the previously quoted passage.

Not, however, without the addition of a few words of critical reflection. It may be asked whether and how far I am myself convinced of the truth of the hypotheses that have been set out in these pages. My answer would be that I am not convinced myself and that I do not seek to persuade other people to believe in them. Or, more precisely, that I do not know how far I believe in them. There is no reason, as it seems to me, why the emotional factor of conviction should enter into this question at all. It is surely possible to throw

[6]From *Beyond the Pleasure Principle* (1920) by Sigmund Freud, pp. 80, 81, by permission of Liveright, Publishers, N.Y., Sigmund Freud Copyrights Ltd., Mr. James Strachey, and The Hogarth Press Ltd. Volume XVIII of the Standard Edition of *The Complete Works of Sigmund Freud.*

oneself into a line of thought and to follow it wherever it leads out of simple scientific curiosity, or, if the reader prefers, as an *advocatus diaboli*, who is not on that account himself sold to the devil ... [p. 81].

What I am trying to express here has intrinsic difficulties. There is the general difficulty which is associated with the clarification of any psychological problem, that of using the psyche for the understanding of the psyche. In the case of the Satanic image, there is the special difficulty in connection with its "reality," which I have already spoken of. In the following pages, I attempt to clarify this image, partly through analysis, in which the agentic is itself involved, partly through the use of metaphor, which is a way of communicating meaning with less of the agentic involved, and partly by availing myself of the assumption that the critical features of existence are essentially developmental. Thus, I distinguish among four stages in the natural history of Satanism. The first is separation. The second is mastery. The third is denial. The fourth is beholding that which has been denied. This last I also refer to as the therapeutic stage. These four stages at once characterize both the normal developmental process at large and smaller developmental episodes within a life history.

SEPARATION

My first analytic notion for understanding the mechanism associated with the Satanic image is that of separation. Cell division may be taken as a model, and perhaps the ultimate biological example, of separation. When cells separate from each other after division, they can live as separate entities, they can be organized to form a larger organismic unity, they can separate for a time and unite temporarily as in conjugation, or they can come in conflict with each other and one can kill or consume or otherwise harm the other. Such biological separations and their consequences take place not only on the cellular level, but also on the multicellular level. In psychoanalytic thought, this fundamental pattern has been taken as important for the understanding of the psychological characteristics of the human being. Thus, for the psychoanalyst, the separation of birth and the subsequent interaction of the various members of the family, their destiny as separate and organized entities, sexual union, and mutual nurturance and harm in the interrelationships have been taken as root experiences of mankind.

Our knowledge is inadequate for the full comprehension of the way in which certain primitive biological processes repeat themselves at various levels of organismic complexity. But the absence of a comprehensive theory need not prevent us from observing parallels, even though we do not understand the dynamics whereby the parallels take place.

I have already referred to the mechanism of projection associated with the Satanic image, which is a separation of the personage of Satan from the psyche which has generated and entertained it. The Devil is characteristically "cast out." He has all of the "reality" of the person who entertains him. The characteristic nature of the struggle with the Devil in the mythology is to try to become separated from him.

The notion of separation is intrinsic to the Satan myth. He is originally an angel with all the other angels. Then he becomes the fallen angel who revolts against God. Freud, in his paper on demoniacal possession, wrote:

Concerning the Evil Demon, we know that he is regarded as the antithesis of God, and yet is very close to him in his nature.... The evil demon of the Christian faith, the Devil of the Middle Ages, was, according to Christian mythology, himself a fallen angel and of a godlike nature. It does not need much analytic perspicacity to guess that God and the Devil were originally identical — were a single figure which was later split into two figures with opposite attributes.[7]

In this paper, Freud argued that the fundamental feature of the human being relevant to this split of God and Devil is the ambivalence between love and hate. Here, within the psyche, is the separation of the affective bond among human

---

[7]Standard Edition of *The Complete Psychological Works of Sigmund Freud,* trans. and ed. James Strachey (London: The Hogarth Press, Ltd., 1953- ), XIX, 85-86. Basic Books, Inc., Publishers, New York.

beings into two components, and this separation is one which is metaphorically expressed in separating God from Devil, one the object of love and the other the object of hate, as well as one being the personification of love and the other the personification of hate.

The notion that we are advancing here, that in the splitting of deities we have an expression of the tendency of the human psyche to separate, can help us understand part of the thrust of monotheistic religion. Basically, the monotheistic injunction is an injunction against the separatistic nature of the human psyche. It is rather interesting that in Freud's *Moses and Monotheism,* a book which he composed with great misgivings, the problem of *mono*theism as such is hardly illuminated. In my earlier treatment of Freud, I pointed out his preoccupation with the image of the Devil and the deviations within his thought from a strict monotheism. As evidence, I cited the way in which he surrounded himself in his study with a variety of works of art associated with "strange gods." The struggle involved in separation and the overcoming of separation was a dominant one in Freud's life; and, indeed, the richness of psychoanalysis for the appreciation of this problem can be viewed as a result of this struggle. I might, at this point, also refer back to the modern theology of Bultmann, in which the separation of man from God is still taken as the essential feature of sin.

The problem of separation as related to sin is a pervasive one in a good deal of Christian thought. Consider the Augustinian vision of the nature of the fall of man, for example. In his introduction to Augustine's *The City of God,* Merton paraphrases the Augustinian position as follows:

God created Adam as a pure contemplative. Material creation was subject to Adam's reason, and the soul of Adam was perfectly subjected to God. United to God in a very high degree of vision and love, Adam would have transmitted to all mankind his own perfection, his own liberty, his own peace in the vision of God. In Adam all men were to be, as it were, "one contemplative" perfectly united to one another in their one vision and love of the One Truth.

Original sin, an act of spiritual apostasy from the contemplative vision and love of God, severed the union with God that depended on the subjection of Adam's will to the will of God. Since God is Truth, Adam's apostasy from Him was a fall into falsehood, unreality. Since God is unity, Adam's fall was a collapse into division and disharmony. All mankind fell from God in Adam. And just as Adam's soul was divided against itself by sin, so all men were divided against one another by selfishness. The envy of Cain, which would have been impossible in Eden, bred murder in a world where each self-centered individual had become his own little god, his own judge and standard of good and evil, falsity and truth.[8]

Here we have a variety of separations: God and Adam, material and nonmaterial creation, "Adam's soul ... divided against itself by sin," God and one's "own little god," man's judgment and God's judgment. In Augustine's thought, there is also the separation of the spirit from the flesh, and of authority from obedience.

We can view the mechanism of repression, which Freud took as a major feature in the development of the neurosis, as a step beyond separation. For analytically, separation is the precondition for repression. The person "decides" between what he likes and what he does not like and represses the latter. The task of psychoanalysis is often precisely the discovery of the inner unity which is behind separation and repression. In a short paper entitled "Negation," Freud told of the clinical situation in which a person may say, " 'You ask who this person in the dream can be. It's *not* my mother'." Freud wrote that in his interpretation he emended this with " 'so it *is* his mother.' In our interpretation, we take the liberty of disregarding the negation and of picking out the subject-matter alone of the association."[9]

The distinction of the unconscious from the conscious is the result of repression. "Egotism," which is the extreme separation of the conscious ego from the rest of being, is characteristically attributed to Satan. And we can thus understand the nihilistic character of Satan, which makes nought of

[8]Augustine, *The City of God*, trans. Marcus Dods (New York: Random House, 1950), p. xii.
[9]Standard Edition, XIX, 235.

everything except the limited conscious ego. Indeed, when Freud wrote of the connection between the ego and the death instinct, which is discussed in greater detail below, he was giving psychological meaning to the words, "the wages of sin is death" (Romans 6:23). As the person grows up, he separates himself from his parents. But this biological separate has, with its very commitment to birth, contracted both to live *for term* and to die. There is a profound psychological meaning in the mythical notion that the contract with the Devil is *for term*, terminating in death. What is being expressed here is precisely the condition of man in which he is committed as a separate for term biologically, and in the development of the ego as separated from the rest of being psychologically. The effort of psychoanalysis is to mitigate such separations as are entailed in the development of the psyche, and yet not to overlook their necessity and value. Similarly, it has been one of the major thrusts of our religious history.

Let me pick up a thread from what has already been said. I have read back the phenomenon of repression from the image of Satan. Yet this image hardly appears regularly with repression. For, if the latter were the case, the image of Satan should occur universally at all times and places, which it certainly does not. We have a hint about the nature of the mechanism in two contemporary minds, Sigmund Freud's and Henry A. Murray's. Freud was preoccupied with the "terminal" nature of life all of his life, that is, he was preoccupied with death. Murray, with whom I have spoken of these things — and I hope that he will forgive my indiscretion in writing this — is also preoccupied with death. In both of these men there is a concern with the emergence of the projected Satan. It is not the case, however, that they have been naive about the psychological character of this image. Murray says that his review of the historical sources allows a "hypothetical model of the initial state of mind" associated with the rise of the Satanic figure. Among the characteristics of this state of mind is the "feeling of extreme distress engendered by the tribulations suffered by their peoples and by the perception of rewarded wickedness on all sides of them ever since the breakup of Alexander's empire."[10] I suggest that it is the sense of despair which comes with a failure to master the world, which then moves over to the despair associated with the awareness of the "terminal" character of the life of the biological organism and its ego, which has been so well described by Kierkegaard in *The Sickness unto Death*,[11] that leads to the projection.

A shred of empirical evidence along these lines has been given by David C. McClelland and one of his students, Ellen Greenberger. They used the Thematic Apperception Test, which was developed by Murray to elicit projections, comparing the projections made by women who were critically ill with cancer with those of women ill with minor illnesses. They found that "the women for whom death was a real possibility thought *almost twice as often* about punishment and illicit sex as the women who were about to go home from the hospital after a minor illness."[12] McClelland has used the data from this study to corroborate what he calls the "Harlequin complex" in women. In the stories these women tell in response to the TAT cards, McClelland identified Harlequin as the illicit lover who carries women to their death. McClelland also cites a considerable amount of mythical material allowing an identification of Harlequin and the Devil. Thus, to put it simply, in the despair over the control of the forces which would maintain life, that is, in the despair associated with the functioning of the ego, the image of the Devil is projected. The possible relationship of cancer and agency is dealt with in greater detail below.

A point which needs to be considered is the dogged manner in which Freud maintained his psychological Lamarckianism in the face of objections from numerous sources, including people who were most friendly to his position. I

[10]*Op. cit.*, p. 41.
[11]Soren Kierkegaard, *The Sickness unto Death*, trans. Walter Lowrie (Princeton, N.J.: Princeton University Press, 1951).
[12]McClelland, "The Harlequin Complex," p. 108.

believe that what Freud was trying to do in his own psyche was to overcome the separation of the ego from the stream of biological continuity. The ego, so to speak, steps out of the stream, lives for term, and dies. The psychological Lamarckianism which Freud advanced is in stark contradiction to the "facts" as the ego knows them. Yet, I believe, Freud was sufficiently aware of the other reality, the reality of the unconscious, to feel that if the ego is "terminal," the unconscious may not be. This sense that the unconscious is not "terminal" is, of course, even more striking in Jung's work.

The central position of the Oedipus complex in Freudian thought is well known. Murray, in his paper on Satan, interprets the image of Satan in terms of the Oedipus complex. He enumerates the views of several of the Church Fathers: Satan wanted to pass himself off as God; he tried to convince his fellow angels that he had created himself; he wished to be his own master; he wanted to be adored as a self-created God; he wished to derive happiness from himself alone; he desired to possess the divine nature. Murray summarizes all of these as, "Satan wanted to be God, period."[13] What underlies all of this is the fact of the separation of the father from the son, and the thrust is to overcome the separation. Freud's elaboration of the notion of the Oedipus complex involves both the desire to be rid of the father *and* to be the father. According to Freud, the development of the superego is precisely the effort to incorporate within the psyche that which is "other" to the psyche. Let us again consider the biological situation. The separated being is destined to die. The only way in which there can be any biological continuity is through the act of sexual intercourse, resulting in the birth of another separate. Freud, in his consideration of the Oedipus complex, made the sexual act central and pressed the point that the wish of the child is to have intercourse with the mother. It is from sexual intercourse that the biological being comes into existence. And it is through

[13]*Op. cit.*, p. 45.

sexual intercourse that he can maintain his biological existence in a nonterminal sense. God, in the thought of man, is immortal. Thus, the fantasy of Satan wishing to be God is a fantastic way of coming to terms with the reality: the Satanic way of overcoming the mortality of existence is to be the father of one's self! To convince the angels that he had created himself is, according to the Church fathers Prudentius and Rupert, the nature of Satan's sin.[14] In one paper, Freud made the dramatic assertion: "All his instincts, those of tenderness, defiance and independence, find satisfaction in the single wish *to be his own father.*"[15] This is precisely the sin of Satan. The abiding reality of the father-son relationship is that they are separated from one another, and there is a struggle between them for prerogative and mastery. Both, by virtue of their separate existences, are psychologically committed to their separate existences. And from this emerges the conflict between them which Freud repeatedly referred to.

The ultimate of sexuality has sometimes been thought of as death, particularly in the romantic literature. This is the death of the ego as it reenters the literally immortal biological stream. Freud's attribution of the child's desire for intercourse with the mother, insofar as we take this at face value, can be interpreted as the child's revolt against the essential untenability of life, against commitment to a terminal existence. Sexual intercourse, according to the psychoanalytic interpretation, is motivated partly by the desire to return to the womb, to reverse the process which is associated with becoming a separate entity. In this, there is an expression of the communion feature of sexuality. Interestingly enough, the figure of Satan rarely, if ever, appears in history as the father of children. If, as Freud suggested, it is the father figure which is separated into two components, one God and the other Satan, the generative function for the creation of human beings is reserved to God.

[14]*Ibid.*
[15]Standard Edition, XI, 173.

Satan, who is nonetheless sexual, is not the father of human beings. He rather represents the agentic feature of sexuality, which I elaborate upon later. In the growth of the child, which proceeds inevitably from the moment of his birth onward, he is forced into a separate existence. He cannot really reenter the womb and reverse the process. He cannot really have intercourse with his mother. Indeed, it is one of the major paradoxes of Freudian thought that it ascribes a desire for sexual intercourse with the mother to precisely those ages in which there is inadequate biological maturity for actually engaging in sexual relations. There is only one reasonable strategy. This is for the child to grow up and become strong, masterful, and as sexually competent as his father; for this is the only way in which he can ultimately fulfill himself so as to ensure his immortality. A major crisis of life is associated with the fact that the organism must develop the ego and must commit itself to the ego. But, in the development of the ego, one is already committed to personal death. To break the shell of tragic existence, one must undermine the superego, which one allowed for the sake of the ego, as a step in mitigating the ego itself in order to permit the communion feature in the psyche to function. To do this, one projects the image of Satan as a step toward the refusion of the two fathers, the father who is master with the father who is generative of life. And one must further fuse the separation of father from son, in order to become a father in turn.

## MASTERY

Mastery is the second stage in the projection of the image of Satan. Three points come to attention in connection with mastery which bear strongly upon each other.

First, mastery of the secular world is characteristically attributed throughout history to the projected Satan. In the New Testament, he is referred to as "the prince of this world" (John 12:31, 14:30, 16:11). Paul even referred to Satan as "the god of this world" (II Corinthians 4:4). When the Devil is trying to tempt Jesus, he takes him to a high mountain, shows him "all the kingdoms of the world, and the glory of them; And saith unto him, All these things will I give thee, if thou wilt fall down and worship me" (Matthew 4:8-9). In Luke, this is narrated even more tellingly, with the addition of the notion of "power."

And the devil, taking him up into an high mountain, shewed unto him all the kingdoms of the world in a moment of time. And the devil said unto him, All this power will I give thee, and the glory of them: for that is delivered unto me; and to whomsoever I will I give it. If thou therefore wilt worship me, all shall be thine [Luke 4:5-7].

Second, it should be noted that it is the ego which is in contact with the external world. According to Freud's characterization of the ego,

The relation to the external world has become the decisive factor for the ego.... the ego must observe the external world, must lay down an accurate picture of it in the memory-traces of its perceptions, and by its exercise of the function of "reality-testing" must put aside whatever in this picture of the external world is an addition derived from internal sources of excitation.[16]

I do not think that I stretch Freud's meaning too far when I say that he related this to the notion of the Devil. For he ended the lecture in which he thus described the function of the ego by saying that the therapeutic efforts of psychoanalysis are to "strengthen the ego, to make it more independent of the super-ego, to widen its field of vision, and so to extend its organization that it can take over new portions of the id."

Where id was, there ego shall be. It is a work of culture — not unlike the draining of the Zuider Zee. [p. 80]

One meaning which this last sentence evidently has is that as the waters covered the land of Holland and then the land was uncovered, so the work of the analyst is that of uncovering the unconscious.

This may also be an allusion to the fourth act of the second part of Goethe's *Faust*, with which we know Freud was well

[16]Sigmund Freud, *New Introductory Lectures on Psychoanalysis*, trans. James Strachey (New York: W. W. Norton & Company, 1965), p. 75.

acquainted. In this act, in which Faust and Mephistopheles arrive on a high mountain range, and in which Goethe was evidently alluding to the temptation of Jesus, Mephistopheles says, "You have surveyed a boundless territory, The kingdoms of the world and all their glory."[17] Faust proposes that the water be pushed back from the shore and the land reclaimed. The critics of Goethe have pointed out that this indeed alludes to Holland; and that on a more symbolic level, it refers to man's mastery over the physical world.

Third, coincident with the development of Protestantism in the modern world there developed a greater degree of mastery over the physical world than at any other time in the history of mankind. That the psychological condition outlined as associated with the projection of the image of Satan prevails in some sense in the development of Protestantism is attested to by the fact that such major figures cited by Weber to explicate the Protestant ethic associated with the development of capitalism—Martin Luther, John Calvin, Richard Baxter, and John Wesley—all believed in the reality of Satan.[18]

These three items, which are closely related to each other, involve the singular factor of mastery over the physical environment.

Much of modern psychology has taken mastery as a central notion. The growth of the ego is intrinsic to the growth of the individual. Unless the ego develops within the individual, he remains as he was originally, dependent and inept in the conduct of life. If the growth of the ego is related to sin, then it is certainly "original" sin, in the sense that the growth of the ego is intrinsic to human development. Such quarrel as we may have with the emphasis on ego development is not one of cancellation, but of balance and perspective. Robert W. White's emphasis on competence[19] or Lois B. Murphy's emphasis on

[17]Johann W. von Goethe, *Faust*, trans. George Madison Priest (New York: Alfred A. Knopf, 1941), p. 290, ll. 10130-31.

[18]Edward Langton, *Satan, a Portrait* (London: Skeffington and Son, 1946), pp. 85-96.

[19]Robert W. White, "Motivation Reconsidered: The Concept of Competence," *Psychological Review*, LXVI (1959), 297-333.

mastery in the development of children[20] are appropriate in a larger context. David C. McClelland, with his interest in the achievement motive, is a case in point. He actually speculates as to whether what he is talking about is not the Faustian spirit.[21] He has taken the amount of electrical production of a nation as the measure of its level of achievement — reminiscent of Faust's project of controlling the water of the world in the service of mankind. The danger is only that overemphasis on the development of the ego will obscure, indeed repress, the communion feature of the psyche.

What is it that makes an individual, or a large group of people, so totally committed to the mastery of the physical world? I shall try to bring to bear these three sets of considerations, the myth of Satan, the nature of the ego, and the history of Protestantism, for the understanding of the development of the agency feature of the human psyche.

1. The Freudian notion is that the growth of the ego takes place largely in the latency period, roughly from about the age of five or six to ten or eleven. It is in this period that the affective, or the communion, feature of sexuality is most highly repressed and the mastery impulse grows. At this stage, too, the individual is incapable of having children. Education is important at this stage, but there are important articulations between the educational process and the intrinsic developmental patterns within the individual:

It is during this period of total or at least partial latency that the psychic forces develop which later act as inhibitions on the sexual life, and narrow its direction like dams. . . . We may gain the impression that the erection of these dams in the civilized child is the work of education; and surely education contributes much to it. In reality, however, this development is organically determined and can occasionally be produced without the help of education. Indeed education remains properly within its assigned domain if it strictly follows the path laid out by the organic, and only imprints it somewhat cleaner and deeper.[22]

[20]Lois B. Murphy, *et al.*, *The Widening World of Childhood* (New York: Basic Books, 1962).

[21]*The Achieving Society*, p. 301.

[22]Sigmund Freud, *Three Contributions to the Theory of Sex*, in *Basic Writings*, p. 583.

Cruelty, which Freud later identified with the death instinct, develops at this time and is related to the mastery impulse, associated with the ego: "... we may assume that the feelings of cruelty emanate from the mastery impulse and appear at a period in the sexual life before the genitals have taken on their later rôle" (pp. 593-94).

2. McClelland, on the basis of his data and the data of others, generalized that high need for achievement, which he sometimes identifies with mastery, is related to "the boy being put on his own" somewhere between the ages of six and eight, precisely within the latency period. He cites data to indicate that "father absence" from around eight years of age onward, facilitates the growth of the need for achievement.[23]

3. In the myth, Satan begins as an angel among all the other angels. At a somewhat later time, and yet early in history after creation, he is expelled from Heaven and "put on his own." Indeed, one of the great paradoxes associated with the notion of Satan, that God is not evil although Satan is created by God and is the expression of God's will, is understandable in these psychological terms: although Satan was created by God, he was "put on his own." The expulsion of Satan from Heaven is parallel to the expulsion of Adam and Eve from the Garden of Eden, and to the condition of a child who is "put on his own" at a relatively early age. Weber, in his effort to communicate the nature of the Protestant mentality, cited the following from Milton's *Paradise Lost*, which describes the *expulsion* from Paradise:

> They, looking back, all the eastern side beheld
> Of paradise, so late their happy seat,
> Waved over by that flaming brand; the gate
> With dreadful faces thronged and fiery arms.
> Some natural tears they dropped, but wiped them soon:
> The world was all before them, there to choose
> Their place of rest, and Providence their guide.[24]

4. Expulsion characterizes the Protestant, especially the American, experience. Historically, the Protestants were often

[23]*The Achieving Society*, p. 376.
[24]*The Protestant Ethic* ..., p. 88.

those people who were expelled from the land, coming into the cities, and developing in the cities. The Protestants who came to American shores were, in many senses, expelled from their homelands. Expulsion was also a common experience associated with childhood in the early Protestant family. Bernard Bailyn, in an astute historical analysis of the social factors associated with the development of American education, points out that there was a radical shift from a fairly extended kinship community which bore the burden of education to a condition in which there was a gross separation of the conjugal unit, the community, and the church. In addition, there was a sharp separation of the generations. He describes the "maimed functions of the family" which were then taken over by formal institutions.[25] Bailyn cites the selling of children of the poor both in England and in the colonies. He quotes from a Massachusetts statute of 1642 which sought to compensate for "the great neglect of many parents and masters in training up their children in learning and labor." Virginia at this time passed a law which ordered county officials to "take up" children whose parents "are disabled to maintaine and educate them" (p. 26). The institution of the apprenticeship, originally a device whereby the master would be *in loco parentis,* in which the master's duties "included all those of an upright father," was downgraded to a condition in which masters found apprentices to be a source of cheap labor (p. 30). Weber has said that the Calvinist created his own salvation. "In practice this means that God helps those who help themselves."[26] The young person who came out of these families was "put on his own." According to Bailyn, education had to become self-education, and this is how to account for the strenuous efforts at self-education exemplified by Benjamin Franklin, who was taken by Weber as the outstanding expression of the spirit he was trying to delineate. Bailyn characterizes both Henry Adams and Benjamin Franklin as follows:

[25]Bernard Bailyn, *Education in the Forming of American Society: Needs and Opportunities for Study* (Chapel Hill: University of North Carolina Press, 1960), p. 27.

[26]*The Protestant Ethic . . . ,* p. 115.

. . . both had fought the same battle of locating themselves in an unfamiliar world, a world for which by early training and normal expectation they had not been prepared. Both early in life had realized that the past no longer held the key to the present or future, that the knowledge, traditions, and responses of their parents would not suffice for their needs, that they would have to undertake their own education into careers whose patterns were not only indistinct but non-existent, mere possibilities whose shape they would themselves determine.[27]

5. If expulsion is a factor in the encouragement of the development of agency, then we ought to be able to find some confirmation in a microcosm of expulsion. Such a microcosm exists in the position of the child in the family. Alfred Adler has suggested that "the first-born is in a unique situation; for a while he is an only child and sometime later he is 'dethroned.'"[28] The Bible presents us with the greater agency of Cain, for he kills Abel. According to Tatian, Satan was a first-born.[29] Dethronement is certainly one of the major characteristics of all stories in connection with Satan, who is initially first among the angels and then "dethroned."

A number of empirical studies on first-born children are extremely telling in this connection. There are a whole series of studies relating eminence and birth order, all showing that the relative frequency of first-born children among eminent people far exceeds chance expectation. Havelock Ellis found this to be the case for the most prominent figures listed in the English *Dictionary of National Biography*.[30] Similar findings have been reported for American men of letters, Italian university professors, men starred in *American Men of Science*, persons listed in *Who's Who*, ex-Rhodes scholars, and eminent

---

[27]*Op. cit.*, p. 34.

[28]Alfred Adler, *The Individual Psychology of Alfred Adler: A Systematic Presentation in Selections from His Writings*, ed. Heinz L. and Rowena R. Ansbacher (New York: Basic Books, 1956), p. 377.

[29]Alexander Roberts and James Donaldson (eds.), *Ante-Nicene Christian Library* (Edinburgh: T. and T. Clark, 1867). "And, when men attached themselves to one who was more subtle than the rest, having regard to his being the first-born. . . . but that first-begotten one through his transgression and ignorance becomes a demon . . ." (III, 11-12).

[30]Havelock Ellis, *A Study of British Genius* (London: Hurst and Blackett, 1904).

biologists, physicists, and social scientists.[31] First-born children are considerably overrepresented among college and graduate students, as compared to high school students whose school attendance is required (pp. 761ff.). Among high school students, however, there is a strong relationship between grades and birth rank, the highest average grades being received by the first-born (p. 767). Atkinson and Miller found that first-born children have a greater need for achievement than later-born children.[32] In addition, there is the observation by Schacter, who found, by analyzing the sociometric structure of fraternities and sororities, that first-borns were considerably less popular than later-borns,[33] this being very suggestive that the communion component is less expressed among first-borns.

It must be pointed out, however, that although I believe the dethronement factor is associated with the encouragement of the agency feature in the psyche, and the objective of agency is mastery, agency does not necessarily express itself in achievement. Later, I discuss suicide as an expression of the agentic. At the moment, it is important to qualify the impression of the data cited above with another observation, that suicides in children are also related to birth rank. In a recent study of suicides among school children in the New Jersey public schools, thirty out of forty-one were first-born. The author of this study writes, "There are also indications that children find it especially intolerable to think they have been replaced by a younger sibling in the affections of significant authority figures — parents, teachers, etc."[34]

6. The association of agentic knowledge with the figure of Satan is patent. Agentic knowledge may be understood as that kind of knowledge associated with the enhancement of the ego, in theological thought characteristically referred to as

[31]Stanley Schacter, "Birth Order, Eminence and Higher Education," *American Sociological Review*, XXVIII (1963), 757.

[32]McClelland, *The Achieving Society*, p. 374.

[33]*Op. cit.*, pp. 767-68.

[34]James Jan-Tausch, *Suicide of Children 1960-1963: New Jersey Public School Students* (Trenton, N.J.: Office of Special Education Services, Department of Education, 1965), p. 7.

pride, and that kind of knowledge which serves the mastery objective of the ego, whether this be mastery of other people or of the materials of the world. Agentic knowledge may be distinguished from communion knowledge, in that the former is instrumental and the latter is not. Communion knowledge entails the opening up of regions of experience to contact. This is exemplified in the use of the word "understanding" when one says that one person "understands" another. This is not in the sense of one person being in a position to control the other, but in the sense that there is openness between their psyches. Two meanings of agentic knowledge, the enhancement of the ego and the mastery of the world and people, have hardly been distinguished in the history of Christian thought; indeed, they are hardly distinguishable in the psyche; and together they have prevailed in the image of Satan as it has been projected. The history of the Judeo-Christian tradition has made eating from the tree of knowledge of good and evil the paradigmatic sin of mankind. Only in very recent times have we come to take knowledge as one thing and good and evil as another. Thus, we embrace science, which is knowledge; and whether knowledge serves good or evil is another question. Perhaps the outstanding insight of modern times is precisely that we have seen that agency knowledge has these two characteristics, and that at times evil itself results from the lack of the development of agency knowledge.

Augustine, whose influence has pervaded the history of Christian thought, was clear on the association of knowledge of this world with demons and the Devil. In *The City of God,* he wrote:

. . . the very origin of the name [demon] suggests something worthy of consideration. . . . They are called demons from a Greek word meaning knowledge. . . . The demons . . . have knowledge without charity. . . . The good angels . . . hold cheap all that knowledge of material and transitory things which the demons are so proud of possessing. . . . [The demons] foresee a larger part of the future than men do, by reason of their greater acquaintance with the signs which are hidden from us. Sometimes, too, it is their own intentions they predict . . . by the aid of things temporal and changeable. . . . [They] conjecture the changes that may occur in time, and . . . modify such things by one's own will and faculty — and this is to a certain extent permitted the demons . . . .[35]

What would appear to be the earliest of the Faust figures[36] involved with the Devil in connection with knowledge is present in Augustine's *Confessions:*

I would lay open before my God that nine-and-twentieth year of mine age. There had then come to Carthage a certain Bishop of the Manichees, Faustus by name, a great snare of the Devil, and many were entangled by him through that lure of his smooth language: which though I did commend, yet could I separate from the truth of the things which I was earnest to learn: nor did I so much regard the service of oratory as the science which this Faustus, so praised among them, set before me to feed upon. Fame had before bespoken him most knowing in all valuable learning, and exquisitely skilled in the liberal sciences. And since I had read and well remembered much of the philosophers, I compared some things of theirs with those long

---

[35]*The City of God,* pp. 298-300.

[36]I might add a footnote here in connection with the Faust scholarship. In William Rose's introduction to *The Historie of the Damnable Life and Deserved Death of Doctor John Faustus 1592* (ed. W. K. Pfeiler [Notre Dame, Ind.: University of Notre Dame Press, 1963]), he says, "The first record of an actual magician or adventurer of the name of Faust occurs in a letter written in Latin by the Abbott Trithemius of Würzburg . . . on the 20th of August, 1507" (p. 3). In this letter there is reference to a man who adopted the title *Magister Georgius Sabellicus, Faustus junior.* Rose writes, "It cannot be explained why Faust should have called himself *junior,* for there is no trace of any earlier magician of the same name" (p. 5). I consulted with several scholars of the Faustian literature and was told that if any connection had ever been made of the Fausts of more recent vintage with Augustine's Faust, it must be very obscure, since the generally available treatments do not mention it. Further probing, however, brought Herman Grimm, "Die Entstehung des Volksbuches vom Dr. Faust," *Preussische Jahrbücher,* XLVII (1886), 445-65; Geneviève Bianquis, *Faust à travers quatre siècles* (Paris: E. Droz, 1935); and Charles Dédéyan, *Le thème de Faust dans la littérature Européenne* (Paris: Lettres Modernes, 1954) to my attention as making this connection.

Under any circumstances, the Faustus of Augustine was well known and was never lost sight of in the Middle Ages. Augustine's books were among the most frequently listed works in the catalogues of medieval libraries and among the most frequently cited works in the writings of medieval scholars. When the first serious heresy appeared in medieval Europe, that of the Albigensians in southern France in the twelfth century, the defenders of orthodoxy sought advice and arguments in the writings of Augustine against the Manicheans.

fables of the Manichees, and found the former the more probable; even although they could only prevail so far as to make judgment of this lower world, the Lord of it they could by no means find out. For Thou art great, O Lord, and hast respect unto the humble, but the proud Thou beholdest afar off. Nor dost Thou draw near, but to the contrite in heart, nor art found by the proud, no, not though by curious skill they could number the stars and the sand, and measure the starry heavens, and track the courses of the planets.

For with their understanding and wit, which Thou bestowedst on them, they search out these things; and much have they found out; and foretold, many years before, eclipses of those luminaries, the sun and moon, — what day and hour, and how many digits, — nor did their calculation fail; and it came to pass as they foretold; and they wrote down the rules they had found out, and these are read at this day, and out of them do others foretell in what year and month of the year, and what day of the month, and what hour of the day, and what part of its light, moon or sun is to be eclipsed, and so it shall be, as it is fore-showed. At these things men, that know not this art, marvel and are astonished, and they that know it, exult, and are puffed up; and by an ungodly pride departing from Thee, and failing of Thy light, they foresee a failure of the sun's light, which shall be, so long before, but see not their own, which is. For they search not religiously whence they have the wit, wherewith they search out this. And finding that Thou madest them, they give not themselves up to Thee, to preserve what Thou madest, nor sacrifice to Thee what they have made themselves; nor slay their own soaring imaginations, as fowls of the air, nor their own diving curiosities (wherewith, like the fishes of the sea, they wander over the unknown paths of the abyss), nor their own luxuriousness, as beasts of the field, that Thou, Lord, a consuming fire, mayest burn up those dead cares of theirs, and re-create them-selves immortally.

But they knew not the way, Thy Word, by Whom Thou madest these things which they number, and themselves who number, and the sense whereby they perceive what they number, and the under-standing, out of which they number; or that of Thy wisdom there is no number. But the Only Begotten is Himself made unto us wisdom, and righteousness, and sanctification, and was numbered among us, and paid tribute unto Caesar. They knew not this way whereby to descend to Him from themselves, and by Him ascend unto Him. They knew not this way, and deemed themselves exalted amongst the stars and shining; and behold, they fell upon the earth, and their foolish heart was darkened. They discourse many things truly concerning the creature; but Truth, Artificer of the creature, they seek not piously, and therefore find Him not; or if they find Him, knowing Him to be God, they glorify Him not as God, neither are thankful, but become vain in their imaginations, and profess themselves to be wise, attributing to themselves what is Thine; and thereby with most perverse blindness, study to impute to Thee what is their own, forging lies of Thee who art the Truth, and changing the glory of the uncorruptible God into an image made like corruptible man, and to birds, and four-footed beasts, and creeping things, changing Thy truth into a lie, and worshipping and serving the creature more than the Creator.[37]

Here we have a clear association between being a "great snare of the Devil" and being "knowing in all valuable learning." It is rather interesting also that the knowledge that Augustine discussed is knowledge of astronomy, the discipline which was so critical in ushering in the present age of science.

Great knowledge has been attributed to Satan and the demons by others as well throughout the history of Christianity. Tertullian, who lived in the second and third centuries, attributed their knowledge to their swiftness and ability to be everywhere in a single moment.[38] Isidore of Seville, who lived in the sixth and seventh centuries, attributed it to their keenness of a more subtle sense, their long life, and access to revelation (p. 64). Joseph Hall, an English bishop of the sixteenth and seventeenth centuries, indicated that the evil spirits have immense power, and that their knowledge is equal to their power. This he attributed also to their long experience and their swiftness of movement (p. 91). Glanvil, in a book published in the eighteenth century, *Sadducismus Triumphatus*, defined a witch as "one who can do, or seems to do, strange things beyond the power of art or ordinary nature by virtue of a confederacy with evil spirits" (p. 76).

In John Milton's *Paradise Lost*, we find the full power and knowledge of Satan portrayed. He is, indeed, Milton's central figure; God, Jesus, Adam, and Eve, all somehow pale com-

[37]From *Confessions of St. Augustine,* pp. 65-67. Translated by Edward B. Pusey, D.D. Copyright, 1951, by Washington Square Press. Reprinted by permission of the publishers.
[38]Langton, *op. cit.,* pp. 49-50.

pared to him. One of the critics of Milton, Gilfillan, even expressed concern of the effect "upon Milton's mind from the long presence of his own terrific creation (to be thinking of the Devil for six or ten years together looks like a Satanic possession)."[39] The serpent is the "subtlest beast of all the Field."[40] He persuades Eve that he himself had eaten of the tree, and that it had the effect of altering him:

> Thenceforth to Speculations high or deep
> I turn'd my thoughts, and with capacious mind
> Consider'd all things visible in Heav'n,
> Or Earth, or Middle, all things fair and good; [IX, 602-5].

Of himself, the serpent says,

> ... hee hath eat'n and lives,
> And knows, and speaks, and reasons, and discerns,
> Irrational till then [IX, 764-66].

One of his final arguments is,

> In plain then, what forbids he but to know,
> Forbids us good, forbids us to be wise?
> Such prohibitions bind not... [IX, 758-60].

Milton is an important representative of Protestantism, and we have already discussed the connection between Protestantism and science. Thus, it is interesting to note that the serpent refers to the tree of knowledge as "Mother of science":

> O Sacred, Wise, and Wisdom-giving Plant,
> Mother of Science, Now I feel thy Power
> Within me clear, not only to discern
> Things in their Causes, but to trace the ways
> Of highest Agents deem'd however wise [IX, 679-83].

These lines in *Paradise Lost* come immediately after a discussion of separation; and in Milton there is a kind of confirmation of my psychodynamic hypothesis concerning the nature of agency, of separation being the precondition of mastery, and of the relationship of mastery to the agency

[39]John Milton, *Paradise Lost*, ed. James Robert Boyd (New York: A. S. Barnes and Company, 1854), p. 150.

[40]John Milton, *Paradise Lost*, ed. Merritt Y. Hughes (New York: The Odyssey Press, 1962), Bk IX, l. 86.

feature of the human psyche. According to Milton, Adam and Eve go forth to their labors in the morning, working side by side. But the work is too much for Eve, and she expresses a wish for child labor to help them. In addition, Eve observes that they distract each other in their labor, so that it would be better if they both divide their labor, and work separately.

> ... Thou therefore now advise
> Or hear what to my mind first thoughts present,
> Let us divide our labors, thou where choice
> Leads thee, or where most needs, whether to wind
> The Woodbine round this Arbor, or direct
> The clasping Ivy where to climb, while I
> In yonder Spring of Roses intermix't
> With Myrtle, find what to redress till Noon:
> For while so near each other thus all day
> Our task we choose, what wonder if so near
> Looks intervene and smiles, or object new
> Casual discourse draw on, which intermits
> Our day's work brought to little, though begun
> Early, and th' hour of Supper comes unearn'd [IX, 212-25].

Here we certainly see the Puritan in Milton! Labor is too important to be disturbed by love. The separation makes it possible for the serpent to approach Eve while she is alone. Adam reluctantly agrees to this separation, but he does not quite see the point. Adam argues:

> Yet not so strictly hath our Lord impos'd
> Labor, as to debar us when we need
> Refreshment, whether food, or talk between,
> Food of the mind, or this sweet intercourse
> Of looks and smiles, for smiles from Reason flow,
> To brute deni'd, and are of Love the food,
> Love not the lowest end of human life.
> For not to irksome toil, but to delight
> He made us, and delight to Reason join'd.
> These paths and Bowers doubt not but our joint hands
> Will keep from Wilderness with ease, as wide
> As we need walk, till younger hands ere long
> Assist us: [IX, 235-47].

The elements we have been discussing are clear. Eve is concerned with controlling nature. There is the urge to separate in order to enhance mastery. The fact that, as Adam points out, there is not much purpose to the labor is unimportant. The objective is mastery, aside from the actual need for mastery. From here, Milton takes us directly to Eve's temptation. He ends *Paradise Lost* with Adam and Eve wiping their tears, as Weber pointed out—"Some natural tears they dropt, but wiped them soon"—and facing the world.

The association of knowledge with ego enhancement and power over the world and people comes out clearly also in Geothe's *Faust*. Faust begins in despair concerning his knowledge. He has studied philosophy, jurisprudence, medicine,

> And even, alas! Theology
> All through and through with ardour keen!
> Here now I stand, poor fool, and see
> I'm just as wise as formerly.[41]

His agentic knowledge has reached the limit of its effectiveness:

> I do not imagine I could teach what might
> Convert and improve humanity.
> Nor have I gold or things of worth,
> Or honours, splendours of the earth [ll. 372-75].

This frustration of what I have been calling the agentic leads directly to suicide: "No dog could live thus any more!" (l. 376).

Following this expression of despair, and one pass at the use of magic, he puts a goblet of poison to his lips. The sound of bells and a song of angels interrupt him. It is after this that he turns to the Devil. In this sequence, we see the psychodynamic pattern I have already outlined: the commitment to the agency feature, the despair over its ultimate ineffectiveness, and the projection of the image of Satan.

In Faust's study, with Mephistopheles present in the form

[41]*Op. cit.*, ll. 356-59.

of a dog, there is transition from word, to thought, to power, to deed.

> 'Tis written: "in the beginning was the Word!"
> Here now I'm balked! Who'll put me in accord?
> It is impossible, the *Word* so high to prize,
> I must translate it otherwise
> If I am rightly by the Spirit taught.
> 'Tis written: In the beginning was the *Thought*!
> Consider well that line, the first you see,
> That your pen may not write too hastily!
> Is it then *Thought* that works, creative, hour by hour?
> Thus should it stand: In the beginning was the *Power*!
> Yet even while I write this word, I falter,
> For something warns me, this too I shall alter.
> The Spirit's helping me! I see now what I need
> And write assured: In the beginning was the *Deed*! [ll. 1224-37].

The ego, Freud wrote, "has dethroned the pleasure principle ... and has replaced it by the reality principle, which promises more certainty and greater success."[42] In Faust's discourse with Mephistopheles, Mephistopheles offers him pleasure. But Faust tells Mephistopheles that that is not what he is seeking. Indeed, Faust says,

> If with enjoyment you can fool me,
> Be that for me the final day![43]

Thus, the agreement which he makes with Satan is not for the purpose of winning pleasure, but entails the functioning of the ego. It is "beyond the pleasure principle."

7. Later in this essay, I discuss the significance of children in the life of the psyche, attempting to indicate that in connection with children there may be a fundamental synthesis of the agency and communion features. I argue that when the agentic is unmitigated by the communion feature, the tendency toward infanticide arises. In Goethe's *Faust* three children are born, in all of whom we see the projection of agency unmitigated by communion. The first is the child that Faust

[42]*New Introductory Lectures on Psychoanalysis*, p. 76.
[43]Goethe, *op. cit.*, ll. 1696-97.

has with Gretchen. She kills it. The second child is Homunculus, a "test-tube baby," who is endowed with great knowledge and perception. His creation is a fantasy of agency,
the creation of a living human being through knowledge
without the necessity of sexual union. In response to the question by Mephistopheles of whether he has a "lovesick pair . . .
shut in the chimney-flue" (ll. 6836-37), Wagner, Faust's
assistant, replies:

> May God forbid! Begetting, as men used to do,
> Both vain and senseless we declare.
> The tender point whence life used to begin,
> The gracious outward urgence from within,
> To take and give, to have its likeness known,
> Near and remote alike to make its own—
> All that has lost its former dignity.
> Whereas delighted with it still the beast may be,
> A man with his great gifts must henceforth win
> A higher, ever higher origin [ll. 6838-47].

And, watching the phial, he says:

> It rises, flashes, gathers on;
> A moment, and the deed is done.
> A great design at first seems mad; but we
> Henceforth will laugh at chance in procreation,
> And such a brain that is to think transcendently
> Will be a thinker's own creation [ll. 6865-70].

This wish, which I regard as the fantasy that issues from
agency, which would seek to procreate without communion, is
also put into Adam's mouth by Milton, after Adam has already
eaten of the tree of knowledge:

> O why did God,
> Creator wise, that peopl'd highest Heav'n
> With Spirits Masculine, create at last
> This novelty on earth, this fair defect
> Of nature, and not fill the world at once
> With Men as Angels without Feminine,
> Or find some other way to generate
> Mankind?[44]

[44]Milton, *op. cit.*, Bk X, ll. 888-95.

Later in this essay, I cite a number of investigations dealing with cancer patients which seem to suggest that there is an excessive agency development in them. It may seem startling, at this point, to introduce the consideration of cancer. But cancer is a peculiar disease. A cancerous growth is a growth of a new "organ" within the organism without heterosexuality. I cannot avoid noting the correspondence of cancer growth to this "dream." This observation, which, at the moment, must appear as rude and uncontextual to the reader, is amplified later. If cancer is, as it seems to be, the creation of life without heterosexuality, it corresponds to the dream of the agentic personality as exemplified in these passages from Milton and Goethe. Indeed, it is with the New Testament, in which the communion feature receives the greater emphasis in the Bible, that even creation by God becomes heterosexual. Adam is *created* by God, but Jesus is *begotten* of woman.

The third child in the *Faust* drama is Euphorion, a male offspring of Helena and Faust. Helena, as Goethe's creation, appears as the communion feature which would mitigate the agency feature. When a prisoner is brought before her who is guilty of having been negligent in his watch, he tells her that because he was watching her, he "forgot the warder's duty."[45] She asks that he go free, aware that her beauty evokes the agentic feature in man, who

> Ravishing,
> Seducing, fighting, harrying hither, thither,
> Demigods, heroes, gods, aye, demons also,
> To and fro they led me ever wandering [ll. 9250-53].

Out of the union of Faust and Helena comes Euphorion. Helena says,

> Love, in human wise to bless us,
> Makes Two One in sympathy,
> But us godlike joy possesses
> When Love forms a precious Three [ll. 9699-9702].

[45]Goethe, *op. cit.*, l. 9242.

Agentic sexuality, in which the objective is mastery and ego enhancement, appears in Euphorion,

> Here I drag the sturdy maiden
> Hither to enforced enjoyment;
> For my rapture, for my zest,
> I press her resisting breast,
> Kiss her lips reluctant still,
> Showing thus my strength and will [ll. 9794-99].

Upon the maiden's managing to escape him, he proceeds to climb higher and higher and to try to fly. He falls and dies. In all three instances, there is in Goethe the representation of agency; in the first and third instances, there is the association of agency and death. In the sequence involving Helena, a synthesis is almost achieved, which, however, fails because of the agentic feature which rises so strongly in Euphorion. In the second, there is the dream of agency to have a child without any communion.

In both Milton's *Paradise Lost,* in which the ending is the wiping of tears and facing the world, and Goethe's *Faust,* which begins with the despair of the agentic and the rise of the projected Satan, and ends with

> The Eternal-Womanly
> Draws us above [ll. 12109-10].[46]

there is a cycle. There is the pattern of the rise of unmitigated agency, the separations which take place in the psyche, the effort at mastery, the projection of the image of unmitigated agency, and, finally, the mitigation of agency through the communion feature. In the next chapter, I attempt to indicate the basis for my assumption of an identification of the communion feature of the human psyche with the feminine.

8. The power of manipulation of the human mind, which includes the necessary psychological knowledge, both in

[46]John Milton's *Paradise Regained* (ed. Merritt Y. Hughes [Garden City, N.Y.: Doubleday, Doran and Company, 1937]), ends similarly:

> Thus they the Son of God our Savior meek
> Sung Victor, and from Heavenly Feast refresht
> Brought on his way with joy; hee unobserv'd
> Home to his Mother's house private return'd (Bk IV, ll. 636-39).

terms of knowing what "stimulus" will produce what "response" and the intimate secrets of its content and workings, is characteristic of the image of Satan. He is tempter (Matthew 4:3), father of lies (John 8:44), deceiver (II Corinthians 11:14), subtle (Genesis 3:1). The image of Satan as a manipulator of the mind is tellingly represented by Hawthorne in the person of Roger Chillingworth of *The Scarlet Letter*. This is a novel about an adulteress and her lover, reminiscent of the Biblical tale of Jesus and the adulteress (John 8:3-11). Chillingworth, in the novel, is a physician who, under the guise of attempting to heal Dimmesdale, the lover of his wife, tries to destroy him by insinuating himself into his confidence. Indeed, Chillingworth plays much the role of the contemporary psychotherapist, but with one important difference. The latter attempts to heal, while Chillingworth is bent on destruction. The association of the power over mind and the Devil is very clear in Hawthorne's depiction. In the following passage, we see Chillingworth very clearly in his role as "psychologist."

Thus Roger Chillingworth scrutinized his patient carefully, both as he saw him in his ordinary life, keeping an accustomed pathway in the range of thoughts familiar to him, and as he appeared when thrown amidst other moral scenery, the novelty of which might call out something new to the surface of his character. He deemed it essential, it would seem, to know the man, before attempting to do him good. Wherever there is a heart and an intellect, the diseases of the physical frame are tinged with the peculiarities of these. In Arthur Dimmesdale, thought and imagination were so active, and sensibility so intense, that the bodily infirmity would be likely to have its groundwork there. So Roger Chillingworth — the man of skill, the kind and friendly physician — strove to go deep into his patient's bosom, delving among his principles, prying into his recollections, and probing everything with a cautious touch, like a treasure-seeker in a dark cavern. Few secrets can escape an investigator, who has opportunity and license to undertake such a quest, and skill to follow it up. A man burdened with a secret should especially avoid the intimacy of his physician. If the latter possess native sagacity, and a nameless something more, — let us call it intuition; if he show no intrusive egotism, nor disagreeably prominent characteristics of his own; if he have the power which must be born with him, to bring his mind into such affinity with his patients, that this last shall unawares have spoken what he imagines himself only to have thought; if such revelations be received without tumult, and acknowledged not so often by an uttered sympathy as by silence, an inarticulate breath, and here and there a word, to indicate that all is understood; if to these qualifications of a confidant be joined the advantages afforded by his recognized character as a physician, — then, at some inevitable moment, will the soul of the sufferer be dissolved, and flow forth in a dark, but transparent stream, bringing all its mysteries into the daylight.[47]

But beyond this, Hawthorne clearly identified the "psychologist" as Satan:

To sum up the matter, it grew to be a widely diffused opinion, that the Reverend Arthur Dimmesdale, like many other personages of especial sanctity, in all ages of the Christian world, was haunted either by Satan himself, or Satan's emissary, in the guise of old Roger Chillingworth. This diabolical agent had the Divine permission, for a season, to burrow into the clergyman's intimacy, and plot against his soul [p. 159].

And, in another place, at the point of climax in Dimmesdale's demise: "Had a man seen old Roger Chillingworth, at that moment of his ecstasy, he would have had no need to ask how Satan comports himself when a precious human soul is lost to heaven, and won into his kingdom" (p. 166).

A number of psychologists of the present generation have taken the "prediction and control" of human behavior as their objective, and strive to achieve this by the determination of the "laws," that is, the regularities, of behavior. Herbert Butterfield, in an analysis of the thought of Machiavelli, one of the arch-manipulators of the human mind in history, asserts that the Machiavellian approach to mankind entails the assumption of the unchanging nature of human beings; that there are certain inexorable regularities associated with this nature.[48]

[47]Nathaniel Hawthorne, *The Complete Novels and Selected Tales*, ed. Norman Holmes Pearson (New York: Modern Library, 1937), p. 157.

[48]Herbert Butterfield, *The Statecraft of Machiavelli* (London: G. Bell and Sons, 1940), pp. 30ff.

9. One specific form of power to manipulate others characteristic of the Satanic image is with respect to sexual access, characteristically without affection. In one contract with the Devil, he promises that "By virtue of thy breath, thou wilt inflame with love of thyself all the girls and women whom thou shalt desire to possess. . . ."[49]

In *Faust,* this is the offer Mephistopheles makes.[50] Upon seeing Gretchen, Faust turns to Mephistopheles and requests immediate sexual access. Mephistopheles says that it will take fourteen days, to which Faust replies that he could manage such an enterprise in seven hours and would not need Mephistopheles.

Mephistopheles' instruction to the student on the conquest of women is interesting:

> Learn chiefly how to lead the women; be assured
> That all their "Oh-s" and "Ah-s," eternal, old,
> So thousandfold,
> Can at a single point be cured;
> And if you half-way decorously come,
> You have them all beneath your thumb.
> A title first must make them comprehend
> That your art many arts doth far transcend.
> By way of welcome then you touch all matters
> For sake of which, long years, another flatters.
> Learn how the little pulse to squeeze
> And then with sly and fiery glances seize
> Her freely round the slender hips to see
> How firmly laced up she may be [ll. 2023-36].

10. Contractual obligation is characteristically associated with the image of Satan, most clearly expressed in the pact with the Devil. Associated with this are two characteristics: the pact with the Devil is *for term,* and the Devil unrelentingly demands that the conditions of the pact be fulfilled. It is certainly the case that obligation by covenant or contract is an essential feature of the Old Testament. However, the Biblical

[49]M. Garcon and J. Vinchon, *The Devil: An Historical, Critical and Medical Study,* trans. S. H. Guest (New York: E. P. Dutton & Company, 1930), p. 68.
[50]Goethe, *op. cit.,* ll. 2605ff.

covenant is not for term but for eternity, and man's part of the covenant is not unrelentingly demanded. After all, Adam does not die after his sin, and the children of Israel were not totally destroyed when they defected.

That contractual obligation for term is closely associated with the image of Satan is exemplified in *Doctor Faustus*, which Christopher Marlowe took almost word for word from the 1592 *The Historie of the Damnable Life and Deserved Death of Doctor John Faustus.*

On these conditions following:

First, that Faustus may be a spirit in form and substance;

Secondly, that Mephostophilis shall be his servant and at his command;

Thirdly, that Mephostophilis shall do for him and bring him whatsoever;

Fourthly, that he shall be in his chamber or house invisible;

Lastly, that he shall appear to the said John Faustus at all times in what form or shape soever he please;

I, John Faustus of Wittenberg, doctor, by these presents do give both body and soul to Lucifer, prince of the east, and his minister Mephostophilis, and furthermore grant unto them that, four-and-twenty years being expired, the articles above written inviolate, full power to fetch or carry the said John Faustus, body and soul, flesh, blood, or goods, into their habitation wheresoever.

By me John Faustus.[51]

In the history of Christianity, it is the Devil who stands on the side of unmitigated contractual obligation, as contrasted with Jesus, who stands for the mitigation of contractual obligation by such ideological manifestations of the communion feature such as mercy, kindness, love, and the like. In order to understand this, let us consider some of the relevant material from both the Old and New Testaments.

The notion of contractual obligation is presented in the Old Testament in several ways. There is the promise of God that Adam could live as long as he did not eat of the tree of knowledge of good and evil. There is the Covenant that God

[51]Christopher Marlowe, *Doctor Faustus*, ed. John D. Jump (London: Methuen and Company, 1962), Scene V, ll. 95ff., pp. 30-31.

makes with Abraham, with the circumcision to "be a token of the covenant betwixt me and you" (Genesis 17:11). Similarly, the Sabbath is a sign of the Covenant between God and Israel. In particular, the gathering of food on the Sabbath is specified as a violation in the Old Testament; for when some of the people attempt to gather manna on the Sabbath, they are specifically rebuked: "And it came to pass, that there went out some of the people on the seventh day for to gather, and they found none. And the Lord said unto Moses, How long refuse ye to keep my commandments and my laws?" (Exodus 16:27-28). The keeping of the Sabbath is among the ten commandments that Moses brings down from the mountain (Exodus 20:9-11; Deuteronomy 5:13-15). The violation of the Sabbath is punishable by death. It is singled out of all the commandments to precede the passage which refers to the commandments as written with the finger of God.

And the Lord spake unto Moses, saying, Speak thou also unto the children of Israel, saying, Verily my sabbaths ye shall keep: for it is a sign between me and you throughout your generations; that ye may know that I am the Lord that doth sanctify you. Ye shall keep the sabbath therefore; for it is holy unto you: every one that defileth it shall surely be put to death: for whosoever doeth any work therein, that soul shall be cut off from among his people. Six days may work be done; but in the seventh is the sabbath of rest, holy to the Lord: whosoever doeth any work in the sabbath day, he shall surely be put to death. Wherefore the children of Israel shall keep the sabbath, to observe the sabbath throughout their generations, for a perpetual covenant. It is a sign between me and the children of Israel for ever: for in six days the Lord made heaven and earth, and on the seventh day he rested, and was refreshed. And he gave unto Moses, when he had made an end of communing with him upon mount Sinai, two tables of testimony, tables of stone, written with the finger of God [Exodus 31:12-18].

The Sabbath was thus a deeply significant symbol associated with the Covenant. It is interesting that it is precisely the Sabbath which should have become a major issue between Jesus and the Pharisees in the New Testament. Jesus' violation of the Sabbath was seen by the Pharisees as a violation of the Covenant, and this was one of the major instigating factors in the hostility to him. "Therefore the Jews sought the more to kill him, because he not only had broken the sabbath, but said also that God was his Father, making himself equal with God" (John 5:18). Indeed, such comments by Jesus as "For the Father judgeth no man, but hath committed all judgment unto the Son" (John 5:22) could not but be inflammatory in the context. Not only did Jesus heal the sick on the Sabbath, in the face of the injunction against healing on the Sabbath except in cases where life was in jeopardy, but also defended his disciples for having taken food from the field: "And it came to pass, that he went through the corn fields on the sabbath day; and his disciples began, as they went, to pluck the ears of corn."[52] Jesus' reply to the rebuke was, "The sabbath was made for man, and not man for the sabbath" (Mark 2:27).

One of Jesus' arguments against the Pharisees entails the two symbols of the Covenant, the circumcision and the Sabbath, since circumcision was permitted on the Sabbath. In the contradiction between them, there emerges a new covenant which is freed from its symbols. He said,

Moses therefore gave unto you circumcision; (not because it is of Moses, but of the fathers;) and ye on the sabbath day circumcise a man. If a man on the sabbath day receive circumcision, that the law of Moses should not be broken; are ye angry at me, because I have made a man every whit whole on the sabbath day? Judge not according to the appearance, but judge righteous judgment [John 7:22-24].

In the later development of Christianity, both of these symbols of the Covenant were dropped. Instead of the Sabbath, it is the Lord's day which is celebrated, the "first day of the week."[53] Since this is the day of the resurrection, the change from the last day of the week to the first day of the week had profound significance for the development of Christianity; for the last day of the week seems to refer backward, but the first day of the week refers forward. Paul, who inter-

[52]Mark 2:23; cf. also Matthew 12:1ff. and Luke 6:1ff.
[53]Matthew 28:1; cf. also Mark 16:2, 9; John 20:1, 19.

preted the Old Testament as unrelenting contractual obligation, undid the symbols of the Covenant, the circumcision, the
Sabbath, and other ordinances of the Old Testament:

But before faith came, we were kept under the law, shut up unto
the faith which should afterwards be revealed. Wherefore the law
was our schoolmaster to bring us unto Christ, that we might be
justified by faith. But after that faith is come, we are no longer under a
schoolmaster [Galatians 3:23-25].

And ye are complete in him which is the head of all principality
and power: In whom also ye are circumcised with the circumcision
made without hands, in putting off the body of the sins of the flesh by
the circumcision of Christ: Buried with him in baptism, wherein also
ye are risen with him through the faith of the operation of God, who
hath raised him from the dead. And you, being dead in your sins and
the uncircumcision of your flesh, hath he quickened together with
him, having forgiven you all trespasses; Blotting out the handwriting
of ordinances that was against us, which was contrary to us, and took
it out of the way, nailing it to his cross; And having spoiled principal-
ities and powers, he made a shew of them openly, triumphing over
them in it. Let no man therefore judge you in meat, or in drink, or in
respect of an holyday, or of the new moon, or of the sabbath days:
[Colossians 2:10-16].

Specific contractual obligations as expressed in the Old
Testament, bound by the Covenant and its "seals," the circumcision and the Sabbath, are removed by Christianity. In
the history of Christianity, specific contractual obligation becomes associated with the Devil, the antagonist of Jesus
Christ, expressed in the notion of the Devil pact, in which the
soul is promised in return for temporal favors by the Devil.
But what Christianity "writes into" or projects into the Devil
pact in addition is the *terminal* feature and the removal of any
kind of "escape clause," the latter to be located in the figure of
Jesus.

Although the reasons associated with the repugnance to
usury during the Middle Ages are many and complicated,
nonetheless the "note" containing a promise to deliver at a
specified time is essentially the model of the Devil pact. If we

think of the usurious promissory note as a major device of the Devil, then it is evident that he should sometimes be referred to as the "god of time,"[54] because time is one of its critical elements. Jesus was opposed to the significance of time, expressed, for example, in his words: "Take therefore no thought for the morrow: for the morrow shall take thought for the things of itself" (Matthew 6:34).

Money and wealth, so often the substance of specific contractual obligation among men, are eschewed in the original Christian doctrine. Jesus said, "Lay not up for yourselves treasures upon earth..." (Matthew 6:19) and "No man can serve two masters: for either he will hate the one, and love the other; or else he will hold to the one, and despise the other. Ye cannot serve God and mammon."[55] Money is that which is commonly given and accepted in exchange for goods or services, or, as has been said, money is a medium of exchange acceptable by a stranger. The power of a contract inheres in its appeal to the impersonal social. The relationship between the people involved in a contract is exhaustively specified in the contract, and the specifics are held to be binding.

The history of Christian thought in connection with usury is extremely complicated, and such writers as Tawney have considered it to have been one of that history's major problems. One historian of the question wrote:

. . . from the days of Moses to our own time, the question of the liceity of usury has had a great attraction for the intellect of man. Construction, destruction; reconstruction, redestruction — such is the historian's summary of the result. So thickly are the ruins of shattered systems piled around us that any attempt to extricate ourselves from the confusion must seem well nigh hopeless.[56]

Yet it is clear that, following the Reformation, specific contractual arrangements of men involving money became in-

---

[54]Langton, *op. cit.*, p. 102.

[55]Matthew 6:24; cf. also Luke 16:9ff.

[56]Patrick Cleary, *The Church and Usury: An Essay on Some Historical and Theological Aspects of Money-Lending* (Dublin: M. H. Gill and Son, 1914), p. 178.

creasingly important. Calvin, in his commentary on Ezekiel, argued that usury was not contrary to divine law, pointing out that in the same way that Jesus had indicated that the specific prohibitions from the Old Testament were not binding neither was the injunction against usury (pp. 150ff.). Thus, it turns out, paradoxically, that the argument used by Jesus for the mitigation of contractual obligation was used by Calvin against that Old Testament injunction which precisely sought to avoid one of the most prominent evils of umitigated contractual obligation, the injunction against usury. It is similarly paradoxical that Milton, who in so many ways represented the thought of the Reformation, reaffirmed the propriety of contractual obligation by putting into the *mouth of the serpent* what is essentially the spirit of the New Testament Jesus. For, in the same way that Jesus addressed the Pharisees when he healed a man with a withered hand on the Sabbath with "Is it lawful to do good on the sabbath days, or to do evil?" (Mark 3:4), so does the serpent challenge Eve, by telling her that prohibitions against what is good are not binding (see p. 65 above). The Reformation tended to strengthen rather than weaken the binding quality of contractual arrangements. That characteristic of Satan was withdrawn from the projected image back into man, and the tendency to mitigate obligation was projected into the serpent by Milton, a dramatic reversion from the New Testament.

11. Weber cited some of Benjamin Franklin's writings as containing "that spirit which contains what we are looking for in almost classical purity,"[57] the spirit of capitalism which emerged from the Reformation. In this passage we see the elements we have been discussing:

"Remember, that *time* is money. He that can earn ten shillings a day by his labour, and goes abroad, or sits idle, one half of that day, though he spends but sixpence during his diversion or idleness, ought not to reckon *that* the only expense; he has really spent, or rather thrown away, five shillings besides.

[57]*The Protestant Ethic . . .*, p. 48.

"Remember, that *credit* is money. If a man lets his money lie in my hands after it is due, he gives me the interest, or so much as I can make of it during that time. This amounts to a considerable sum where a man has good and large credit, and makes good use of it.

"Remember, that money is of the prolific, generating nature. Money can beget money, and its offspring can beget more, and so on. Five shillings turned is six, turned again it is seven and threepence, and so on, till it becomes a hundred pounds. The more there is of it, the more it produces every turning, so that the profits rise quicker and quicker. He that kills a breeding-sow, destroys all her offspring to the thousandth generation. He that murders a crown, destroys all that it might have produced, even scores of pounds."

"Remember this saying, *The good paymaster is lord of another man's purse.* He that is known to pay punctually and exactly to the time he promises, may at any time, and on any occasion, raise all the money his friends can spare. This is sometimes of great use. After industry and frugality, nothing contributes more to the raising of a young man in the world than punctuality and justice in all his dealings; therefore never keep borrowed money an hour beyond the time you promised, lest a disappointment shut up your friend's purse for ever.

"The most trifling actions that affect a man's credit are to be regarded. The sound of your hammer at five in the morning, or eight at night, heard by a creditor, makes him easy six months longer; but if he sees you at a billiard-table, or hears your voice at a tavern, when you should be at work, he sends for his money the next day; demands it, before he can receive it, in a lump.

"It shows, besides, that you are mindful of what you owe; it makes you appear a careful as well as an honest man, and that still increases your credit.

"Beware of thinking all your own that you possess, and of living accordingly. It is a mistake that many people who have credit fall into. To prevent this, keep an exact account for some time both of your expenses and your income. If you take the pains at first to mention particulars, it will have this good effect: you will discover how wonderfully small, trifling expenses mount up to large sums, and will discern what might have been, and may for the future be saved, without occasioning any great inconvenience."

"For six pounds a year you may have the use of one hundred pounds, provided you are a man of known prudence and honesty.

"He that spends a groat a day idly, spends idly above six pounds a year, which is the price for the use of one hundred pounds.

"He that wastes idly a groat's worth of his time per day, one day with another, wastes the privilege of using one hundred pounds each day.

"He that idly loses five shillings' worth of time, loses five shillings, and might as prudently throw five shillings into the sea.

"He that loses five shillings, not only loses that sum, but all the advantage that might be made by turning it in dealing, which by the time that a young man becomes old, will amount to a considerable sum of money [pp. 48-50].

Here we have the significance of time, a major feature of both the promissory note and the Devil pact, the significance of money, which is eschewed in the New Testament, and the relationship between them. Interest is defended much as it was by Calvin. The notion that money is not sterile, which is so pointedly expressed by Franklin, reflects Calvin's quarrel with Aristotle. For Aristotle had argued that usury is against Natural Law, since metals are barren, making the begetting of money by money illegitimate. This opinion Calvin did not agree with.[58] Not only did Franklin urge the full acceptance of the binding character of a promissory note, but urged going even beyond this: to impress the creditor, let the hammer sound at five in the morning, and stay away from the billiard-table and the tavern! This, and the remainder of the passage, is an injunction for the ego to manage and control the whole of life, and thus to spend that life, to old age, "laying up treasures," which was enjoined against by Jesus.

The contract was the basis for feudal government, and certainly the contract was not novel to the Reformation. However, following the Reformation, contractualism became much more pervasive as the basis for the regulation of inter-personal relationships. In the thought of some of the political philosophers, contractualism became the dominant basis for the analysis of the nature of government. In modern times, some social scientists, evidently still under this influence, have taken it as the essence of social interaction. This is, for example, explicitly stated in a paper by George C. Homans.

[58]Cleary, *op. cit.*, pp. 28ff., 150ff.

In this paper, Homans asserts that all social behavior is illuminated by "adopting the view that interaction between persons is an exchange of goods, material and non-material."[59] He would attempt to understand all interactions among people in terms of the formula: "Profit= Reward − Cost." Historically, this is the basis for interaction which is associated with the image of the Devil. As Goethe put it,

> The Devil is an egoist
> And not "for God's sake!" only will he do
> What will another's needs assist.[60]

This characteristic of the "egoist" was made a general characteristic of mankind by Adam Smith, rather than just a characteristic of economic arrangements. In the passage from Smith quoted above (see p. 34), this is very clear. That a contemporary sociologist such as Homans can be tempted into making this the basis for all social interactions is indicative of the degree to which this general condition which we have been describing is prevalent in the contemporary world, the world which has issued out of the Reformation, and the corresponding rise of the significance of economic relationships, the connection between the latter two having been so well pointed out by Weber.

12. Our considerations concerning the development of mastery as a stage in the history of Satanism bring us to a consideration of one of the critical developmental stages in the life of the individual, that which Freud referred to as the anal stage. Characterisics such as thrift, methodicalness, orderliness, punctuality, reliability have characteristically been noted in psychoanalytic literature as associated with the anal personality, essentially the characteristics associated with the spirit of capitalism which Weber described. In the vernacular, a large sum of money is referred to as a "pile." Freud expressed the relationship between feces and gold in a letter to

---

[59]George C. Homans, "Social Behavior as Exchange," *American Journal of Sociology,* LXIII (May, 1958), 597.

[60]*Op. cit.,* ll. 1651-53.

Fliess in connection with the Devil.[61] The Devil is characteristically "cast out," and resistance to the Devil is to tell him, "Get thee behind me" (Luke 4:8). In two recent treatments dealing with the development of Protestantism, Erikson's *Young Man Luther* and Brown's *Life Against Death*, there is material which strongly indicates that, in the way human history at large is related to the intrinsically human qualities of the individuals involved, there are deep relationships between the development of Protestantism and the residua of the anal stage of development.[62] Brown, for example, cites the passage from Luther which includes the words: "Therefore it is God's justice which justifies us and saves us. And these words became a sweeter message for me. This knowledge the Holy Spirit gave me on the privy in the tower" (p. 202). He develops at length the "hypothesis . . . that there is some mysterious intrinsic connection between the Protestant illumination and the privy" (p. 206). He cites material which indicates that there is a strong relationship between Luther's preoccupation with the Devil, the completely anal character of the Devil, the this-wordliness of the Devil, and the way in which these character traits became dominant in the Protestant world.

At this point, let me introduce some considerations from psychoanalysis. In a paper entitled *Character and Anal Erotism*, Freud drew attention to the relationships of adult personality and certain features of the anal stage of development.

Among those whom we try to help by our psycho-analytic efforts we often come across a type of person who is marked by the pos-

[61]From *The Origins of Psycho-Analysis, Letters to Wilhelm Fliess, Drafts and Notes: 1887-1902*, by Sigmund Freud, ed. Marie Bonaparte, Anna Freud, and Ernst Kris; trans. Eric Mosbacher and James Strachey, pp. 188-89, © 1954 by Basic Books, Inc., Publishers, New York.

[62]Erik H. Erikson, *Young Man Luther: A Study in Psychoanalysis and History* (New York: W. W. Norton Company, 1958); Norman O. Brown, *Life Against Death: The Psychoanalytical Meaning of History* (Middletown, Conn.: Wesleyan University Press, 1959).

session of a certain set of character-traits, while at the same time our attention is drawn to the behaviour in his childhood of one of his bodily functions and the organ concerned in it. . . .

The people I am about to describe are noteworthy for a regular combination of the three following characteristics. They are especially *orderly, parsimonious* and *obstinate*.[63]

In a later part of this paper, he tied this in with the reactions of the latency period and referred to "cleanliness, orderliness, and reliability" (p. 48) and "shame, disgust, and morality" (p. 47).

During the period of life which may be called the period of "sexual latency"—i.e. from the completion of the fifth year to the first manifestations of puberty (round about the eleventh year)— reaction-formations, or counter-forces, such as shame, disgust and morality, are created in the mind. They are actually formed at the expense of the excitations proceeding from the erotogenic zones, and they rise like dams to oppose the later activity of the sexual instincts. Now anal erotism is one of the components of the [sexual] aims. It is therefore plausible to suppose that these character-traits of orderliness, parsimony and obstinacy, which are so often prominent in people who were formerly anal erotics, are to be regarded as the first and most constant results of the sublimation of anal erotism [p. 171].

If we take this characterization seriously, as I think we should, and, in addition, take seriously the historical association of the Devil with excrement and the anal region, these characteristics in the Protestant personality, and the relationship of all of this to the mastery feature of the human organism, we need to consider the relationship of the anal stage to the nature of the human psyche.

Turning away from excrement is paradigmatic of repression. One of Freud's early formulations of the nature of repression was to regard it as the nose turning away from what smells bad. The anal region is precisely the region that is not "faced." This paradigmatic repression is associated first with the anal stage and then with the latency period, periods of repression

[63]Freud, *Standard Edition*, IX, 169.

and growth of the ego in which the individual is committed to the mastery of the world, and in which he is, because of forces within him, most "educable."

The anal stage is related to mastery in several ways. First, it is related to self-mastery. The urge to defecate is, in the earlier stage of life, one which is in no way related to any self-mastery. "Toilet-training" consists in the individual becoming a master over the urge, learning to delay the defecation until the time and the place are appropriate, to put the urge to defecate under the control of the will.

Second, it is related to the separation of the individual from other people. Defecation is done in "private." If, indeed, there are relations between privacy, Protestantism, and individualism, as I have suggested, the earliest learning of privacy is in connection with the act of defecation. The early Puritan churches, such as the Old North Church in Boston, were arranged in private cubicles, called "pews," between which there were walls. It might be pointed out that the word "pew" as referring to the furniture of a church does not occur, according to the *Oxford Universal Dictionary*, until 1631, soon after the beginning of the Reformation. One cannot avoid the observation that the word is also indicative of foul odor. In the act of defecation, the individual receives his first lessons in independence from other people.

Third, in the act of defecation the individual learns some of his first lessons in distinguishing between the self and the inorganic not-self, a distinction which is critical in becoming a master. For feces constitute the margin between the organic and the inorganic world. Material which has been part of the self becomes material which is part of the not-self. It is that part of the individual which regularly becomes part of the inorganic world. Erikson, in *Childhood and Society*, tells the story of Peter, a four-year-old boy whom he treated.[64] The boy had retained fecal matter for a week and was unwilling to

[64]Erik H. Erikson, *Childhood and Society* (New York: W. W. Norton Company, 1950), pp. 49-54.

defecate. Investigation by Erikson revealed that the child was of the opinion that the fecal matter was alive, that it was a baby with which he was pregnant. The therapy consisted, in part, in making the child aware that the fecal matter was not alive and not a part of his living body.

Fourth, anality is related to defiance of other people. As Freud pointed out in this essay, the exposure of one's buttocks is a characteristic gesture of defiance. It is an act associated with the arrogation to one's self of agency, against any deference to others. An astute psychological observation by Ferenczi is that the emission of flatus by a patient during analysis signifies that the patient would arrogate to himself this "adult prerogative."[65] Brown cites a passage in which Luther said that he routed the Devil with this "same weapon."[66]

Fifth, the anal stage is the stage in life in which the child apprehends himself as a separate *living* creature; and with the emergence of the sense of self as alive, there is necessarily the corresponding sense of the possibility of death. Feces, the concrete part of the body which is closest to death, must be mastered. In "turning away" from the feces, the individual is turning away from "facing" death as a possibility. The individual develops a repressive ego whose function it will be to help the individual "face" life, that is, to master it, and he does so, in part, by "turning away" from that which is critically symbolic of the death of the individual. The way the ego has of turning toward the inorganic world is then, in part, a way of mastering death, but has within it the very thing which it would avoid. It has converted the whole world which it faces into a world of the inorganic and lifeless, the world of the feces it would reject. Later, I discuss the problem of the differentiation of the sexes and the having of children. I might say at this point, however, that infant care requires the ability to overcome the repression associated with the repugnance to feces.

[65]Sandor Ferenczi, *Further Contributions to the Theory and Technique of Psychoanalysis,* comp. John Rickman, trans. Jane Isabel Suttle (New York: Basic Books, 1953), p. 325.
[66]*Op. cit.,* p. 208.

DENIAL

The third stage in the natural history of Satanism after separation and mastery is denial. The neurosis is very important, because it is the central phenomenon out of which a number of considerations of which I have spoken emerge. It was out of the considerations associated with the neurotic individual that Freud came to his particular approach. Denial, in the Freudian framework, is the nub of neurosis. The neurosis arises out of the separation within the individual, the effort of mastery, and the denial of elements resulting from separation. One of the most significant lessons of psychoanalysis is that what has been denied does not go out of existence, but remains active and makes for mischief. Let us consider the kinds of mischief which are thus wrought.

Denial leads to deviousness. The demonstration of this thesis is the major burden of Freud's writings, particularly clearly presented in *The Interpretation of Dreams*. The repressed material seeks expression, and, being blocked in direct expression, disguises itself in various forms so that it may be expressed, and at the same time elude recognition. The very denial of the diabolic within ourselves is precisely the condition that produces the projection which is the fundamental mechanism which makes for the existence of the Satan image.

Denial leads to the repetition compulsion. In Freud's effort to explicate the death instinct, he took the compulsion to repeat as a prime manifestation of the work of the ego and the major hint of the existence of the death instinct. The ego attempts to convert the flow of existence into things which are of an unchanging nature, so that repetition brings mastery and surprise is ruled out. With this comes a cessation of growth, a denial to consciousness of much that would enrich existence. There is fear of all that is repressed, for it has not been managed, and this fear manifests itself in anxiety. Fenichel saw repetition as the essential feature of the neurosis: the "patients, instead of reacting vividly to actual stimuli according to their specific nature, react repeatedly with rigid patterns."[67] Much of the contemporary hunger for meaningfulness is based on the monotonousness of what the ego will allow and the deep but unacknowledged fear of what is not acknowledged.

Denial makes for behavior which is out of control. This is one of the great paradoxes associated with the development of the ego. Mastery is the function of the ego. In order to master, the ego rules things out of existence. Yet it is often what is ruled out that arises and asserts itself, so there is no mastery precisely where mastery was sought. Crimes of violence and passion are committed daily by people of whom it might be said, in a sense, that the egos are strong. In the political sphere there are people like Adolf Hitler, in whom, although the ego appeared strong, there was an eruption of things which we regard as abhorrent. In a study of delinquents done under the direction of Carl R. Rogers, it was found that the single best predictor of later behavior, to the surprise of even the investigators, was the degree of self-understanding.[68] The romantic ideal of innocence can become diabolical, in the sense of evil, as in the case of Hitler. For the protest of innocence is closely connected with the effort to destroy that which one finds repugnant, resulting as it did in Nazi Germany in an interminable sequence of murders that stopped only when the ego which perpetrated those murders was itself destroyed.

## TO BEHOLD THAT WHICH HAS BEEN DENIED

Let us now turn to the fourth, and what we may consider to be the most paradoxical stage in the natural history of Satan-

---

[67]Otto Fenichel, *The Psychoanalytic Theory of Neurosis* (New York: W. W. Norton Company, 1945), p. 542.

[68]Cited by Rogers in Rollo May, *Existential Psychology* (New York: Random House, 1961), p. 91; C. R. Rogers, Bill L. Kell, and Helen McNeil, "The Role of Self-Understanding in the Prediction of Behavior," *Journal of Consulting Psychology*, XII (1948), 174-86.

ism, the beholding of that which has been denied. As death is intrinsic to the ego, as Freud pointed out, so is the termination of the agentic, the final stage in the natural history of Satanism. In this last stage, the diabolical can pass into healing. The major difficulty associated with this stage is that it *appears* to be diabolical; and it is precisely for this reason that many of the paradoxes associated with the myths and psychological conditions associated with Satanism arise. *For when separations are made and parts denied, diabolical qualities are attributed to the denied parts, rather than to the separation itself.* Thus, we have the paradox that to behold what was denied appears to be diabolical; and yet it is the necessary way in which the diabolical is overcome. It is in this way that we can understand the various features of the psychoanalytic approach which give it the appearance of being diabolical. "Playing the Devil" enables one to overcome the evil consequences of repression. One of the major contributions of psychoanalytic thought was the recognition that thinking of evil is different from evil action, and that bringing into consciousness that which is denied as evil is a device whereby the individual may be prevented from "acting out." This fourth stage in the natural history of Satanism, appearing diabolical, undoes the actual evil that the unmitigated agency in the individual might lead him to engage in. It is in this way that we can understand the various references that Freud made to himself as diabolical. The title page of Freud's *The Interpretation of Dreams* contains the motto *"Flectere si nequeo superos, Acheronta movebo"* (If the gods above are no use to me, then I'll move all hell) from Virgil's *Aeneid*. In a letter to Fliess, written while he was working on *The Interpretation of Dreams,* he wrote, "It is an intellectual hell, layer upon layer of it, with everything fitfully gleaming and pulsating; and the outline of Lucifer-Amor coming into sight at the darkest centre."[69] In talking to his associates, he once commented, "Do

[69]Freud, *The Origins of Psycho-Analysis*, p. 323.

you not know that I am the Devil? All my life I have had to play the Devil. . . ."[70] To "play the Devil" turns on the paradox of the way in which "nothing is holy" becomes "nothing is profane." To "play the Devil" means to allow thought to go as it will, fully to face the fact that human thought can be devious, and thereby to overcome the evil which is associated with deviousness. To "play the Devil" means to enter into the realm of the Devil, and to understand that realm. To "play the Devil" means that we enter into the deepest portions of the psyche to overcome the psychophobia which is associated with diabolism, even though such entry into the psyche itself appears to be diabolical. To "play the Devil" means to try to behold that which is "behind," for, as we saw in the discussion of anality, the fear of beholding is associated with the projection of the Devil.

In this fourth stage of the natural history of Satanism, the objective of mastery is surrendered. The evil associated with Roger Chillingworth was that he entered upon the psyche of Arthur Dimmesdale to destroy him. He used his knowledge of the intrapsychic processes of Dimmesdale for the purposes of his own ego and its urge to master. In the psychoanalytic process, we can see the surrender of the urge to master take place in two ways. First, the surrender of mastery is essential for free association. To engage in free association, one must surrender the faculty associated with the ego and its business of mastery. Second, understanding is substituted for mastery. The objective of the psychoanalytic process is insight, which means understanding in the literal sense of "seeing within." Mastery emerges, but it is a mastery which is not based on the restriction of that which is to be beheld. Here is contained the paradox that the surrender of mastery in the ego's sense results in a more profound mastery.

In the Christian concept of salvation, there is a partial

[70]R. Laforgue, "Persönliche Erinnerungen an Freud," *Lindauer Psychotherapiewoche* (1954), p. 49. (Quotation translated by the present author.) Cf. Bakan, *Sigmund Freud and the Jewish Mystical Tradition*, pp. 187ff.

understanding of this process, involving the surrender of the ego. It recognizes the limitations of attempting to manage life completely on the basis of the ego, recognizes that there is no way of being on earth which is completely safe and provided for. It acknowledges the existence of regions which have been denied by the ego. It encourages openness, receptivity, trust, and faith, which entail the surrender of the dominion of the ego. What has characteristically been lacking in the notion of salvation is the recognition of the increase of understanding through salvation. The Christian notion of salvation acknowledges a realm of understanding but falls short in penetrating it. It recognizes the partiality of knowledge, but attempts to complete this knowledge by faith alone. In *The City of God*, we read that "in the case of things which are perceived by the mind and spirit, *i.e.* which are remote from our own interior sense, it behooves us to trust those who have seen them set in that incorporeal light, or abidingly contemplate them."[71] Augustine saw the way to a fundamental *reconciliation* of the split in man which should be overcome. But he rested too comfortably in the image of the Christ, seeing it as part of the divine wisdom and not sufficiently in his own power.

But since the mind, itself, though naturally capable of reason and intelligence, is disabled by besotting and inveterate vices not merely from delighting and abiding in, but even from tolerating His unchangeable light, until it has been gradually healed, and renewed, and made capable of such felicity, it had, in the first place, to be impregnated with faith, and so purified. And that in this faith it might advance the more confidently towards the truth, the truth itself, God, God's Son, assuming humanity without destroying His divinity, established and founded this faith, that there might be a way for man to man's God through a God-man. For this is the Mediator between God and men, the man Christ Jesus. For it is as man that He is the Mediator and the Way. Since, if the way lieth between him who goes, and the place whither he goes, there is hope of his reaching it; but if there be no way, or if he know not where it is, what boots it to know whither he should go? Now the only way that is infallibly secured

---

[71]Augustine, *The City of God*, p. 347.

against all mistakes, is when the very same person is at once God and man, God our end, man our way [pp. 346-47].

I suggest that Augustine lacked full faith in the possibility of understanding and stopped short at Christ Jesus; that he was too much possessed of the sense of the split between God and man, and attempted to overcome the split not by actually overcoming it, but by a *Mediator,* a notion which presumes the validity of the separation. I might again refer to the notion that sinfulness inheres in the separation of man from God.

In the fourth stage of the natural history of Satanism, it is important to be able to overcome repugnance and bear the anxiety which is associated with overcoming separation. Theologically, this is to recognize that there are not two "cities" such as Augustine conceived of, but one, that the divine is not multiple but singular. Psychologically, this requires overcoming repugnance, bearing anxiety, beholding what has been repressed, and increasing understanding. The myth of the holy sparks to which I alluded earlier is helpful, for in this myth the holy sparks were completely dispersed and might be discovered anywhere. The corresponding myth in Protestant theology has been that the dispersal of God's grace is unknown, although it still defers to the separation of those in and out of grace and makes the source of grace something "other" than man. It should perhaps be noted at this point that Freud was Jewish, in the sense that he was within a tradition that regarded the Jews as the "chosen people," much as he felt the notion was artificially imposed upon the Jews by a renegade Egyptian.[72] That he was the favorite child of his mother is also relevant. Implicit in his thought was the notion that all of mankind was in grace insofar as the unconscious, which was universal, was divine.

Grace is both precondition and result. Grace, in the Christian tradition, is God's favor to man: But "God commendeth his love toward us, in that, while we were yet sinners, Christ died for us" (Romans 5:8). It is completely independent of man's

[72]Sigmund Freud, *Moses and Monotheism* (New York: Vintage Books, 1955).

agency. It is the spontaneous gift of God to man. Psychologically, it is something like the unqualified satisfaction of dependency which a child might experience in the hands of its parents; and I might make the banal yet important observation that he who has experienced the proper satisfaction of his dependency in childhood would be the person most likely to feel "in grace." The Christian notion of grace is closer to the infantile and invites the psychoanalytic theory which is concerned with the infantile. In adulthood, it is understanding which is associated with grace. To "play the Devil" in adulthood is to try to understand, in full confidence that this can be done without ultimate catastrophe.

"Playing the Devil" entails the suspension of belief. As has been indicated, Freud distinguished between his being *advocatus diaboli* and the possibility of having sold himself to the Devil; and this means following a line of thought wherever it leads, without necessarily believing. Being in grace allows the suspension of belief; for suspension of belief entails suspension of mastery. Psychologically and sociologically, belief is associated with belonging to a group, to sharing its ideology in a profound manner. When one embarks upon investigation, there is a threat to this fundamental belonging, but it is a threat which may be mitigated by the suspension of belief.

Investigation also involves distinction, criticality, and the like, which I have associated with the growth of the ego and the development of Satanism. Whereas, however, in the development of ego-knowledge associated with the mastery of the world in a direct purposeful manner belief is not suspended, it is suspended in this fourth stage. In this stage, there is always the full recognition of the partiality of intellectual pursuit, the full recognition of its diabolic character in the sense of split. One "goes along" with the Devil, but does not sell one's self to him, that is, one suspends belief. One allows the thought to go where it will, in full confidence that thought does not lead to ultimate catastrophe. One of the reasons for the anti-intellectuality which has sometimes been associated with Christianity is that Christianity, which allowed itself to distinguish between faith and reason and to ask for a decision as to which to believe in, did not effectively suspend belief to be able to enter into this stage. Belongingness and the associated commitment to belief have generally been too strong to allow this. The suspension of belief not only makes it possible to enter upon the diabolical paths of ego knowledge and mastery, but also to enter upon a realm in which surprise is never threatening; and, as Theodor Reik has maintained, surprise is a central feature of the method of psychoanalysis.[73] It provides a way of encountering a universe of human existence which is not necessarily "clean, orderly, and reliable."

HEALING

The major validation associated with the last stage of the development of Satanism is healing. In this stage, Satanism fuses with Messianism. Historically, the Devil appeared when *all else failed,* which we can translate into psychological terms as the failure of the ego to master; when, in spite of all the efforts of the ego, hopelessness prevailed. The Devil is projected in despair when the agentic has failed. But it is also a beginning of overcoming the aversion to that which has been denied, of facing the projection. One of the paradoxes of our religious history has been that the healing role of the Devil is taken over the by the Messianic figures, a paradox which we can now understand. For, in both instances, the effort involves the surrender of the mastery feature of the ego and the reuniting of that which has been split apart. It is fully understandable that the growth of the whole of the psychoanalytic mode of thought should have been in the context of healing; and that, furthermore, it should be regarded by some as the work of the Devil.

There is tension today within psychology and psychiatry

[73]Theodor Reik, *Surprise and the Psycho-Analyst; On the Conjecture and Comprehension of Unconscious Processes* (London: Paul, Trench, Trubner and Company, 1936).

with respect to what is the best strategy in the matter of healing, between an ever greater commitment to the ego and its functioning, or to the suspension of the ego and the reuniting of the separations which are associated with the ego. This tension reflects itself in enormous conflict with respect to role models for the people engaged in the effort to heal others. This conflict is very well expressed by Carl Rogers in his paper "Persons or Science? A Philosophic Question."[74]

One role model which has a strong hold over therapists is that of the "scientist." In this role, one is a discoverer by careful methodological canons, a writer and reader of technical papers, a studied unbeliever in that which is not carefully demonstrated to the senses, vision in particular, and an intense effacer of features of the personality not closely connected with the ego functions. The word "control" is important, not only as designating certain procedures with respect to the investigatory enterprise, but much more largely. The therapist in this sense is very much the "repairman."[75] He is a personage familiar enough in modern times. When the role is not corrupt and vulgar, it is self-effacing, polite, formal, pleasant. Technical competence dominates all other aspects of personality. Everything is subservient to efficient performance and competence. Interest is limited to matters of fact. The repairman has license to investigate as thoroughly as the situation demands, but only with respect to the impersonal. He is supposed to get little pleasure from his work except that of having done a job well. He proceeds systematically, methodically, efficiently, parsimoniously, economically, and deferentially toward the clearly and unambiguously previously defined objective. Unfortunately, there are few clear and un-

---

[74]Carl R. Rogers, *On Becoming a Person: A Therapist's View of Psychotherapy* (Boston: Houghton Mifflin Company, 1961), pp. 199-224.

[75]This part of the discussion is essentially the same as a set of ideas earlier presented in a paper, David Bakan, "Psychotherapist: Healer or Repairman," *Merrill-Palmer Quarterly of Behavior and Development,* VIII (April, 1962), 129-32.

ambiguous predecisions concerning man's thoughts, feelings, and wishes in psychotherapy. Also unfortunate for this strategy is the fact that objectives for the kind of being one wishes to become comprise the intrinsically unfinished business of life. The behaviorists have boasted that they could produce any kind of human being one might specify. Suffice it to say that in spite of the strained efforts along these lines, there is little promise in this kind of approach in connection with psychotherapy.

Consider the healer-role. For the reasons already indicated, there is always the danger that this will be seen as a form of diabolical charlatanry. The healer is a personage who abides in Western civilization. For almost two thousand years, Jesus as healer has been imitated. Characteristically, the healer is religiously involved but is outside the formal religious institutions, the latter tending to enter into the service of the ego. The first step in healing is to ask for the suspension of the ego, to ask for faith or to ask the patient to say everything that comes into his mind, or to seek to form a "transference" in the relationship, or, as Carl Rogers would do, to suspend his own ego functions as a way of encouraging the client to do the same.

The healer attempts in one way or another to untie sin from suffering. He attempts to create an atmosphere in which it is "alright" with respect to what is denied and rejected. The healer attempts to break up the sense of the relationship between suffering and sin, aware that by overcoming barriers, healing is made possible. The ways of overcoming the sense of the relationship between suffering and sin are multiple. The healer may take the sins upon himself, point out that Jesus takes the sins upon himself, locate the evil in the alien, stress the mercy of God; he may assert a deterministic metaphysics in the form of religious predestination or secular determinism; he may assert that the suffering is lodged in the infantile and therefore the unresponsible; he may remove it from the ego and locate the difficulty in the unconscious. This is in contrast to the method of atonement, in the sense of voluntarily appeasing and giving "satisfaction" to God by punishing oneself. Atonement presupposes the connection between sin and suffering and is an ego-method for coming to terms with them. It is an effort to make correction of agency through agency. One of the significant features of the Christian notion of the crucifixion of Jesus as a way of salvation is that it has separated the agency feature from the process of atonement, ascribing agency to God. In order for the individual to benefit from this atonement, it is only necessary that he be open to salvation; that is, he should surrender his agency and be saved through God's mercy.

The healer assumes that the forces for healing are already inherent in the sufferer, and these forces are to be released. In contrast to the repairman, the healer does not attempt to supply the efficient cause, but only to permit the existing forces to operate. One of the important issues in connection with psychotherapy has been precisely the question of the role of agency on the part of the therapist. In his early thinking, Freud believed that if the therapist were simply to supply the interpretations, somehow the patient would be healed. Rogers, on the other hand, has attempted to be meticulous in not taking over agency, believing firmly in the existence of the healing forces within the individual. It must be pointed out, however, that Freud had indicated some misgivings about the possibility of "inducing [the patient] by human influence ... to abandon his resistances,"[76] and in this respect, Rogerian therapy, is more consonant with the healer role than classical Freudian therapy.

The healer cognizes and indicates the cosmological and existential entailment of the suffering. This is the burden of much of Freud's nonclinical writings. The healer points out the meaning of the individual's life in regions which extend

[76]*Beyond the Pleasure Principle,* p. 18.

far beyond the highly circumscribed life of the ego in every-day consciousness.

The major device which the healer uses is communication. He enhances communication between himself and the person who is to be healed; and he enhances communication among the regions of existence, the holy and the mundane, the unconscious and the conscious. The objective of healing is overcoming despair, overcoming alienation, and eliminating anxiety. It seeks in the Christian tradition to produce holiness, which word, in its Anglo-Saxon root, means whole and well. And it does this by attempting to open communication with all of the lost material associated with the denials which have previously been exercised.

The healer in his healing relationship runs the great risk, or what is sensed as risk, associated with the surrender of the mastery of the ego. Rogers is very aware of this and indicates that courage is a necessary element in the personality of the therapist.

. . . to carry on psychotherapy . . . is to take a very real risk, and that courage is required. If you really understand another person in this way, if you are willing to enter his private world and see the way life appears to him, without any attempt to make evaluative judgments, you run the risk of being changed yourself. You might see it his way, you might find yourself influenced in your attitudes or your personality. The risk of being changed is one of the most frightening prospects most of us can face. If I enter, as fully as I am able, into the private world of a neurotic or psychotic individual, isn't there a risk that I might become lost in that world? . . . The great majority of us could not *listen;* we would find ourselves compelled to *evaluate,* because listening would seem too dangerous. So the first requirement is courage, and we do not always have it.[77]

The healer-role is one which entails understanding. But we need again to distinguish between the two meanings associated with this word. The first meaning is that which is associated with the ego. It entails the separation of the knower

[77]Rogers, *On Becoming a Person*, p. 333.

from the known, tending to make an object of that which is known, distinguished from the subject, the knower. The second meaning of the word "understanding" is that of coming into intimate contact with. The latter is the sense of the word which Rogers employs when he says that he launches himself into the clinical relationship "having a hypothesis, or a faith, that my liking, my confidence, and my understanding of the other person's inner world, will lead to a significant process of becoming" (p. 201).

The first sense of the word "understanding" is related to splitting. It is this which has been the object of attack by Alfred Korzybski in *Science and Sanity*[78] and in the general semantics movement. Korzybski indeed saw the Devil in Aristotle's highly ego-oriented philosophy, a philosophy which made split, the distinction between A and not-A, its distinguishing mark. It was precisely in the tendency of the mind to make varieties of separations which Korzybski saw as related to the major psychological difficulties of our time. The objective of psychotherapy which emerged from Korzybski's thought is the development of understanding which, in his way of thinking, would transcend the artificial splits of mind. As but a single example of this way of thinking, I might cite Wendell Johnson's work on stutterers, in which he sees the cultural splitting of stutterers from nonstutterers as critically involved in the genesis of the stuttering condition itself.[79]

In the healing relationship there is a suspension of judgment, the characteristic of the ego which decides what it will entertain and what it will not, what it will allow and what it will deny. Since from the very beginning of the development of the ego the separations which took place within also

[78]Alfred Korzybski, *Science and Sanity: An Introduction to Non-Aristotelian Systems and General Semantics* (New York: The International Non-Aristotelian Library Publishing Company, 1933).

[79]Cf. "The Indians Have No Word for It (The Problem of Stuttering)," in Wendell Johnson, *People in Quandaries: The Semantics of Personal Adjustment* (New York: Harper and Brothers, 1946), pp. 439-66.

entailed the separation of the person from other persons, in the healing relationship the separation between the two people is overcome as the paradigm of the overcoming of all other separations. This is the meaning of the transference in psychoanalytic psychotherapy. Understanding of the person by the healer is the model and beginning for opening understanding within the individual. But, as Rogers has indicated, this requires great courage — the sense of being in grace, as the religious tradition would have it.

# CHAPTER IV

# AGENCY AND COMMUNION IN HUMAN SEXUALITY

Thus far, I have sought to develop our understanding of agency and communion through the history of Protestantism and science and through the image of Satan. In this chapter, I seek to deepen our understanding by yet another tack, the examination of human sexuality and sex differences. In the last chapter, I indicated that there was some connection between agency and the anal and latency stages of development, thus suggesting the possibility of enhancing our understanding by dealing with sexuality, and, more particularly, with the Freudian view of the nature of sexuality.

## SEXUALITY AS A TOUCHSTONE

I believe, with Freud, that sexuality can be considered a touchstone for understanding the nature of man. The objection of both the neo- and anti-Freudians to the Freudian point of view has largely been to the significance he attributed to sexuality. Freud expressed the belief that those who were critical of psychoanalysis were those who could not overcome their own repression sufficiently to see the validity of what he said. But this is merely a rhetorical way of meeting these objections.

There is the manifest objection that the problems of sexuality are but one area of human concern, and that there are many other important problematic concerns which can be related to sexuality only by stretching the imagination. In face of the fact that human beings are concerned with many other things which are indeed problematical, the emphasis on sexuality has seemed to call forth a sense that Freud himself was obsessive about it. The latter answers Freud's charge of psychopathology with a similar charge of Freud's psychopathology — a pointless style of debate.

Another objection to Freud is based on his stress on *infantile* sexuality. Sexuality, in any "meaningful" sense, seems to be something which does not emerge until puberty. The ascription of sexuality to infants and to children would appear to be a "projection" by Freud of pubertal and postpubertal sexuality to the earlier stages of development. The case of Little Hans, or other instances of sexual types of reactions on the part of children, especially children who were in need of psychological help, might well be regarded as anomalies or precocities, rather than as conditions which invite generalizations concerning the nature of man or his development.

One way of answering these objections is to regard the significance of sexuality in adult life and the sexual nature of development as *theory*. The measure of the value of a theory is the extent to which it can explain phenomena better than other theories, the sense of understanding it provides concerning what is otherwise mysterious, and the power it has to lead to other, and otherwise unexpected, findings. I believe, that using such criteria, a very good case can be made out for the value of the notions of the centrality of sexuality in the human psyche and significance of sexuality in prepubertal development. Yet, this judgment is one which is disputable; and certainly the research which is yet to be done may force the qualification of this judgment.

There are, however, a priori bases for the acceptance of the significance of sexuality in human functioning and development. One is that *sexuality is the function of the human organism which is most closely related to his very existence;* and one might therefore expect it to play an extremely important role in all facets of his existence. I am, of course, alluding to the banal fact that human existence is the result of sexuality.

The "first" question, what we may call the existential question, can be roughly formulated as, What's this all about, anyhow? This formulation is already too particularized, a rough expression of some condition of wonder which precedes all questions. Even though this formulation, embodied as it is in a syntactical form which already goes beyond that condition of wonder, is rough, it is in some way the mother of all questions. It lies behind all of our religious and scientific quests. It precedes all of the categories we use in the formulation of our questions; and the categories themselves, although they move us toward answers, sometimes work to defeat the condition of wonder which preceded all questions. In times of crisis or loneliness, or when witnessing some telling phenomenon, we are occasionally brought back to this original condition of wonder and ask, in some way, What's this all about, anyhow?

For Freud the "first" question was put somewhat differently:

... the first problem with which [the child] occupies himself is ... the riddle: Where do children come from? In a distorted form which can easily be unravelled, this is the same riddle which was proposed by the Theban Sphinx.[1]

We may, perhaps, quibble with Freud as to whether the question, Where do children come from? is not a "second" question after What's this all about, anyhow? There is little doubt, however, that at some early stage of development the existential question moves to the question of the origins of being and to the sexual. Wonder must quickly become wonder about the origins of human existence. Curiosity must soon become sexual curiosity.

We might even quarrel with the way in which Freud proceeded to make this concrete in the notion of the Oedipus complex, of the dominant father, the submissive mother, the child's desire to "possess" the mother, and the conflict between child and father. The anthropological data may not quite

[1] Sigmund Freud, *The Interpretation of Dreams*, in *Basic Writings*, p. 595.

substantiate Freud's construction of the matter, as Malin-owski,[2] for example, has indicated, but the basic feature of the arousal of something involving sexuality can reasonably be assumed.

A second a priori basis for regarding sexuality as a touch-stone of human existence relates to the mind-body distinction. The phenomenological basis for this distinction inheres in the fact that many thought processes, feelings, and wishes take place in the human psyche without any conspicuous changes in the physical operations of the body; and that many body proc-esses take place without any conspicuous manifestations in the psyche. Certainly, modern techniques of investigation have been able to demonstrate psychological changes in connec-tion with physiological changes, and physiological changes in connection with psychological changes, where they are not evident in the simple phenomenological sense. But these are based on refined techniques of observation which are not ordinarily present to the functioning individual himself. In the case of sexuality, however, the phenomenological bondage of the psychological and physical is patent. Thus, for example, the psychological and physiological aspects of sexual arousal correspond so closely that there is little invitation to conceptu-alize them in terms of any mind-body distinction. If we regard the mind-body distinction as conceptually mischievous, as many modern investigators do, then sexuality commends itself to our attention methodologically because here the relationships between mind and body are least hidden. This does not mean that in the investigation of the sexual we are limited to that which is phenomenologically manifest in the simple sense. Quite to the contrary, as witness the fact that, of all the psychological systems, psychoanalysis, which perhaps is least guilty of the mind-body fallacy, has also been strongest in making discoveries of that which is com-monly hidden from view. Indeed, it was in the hysterias, where

[2]Bronislaw Malinowski, *Sex and Repression in Savage Society* (New York: Meridian Books, 1955).

the patient attempts to persuade himself and others that his difficulty is physical rather than psychological, that psycho-analysis had its beginnings; and the understanding of the nature of hysteria was made possible by overcoming the distinction between mind and body.

A third a priori basis for regarding sexuality as a touch-stone whereby we can enhance our understanding of the nature of human existence inheres in the great discrepancy between human sexual and reproductive potentiality. Perhaps because of this discrepancy, human sexuality expresses itself metaphorically and symbolically. If we assume that, in some "original" sense, the function of sexuality is reproduction, then the discrepancy between overendowment of sexuality and underendowment of reproductive ability in the human forces expression in ways which are not reproductive, since the sexual in the human being must be largely "frustrated." Even that which might be the fullest possible "sexual satisfaction" in the human being is only partial. The overendow-ment of the human is manifest in many ways. There is, in the first instance, the actual enormous overproduction of sperm cells in the male. This overproduction is not only in terms of the vast number of cells which are present at any one time, but also in terms of the continuous production over a period of life of the adult male, in whom ejaculation can take place several times a week. In the female, too, ova are produced far in excess of the number of children that any one woman could possibly bear and take care of. If we give any credence at all to observations of psychoanalysts in connection with sexuality in children, then sexual capacity, as contrasted with reproductive capacity, precedes puberty. If we consider data that Kinsey has provided, the capacity for orgasm both precedes puberty and, in the female, succeeds the menopause, when reproduction is no longer possible. Sexual desire in the female pervades the whole of the menstrual cycle and is not restricted to the time when conception is possible. There is even some reason to believe that sexual desire in the female is higher at those times when conception is least likely, a phenomenon that appears to be unique among humans.[3]

## THE HEURISTIC VALUE OF CONSIDERING SEX DIFFERENCES

We can differentiate among four "levels" of sexual differentiation. Biologists distinguish between the sexes in terms of their specific contribution to the reproductive process. A distinction between the sexes can be made in terms of the secondary sex characteristics, such as more facial hair and deeper voice in the male, and larger breasts and hips in the female. Distinction is also made in terms of place in the social structure, males taking male "roles," and females taking female "roles" in the society. Finally, there are presumptive differences in the psychological makeup of the two sexes.

When close and careful investigation of each of these levels of sexual differentiation is conducted, any simple male-female dichotomy breaks down. There are the varieties of intersex (hermaphroditic) individuals, based on structural and physiological characteristics. The distributions of secondary sex characteristics, social role, and psychological measures characteristically show overlap of at least some degree, sometimes quite extensive. Culture affects "role" greatly. Correlations among indices from these four levels are far from perfect, so that given individuals may be extremely "masculine" at one level and extremely "feminine" at another.

Yet the distinction between male and female as a simple dichotomy prevails in all cultures and plays an important role in the psychological life of all individuals. In some cultures, this dichotomy has been the model for extensive cosmological, philosophical, and theological ramification. There are the male-sky, female-earth distinction, and the male-sun, female-moon distinction. There are the Chinese Yang and Yin, the Hindu Lingam (Shiva) and Yoni (Shakti),

---

[3]This phenomenon concerning the heightening of sexual desire pre- and postmenstrually is discussed in greater detail below. See pp. 144ff.

the Tantric Buddhist Jewel and Lotus. Among psychoanalysts, a sharp distinction is made between male and female sexuality in the total life of the psyche; and of special significance are the *animus* and *anima* in Jungian psychology.

We must, then, distinguish between an abstract set of male and female "principles" and the assignment of individuals to the male or female category. We could, of course, simply reject the notion of male and female principles and limit all our considerations to the various types of data of the four levels enumerated above. This would be a very tough-minded approach to the problem of sex differences. We would essentially eliminate male and female as very good scientific categories and limit ourselves to individual differences of various types and the correlations that may prevail among them. But to do this would be to give up something which we know is a very important aspect of human life. With all of the difficulties the various empirical data present, there is a validity to the dichotomy which we must accept. And there is a certain truth associated with the male and the female principles, present in both men and women, which we cannot ignore.

How may we approach the problem of the relationship of the male and female principles, on the one hand, and the problem of individual differences, on the other? We can make the assumption that *what differentiates the aggregate of males from the aggregate of females reflects the male and female principles, respectively.* This assumption is entailed in some sense in most studies of sex differences. For example, in their classic study of the relationship of sex and personality, Lewis M. Terman and Catherine C. Miles administered a large number of test items to males and females. They then culled these items to find those which "discriminated" between the males and the females, that is, items which *in the aggregate* were answered one way by males and another way by females. It was out of these items that they constructed their test of masculinity-femininity. Having thus isolated their items, they were in a position to compare males and females carefully and make

inferences concerning the difference between the "sex temperaments," as they do in Chapter 16, "Sex Temperaments as
Revealed by the M-F Test."[4]

This method cannot be employed without misgivings;
and generalizations from it need to be evaluated with respect
to such doubts. The aggregate may not immediately be identified with the general, especially with trend data or functional relationships.[5] Furthermore, there is always the possibility that the single datum is paradoxical with respect to the
phenomenon that it is presumed to assess, for example, that a
"masculine" reaction may be engendered by an underlying
"feminine" tendency as "compensation" or "reaction formation." The method, as Terman and Miles are very aware, does
not distinguish between biological and cultural determination; although one needs always to ask to what degree culture
may reflect and defer to constitutional differences between the
sexes. A difficulty in attempting to read only the central
tendencies without more careful inspection shows up in the
Terman and Miles study of preferences for occupations. Here,
not only do the data indicate differences in preferences for
specific occupations, but also that females more frequently than
males express preference for the cross-sex occupations.[6] It
may be that males differ from females in their central tendencies, but that there is also a difference between the sexes in
the extent of androgynicity, that females are more bisexual
than males, a point which we will presently return to.

Yet, if we keep these objections in mind, the heuristic
assumption may help us to clarify the nature of such male and

[4]Lewis M. Terman and Catherine Cox Miles, *Sex and Personality: Studies in
Masculinity and Femininity* (New York: McGraw-Hill Book Company, 1936),
pp. 371-450.

[5]The technical problems associated with this distinction of the general and the
aggregate have been dealt with by the author in two papers: David Bakan,
"The General and the Aggregate: A Methodological Distinction," *Perceptual
and Motor Skills*, V (1955), 211-12; "A Generalization of Sidman's Results on
Group and Individual Functions, and a Criterion," *Psychological Bulletin*, LI
(1954), 63-64; cf. Murray Sidman, "A Note on Functional Relations Obtained
from Group Data," *Psychological Bulletin*, XLIX (1952), 263-69.

[6]*Op. cit.*, pp. 423-24.

female principles. Actually, this is simply a method of refinement of intuitive and primitive dimensions such as prevails in science at large. Consider, as an example, the refined techniques for the measurement of weight. The measurement of weight begins with the primitive observation that some things are "heavier" than others. Starting from this, it is observed that, when two objects are placed on opposite sides of a balance, the one which was primitively identified as the "heavier" *descends*, and the other *ascends*. From this, we proceed to develop a notion of weight by which weight determinations are possible in instances in which the primitive sense of "heavier" could not serve at all. But the primitive sense of "heavier" remains the basis for the more refined methods of measurement of weight which we have today. Similarly, we start with the primitive and almost, but not quite, tautological observation that males are more masculine and females are more feminine as the basis for the refinement of our concepts. *I propose for consideration that what we have been referring to as agency is more characteristically masculine, and what we have been referring to as communion is more characteristically feminine.* Let us now consider some of the empirical data on sex differences to gain further refinement and clarification of these concepts.

## SEX DIFFERENCES IN ACHIEVEMENT

One of the major differences between the sexes concerns achievement. Achievement is a function of many factors, including the degree to which social structure, social expectations, and both formal and informal education play a part. The very concepts that the society has concerning sex differences in achievement determine such differences, with the mechanism of the "self-fulfilling prophecy" possibly playing a very important role. Even our notion of "achievement" itself may be a biased one in that, assuming there are constitutional differences whereby men and women function better in different types of enterprises, the society may look upon success in one kind of enterprise as "achievement" and not in another.

By usual criteria, there is little doubt that in the history of Western civilization, men have been the major achievers. Havelock Ellis had only 55 women in his group of 1030 persons judged as geniuses in *A Study of British Genius*.[7] Ellis even had some misgivings about whether, had they not been women, they would have attained eminence, since the standards for eminence in women appeared to be lower than for men. James McK. Cattell's list of 1000 eminent persons contains 32 women, and a substantial number of these are eminent by virtue of heredity, as in the case of sovereigns, or other circumstances not closely associated with their actual ability.[8] S. S. Visher's study of persons "starred" in *American Men of Science* shows 50 women among 2607 scientists.[9] Alice I. Bryan and Edwin G. Boring made a very close examination of men and women psychologists. Careful matching of the men and the women in terms of their backgrounds and academic levels showed the productivity of the men to be higher.[10] Cora S. Castle's study of 868 eminent women over history reports that 38 per cent had achieved their eminence in literature, but that the highest degree of eminence was associated with being sovereigns, political leaders, mothers of eminent men, and mistresses. Others were eminent by their marriages, religion, birth, philanthropy, tragic fate, beauty, and being immortalized in literature.[11] With the single exception of literature, eminence among women in history seems largely to be asso-

[7]*Op. cit.*

[8]James McKeen Cattell, "A Statistical Study of Eminent Men," *Popular Science Monthly*, LXII (1903), 359-77.

[9]S. S. Visher, *Scientists Starred, 1903-1943, in "American Men of Science"* (Baltimore: The Johns Hopkins Press, 1947).

[10]Alice I. Bryan and Edwin G. Boring, "Women in American Psychology: Prolegomenon," *Psychological Bulletin*, XLI (1944), 447-54; "Women in American Psychology: Statistics from the OPP Questionnaire," *American Psychologist*, I (1946), 71-79; "Women in American Psychology: Factors Affecting Their Professional Careers," *American Psychologist*, II (1947), 3-20.

[11]Cora S. Castle, "A Statistical Study of Eminent Women," *Archives of Psychology*, XXII (1913), 1-90.

ciated with circumstantial factors. John Stuart Mill argued that women could not be said to be without the ability to achieve, since they had hardly been allowed to. He was particularly impressed with the talent that women appeared to have in government when they had the opportunity, citing Queen Elizabeth I, Deborah, and Joan of Arc. "We know," he wrote, "how small a number of reigning queens history presents, in comparison with that of kings. Of this smaller number a far larger proportion have shown talents for rule; though many of them have occupied their throne in difficult periods."[12] The role of women in history has been dealt with in some detail by Mary R. Beard. She outlines how "from modern times running back into and through the medieval ages of Western feudalism and Christian contests with barbarism, the force of woman was a powerful factor in all the infamies, tyrannies, liberties, activities, and aspirations that constituted the history of this stage of humanity's self expression." But the most important feature of the history for her is the role of women in connection with the civilizing forces of the world:

Despite the barbaric and power-hungry propensities and activities in long history, to which their sex was by no means immune, women were engaged in the main in the promotion of civilian interests. Hence they were in the main on the side of *civil*-ization in the struggle with barbarism.

If this phase of woman's force in history is to be capitalized as against barbaric propensities and activities, then an understanding of women's past history in both connections must be regarded as indispensable to the maintenance and promotion of civilization in the present age.[13]

These findings and interpretations with respect to achievement lead me to the opinion that eminence itself, in the history of the world, has been linked with those characteristics associated with men. Thus, rather than taking the notion of eminence as a *criterion* by which to evaluate the difference

[12]John Stuart Mill, *The Subjection of Women* (New York: Longmans, Green and Company, 1924), p. 81.

[13]Mary R. Beard, *Women as a Force in History: A Study in Traditions and Realities* (New York: The Macmillan Company, 1946), pp. 331-32.

between men and women, we should consider the possibility that the society tends to ascribe eminence in accordance with some principle already based on sex differences.

Perhaps the difference with respect to achievement orientation which may be reflected in these data is the result of differences in the *locus* of achievement rather than in achievement itself. Such a possibility is clearly rendered by a series of studies by David C. McClelland and his co-workers. McClelland has found that achievement motivation as assessed by responses to Thematic Apperception Test pictures can be increased by the manipulation of the situation before the taking of the test. In one such study, in which the subjects took the TAT test before and after an "intelligence" test, there was a significant gain in the achievement scores for males but not for females. However, when the intervening experience was one which involved a "rather lengthy discussion concerning the importance of their social acceptance by the group as the most important determiner of ultimate satisfaction with life," and subjects were told that all members of the group were being "secretly rated . . . on the basis of their social acceptability" by a research committee, there were significant differences in the achievement scores for the females, but not for the males. McClelland summarizes these findings as follows:

In short, the data unequivocally support the hypothesis that women's *n* Achievement is tied up with social acceptability, men's with leadership capacity and intelligence. To put it in another way, if you want to arouse *n* Achievement in women, refer . . . to their social acceptability; if you want to arouse *n* Achievement in men, refer . . . to their leadership capacity and intelligence.[14]

SEX DIFFERENCES IN PSYCHOLOGICAL "CENTERING"

The concept of the "life space," advanced by Kurt Lewin, can be helpful in illuminating the nature of the difference between males and females. Within the life space, one can

[14]From *The Achievement Motive*, by David McClelland, John W. Atkinson, Russell A. Clark, Edgar L. Lowell, p. 181. Copyright, 1953, by Appleton-Century-Crofts, Inc. Reprinted by permission of Appleton-Century-Crofts.

differentiate between that which is the "self" and that which is "other." Furthermore, one can conceptualize a degree of differentiation of the self from the "other." The self is the "center"; it is the figure against the ground of that which is "other."

A difference between the sexes in terms of such "centering" of the self appears to have some validity. In an extremely interesting treatment by Gina Lombroso, the daughter of the famous Cesare Lombroso, this distinction in centering is taken as the critical one by which to differentiate the sexes. Although her treatment is anecdotal, and not empirical in the usual sense, there is some interesting correspondence between her notion and some of the more empirical data on sex differences. She writes as follows:

The fundamental fact which determines woman's attitude toward life is that woman is *alterocentrist,* that is to say, she *centers her feelings, her enjoyment, her ambition in something outside herself; she makes not herself but another person, or even things surrounding her, the center of her emotions*....[15]

Man, on the other hand, is "...*egocentrist,* that is to say, *he makes himself and his pleasures and his activities the center of the world in which he lives*" (p. 6).

A difference between the sexes in terms of the degree of self-other distinction is confirmed in an interesting series of experiments on perception by H. A. Witkin and his associates. In a variety of studies involving the ability of the individual to separate himself from a visual stimulus, Witkin found that such psychological separation is characteristically more easily made by male than female subjects. In Witkin's terminology, men are more "field-independent" than women, where by "field" Witkin means the situation presented visually to the subject.

For example, in one of the conditions, the Tilting-Room-Tilting-Chair Test, the subject sits in a narrow chair with sides

[15]Gina Lombroso, *The Soul of Woman* (New York: E. P. Dutton & Company, 1923), p. 5.

against which the hips and shoulders are pressed. This chair is mounted on an axle so that it can be tipped to either side. It is inside a large box, fitted out as a room, which is also mounted on an axle and which can be rotated to either side. By this means, both the chair and the room can be modified with respect to the gravational upright. The subject judges the true upright under various conditions of tilt of the chair and the room. This is done by having the subject control the movement of the chair to make himself straight.

Witkin found that in this situation, as well as a number of other similar ones, women tend to "go along with" the field, that is, they "accept" the position of the room as indicative of the true upright to a much greater extent than men do. In addition, Witkin found that the judgments of women are more variable than those of men, depending on the situation. "Men," writes Witkin, "are more concerned than women with sensations from their bodies. Women . . . are more likely to regard them in terms of their relation to the prevailing visual field."[16]

Lombroso relates the alterocentric tendency in women to its function in connection with child-rearing.[17] Witkin relates it to the difference between women and men in their sexual functioning, in that the male's erection comes from him, but "In a woman, dependence on the male's erection for her mature sexual pleasures may foster a generalized attitude of greater reliance on factors outside herself."[18] But whatever the explanation, Witkin's data strongly suggest that the "centering" of the self is more labile in the female and more often likely to be outside of the physical self, and that the "separation" of the self from the environment is greater in the male. The related question of differences in eroticism between men and women is dealt with later in this chapter.

[16]H. A. Witkin, *et al.*, *Personality Through Perception: An Experimental and Clinical Study* (New York: Harper and Brothers, 1954), p. 171.

[17]*Op. cit.*, p. 11.

[18]*Op. cit.*, p. 488.

A number of sex differences in interests which have been discovered seem to fall in line with the notion of a degree of self-other distinction and "centering." Terman and Miles found clear evidence in their data of greater gentleness, punctiliousness in dress, personal appearance, manners, language, maternal tenderness, compassion, and active sympathy for palpable misfortune and distress in females. Anne Anastasi, in her review of sex differences, concludes that the data on interests, preferences, attitudes, and values characteristically point to a "greater *social orientation* of women."[19] She cites data which show that in play activity girls tend to use more furniture and family figures, instead of blocks and vehicles; girls prefer stories of love and romance, children and family life, to adventure, travel, and exploration; girls are more interested in personal attractiveness, personal philosophy, planning the daily schedule, mental health, manners, personal qualities, and home and family relationships than in physical health, safety, and money, which are more interesting to boys; women talk more about clothes and people, whereas men talk about money, business affairs, and sports. On interest tests, men prefer the mechanical, persuasive, computational, and scientific; women prefer the literary, musical, social service, and clerical. Women's interests run high in the esthetic, social, and religious; men's in the theoretical, economic, and political. Girls tend to play "social games" and show more "motherly behavior." They tend to have more nicknames of an affectionate nature. Their fantasy life more often concerns people. In one study on old people, sociability was related to happiness in women, but not in men (pp. 478-82).

Girls characteristically receive better school grades. However, the difference is usually more marked when the grades are based on the judgments of teachers than on the basis of achievement tests. Leona E. Tyler explains this partly on the basis of attitudes and personality.

[19]Anne Anastasi, *Differential Psychology: Individual and Group Differences in Behavior* (New York: The Macmillan Company, 1958), p. 481.

Docility and submissiveness, usually considered feminine traits, enable girls to make a better impression on teachers than boys do. This inevitably shows up on report cards in other places besides the deportment column. These same traits would, to some extent, *prevent* their possessors from assuming positions of leadership in the world of affairs.[20]

In those intellectual functions which involve *communication*, on the verbal parts of intelligence tests, and in English courses, females tend generally to be superior; and, as indicated before, the largest category of female eminence has been in literature. Girls learn to talk earlier and are superior in articulation, intelligibility, and correctness of speech. Their scores are higher in verbal fluency, although boys are higher in the grasp of verbal meanings. Girls are less likely to become stutterers (p. 252). The incidence of reading difficulty is about twice as high in males as in females.[21]

If we can accept the conclusion indicated by such data, that females have a greater social orientation and a greater tendency to be communicative, an interesting possibility is suggested concerning the relative roles of biology and culture in the determination of sex differences. This is that *males and females are differentially affected by culture.* There is some evidence that there is a greater tendency for girls to be influenced at an earlier age by their parents, indicated by the fact that significant parent-child correlations (between years of parents' schooling and child's I.Q.) appear at younger ages for girls than for boys.[22] There can be little doubt that the degree of influence of culture is contingent upon constitutional factors. This is patent when we compare humans to lower animals. Humans are certainly more educable, that is, subject to the influence of cultural factors, and this surely has its ground-

[20]From *The Psychology of Human Differences*, Second Edition, by Leona E. Tyler, p. 250. Copyright © 1956, by Appleton-Century-Crofts, Inc. Reprinted by permission of Appleton-Century-Crofts.

[21]John Money, *Reading Disability: Progress and Research Needs in Dyslexia* (Baltimore: The Johns Hopkins Press, 1962), p. 31.

[22]Majorie P. Honzik, "A Sex-Difference in the Age of Onset of the Parent-Child Resemblance in Intelligence," *Journal of Educational Psychology*, LIV (1963), 231-37.

ing in constitutional factors. We can extend this to humans by pointing to the various evidences of variation in educability. If, in addition, we now find that females are more directly educable than males, it would strongly point to the possibility I have indicated. Thus, although such a form of argument should be conducted with restraint, the feminist position that the culture makes for sex differences needs to be tempered by the possibility that the very influence of culture is differential with respect to the sexes. Women may not only have provided the leadership for "civilization" as Mary R. Beard has suggested, they may also be more *civilizable*.

Work on the vocational interests of men and women has indicated rather clear-cut differences between them. What is of considerable interest to us, however, is the finding of less variation among women than men. Factor analysis of some of these data has shown that one thing which appears to characterize the various scales for female occupations is "Interest in Male Association."[23] Tyler comments on this finding as follows:

The name was chosen to represent what housewives, office workers, stenographers, and nurses have in common. It would be simpler and probably more correct to call the factor "Typical Feminine Interests," since it includes elementary teachers as well as housewives and office workers. It doubtless represents the general attitude and outlook of the woman who does not want a career for its own sake, but who is satisfied to pursue any pleasant congenial activity that offers itself until marriage, and perhaps afterward. One can get a fairly good idea of what it is by examining the content of one of the standard women's magazines—home, personal attractiveness, amusements, direct relationships with people. The comparative rarity of specialization of interests in women might well be one of the reasons for the dearth of high-level professional achievement which has been mentioned earlier [p. 260].

Recently, there have been some interesting writings, such as those by Betty Friedan, whose book has entered the ranks of best-sellers, and Alice S. Rossi, which clamor for greater in-

[23]*Op. cit.*, pp. 207, 260.

volvement of women in the world of occupations, away from the bondage associated with home, marriage, sexuality, and child care.[24] The lack of fulfillment for women outside of occupational involvement is cogently argued by both of these writers. However, I believe that neither has seen that the problem inheres in differences between men and women, rather than in their equality or identity. Contemporary life, with its comforts, its great social isolation in any but trivial senses, and its growing trend to satisfy needs outside the household, makes centering outside the limited physical self in the home very difficult to achieve. The urge for vocational involvement may arise in women more from the need to find more adequate loci outside of the physical self for centering than from the need for mastery, achievement, and independence. Furthermore, the world of occupations is moving in the direction of much larger, collective types of enterprises rather than individual enterprises, thus becoming more attractive for women who are frustrated in finding loci for centering in the context of domestic life.

A relative lack of differentiation between self and "other" throws some light on the meaning of the assertion of a greater degree of "intuition" in the female. Sidney M. Jourard, in an interesting series of investigations involving a test of "self-disclosure," has found that there is a difference between males and females. "Men typically reveal less personal information about themselves to others than women." "Men keep their selves to themselves."[25] Women are also greater recipients of self-disclosure by others (p. 49). He speculates that the somatic responses associated with this condition are related to the shorter life span of the male, a matter which is discussed below. We can easily reinterpret Helene Deutsch's exposition of woman's "intuition" as the tendency for the life space of the

[24]Betty Friedan, *The Feminine Mystique* (New York: W. W. Norton Company, 1963); Alice S. Rossi, "Equality Between the Sexes: An Immodest Proposal," *Daedalus* (Spring, 1964), pp. 607-52.

[25]Sidney M. Jourard, *The Transparent Self: Self-Disclosure and Well-Being* (Princeton, N.J.: D. Van Nostrand Company, 1964), p. 47.

woman to center in another person. She writes on this as follows:

> Woman's understanding of other people's minds, her intuition, is the result of an unconscious process through which the subjective experience of another person is made one's own by association and thus is immediately understood. . . .
>
> What we see in intuition is not a logical concatenation of impressions; on the contrary, in each intuitive experience, the other person's mental state is emotionally and unconsciously "re-experienced," that is, felt as one's own. The ability to do this will naturally depend on one's sympathy and love for and spiritual affinity with the other person. . . .[26]

The nature of this intuition is precisely contingent upon the lack of making the distinction between subject and object, between the self which is the onlooker and that which is being looked at.

### SEX DIFFERENCES IN AGGRESSION

Corresponding to the finding of a greater social orientation in the female is the consistent evidence of greater aggressiveness in the male. This is found not only at the adult level, but even in the nursery school and in many lower animals. Various studies at the preschool levels show that boys display "more anger, aggression, destructiveness, and quarrelsome behavior" than girls.[27] The ratio of boys to girls referred to child guidance clinics for aggressive and antisocial behavior is almost four to one, and a similar ratio is obtained on studies of teachers' reports of problem children (p. 487). The kinds of problems which children manifest also suggest a greater aggressive component in males. In boys, it was found that the following are more prevalent: "overactivity, attention-demanding behavior, jealousy, competitiveness, lying, selfishness in sharing, temper tantrums, and stealing." On the other

[26]Helene Deutsch, *The Psychology of Women: A Psychoanalytic Interpretation* (New York: Grune and Stratton, 1944), I, 136.

[27]Anastasi, *op. cit.*, p. 487.

hand, "Girls were more likely to suck their thumbs; be excessively reserved; fuss about their food; be timid, shy, fearful, oversensitive, and somber; and have mood swings" (p. 484).

Data collected from college students seem to show evidence of a greater "urge to destroy" in males (p. 487). Erikson, on the basis of observation of the kinds of scenes constructed out of toys of 150 boys and 150 girls found that *"ruins* were exclusively boys' constructions."[28] In one study of preferences in wit, it was found that the outstanding feature which distinguished male from female appreciation was the amount of hostility expressed in the particular jest.[29] One of the major conclusions that Terman and Miles drew from their data was that there was a greater degree of "aggressiveness" in males, in contrast to the greater amount of "maternal tenderness" in females.[30] Even though the antagonism between the sexes at the preadolescent levels exists for both sexes, the hostility of boys toward girls is greater than the hostility of girls toward boys.[31] The statistics on crime and delinquency show an overwhelming discrepancy between the sexes, with the ratio of men to women sent to prisons and reformatories being about twenty-five to one.[32] Although there may well be other factors which lead to more men being imprisoned, they could hardly account for the figure being this high. The exact nature of this greater tendency to aggressiveness in males is not understood. However, there are several factors which appear to be related to it.

First, the musculature of the male is larger and stronger. Although we may perhaps define our civilization in terms of

[28]Erik H. Erikson, "Inner and Outer Space: Reflections on Womanhood," *Daedalus* (Spring, 1964), p. 591.

[29]Walter O'Connell, "An Item Analysis of the Wit and Humor Appreciation Test," *Journal of Social Psychology*, LV-LVI (1961-62), 271-76.

[30]*Op. cit.*, p. 449.

[31]Elizabeth B. Hurlock, *Child Development* (New York: McGraw-Hill Book Company, 1950), p. 314.

[32]Amram Scheinfeld, *Women and Men* (New York: Harcourt, Brace and Company, 1944), pp. 244ff.

the degree to which we have suspended the use of the musculature in personal interaction as a source of interpersonal influence, it still plays a significant role in the politics of the playground, and its usefulness is a characteristic early lesson in the lives of most children. From birth onwards, with the differences increasing with age, the averages for males in body weight, height, muscular strength, physical restlessness, vigorous muscular activity, and vital capacity, which is a factor in sustained energy output, are higher.[33]

Second, various homeostatic mechanisms operate within narrower limits in the male than in the female. The range of body temperature, basal metabolism, acid-base balance of the blood, and blood sugar level of males is less than that of females. The bodily reaction of females to stress is greater.[34] This factor may actually be more important than has generally been recognized in the determination of other sex differences. It would suggest that females are better able to "go along with" changes in the environment in terms of some of these basic physiological functions. Where the homeostatic range is more restricted, we might expect a greater tendency to make the adjustment by *modifying the environment,* by changing the world rather than the physiological levels. We might even speculate that this would contribute to a sharper psychological distinction between self and not-self, resulting from the more frequent tension between the state of the environment and the state of the body. The data from Witkin that "men are more concerned than women with sensations from their bodies"[35] may be associated with men's tendency toward lower automatic physiological responsiveness. It may well be that women are more "comfortable" in their environments, and that men are less "comfortable" and are thus impelled to act upon the environment to modify it. This would suggest that

[33]Anastasi, *op. cit.*, p. 462.

[34]These data are summarized in Lewis M. Terman and Leona E. Tyler, "Psychological Sex Differences," in Leonard Carmichael (ed.), *Manual of Child Psychology* (2nd ed.; New York: John Wiley and Sons, 1954), p. 1066.

[35]*Op. cit.*, p. 171.

men are more forced to use the musculature to compensate for their lower adjustability in terms of other physiological processes.

Third, there may be some relationship, at least on the adult level, between the androgen—the "male" hormone—level and aggression. The androgens have a strong positive influence on the metabolism of nitrogen and thus on muscular strength and energy,[36] as well as on the development of the male sex organs and other secondary sex characteristics. In adults, the androgen levels of females are about two-thirds those of males.[37] What is also of significance is the accumulation of evidence that "the level of sex drive or libido is hormonally influenced, and androgen is probably the libido hormone in both men and women."[38] This comes as an interesting confirmation of Freud's assertion that "libido is regularly and lawfully of a masculine nature, whether in the man or in the woman,"[39] a proposition which was originally presented in spaced type for emphasis. Similarly, there is some evidence that the administration of estrogen—the "female" hormone—to men decreases the sex urge.[40] In contemporary medical practice topical administration of androgenic creams on the clitoris in the treatment of diminished libido in the female may be prescribed.[41] Later in this essay, I deal with the

[36]John Money, "Sex Hormones and Other Variables in Human Eroticism," in William C. Young (ed.), *Sex and Internal Secretions* (Baltimore: The Williams & Wilkins Company, 1961), p. 1387.

[37]Alfred C. Kinsey, *et al.*, *Sexual Behavior in the Human Female* (Philadelphia: W. B. Saunders Company, 1953), p. 730.

[38]John Money, "Components of Eroticism in Man: Cognitional Rehearsals," in Joseph Wortis (ed.), *Recent Advances in Biological Psychiatry* (New York: Grune and Stratton, 1960), p. 223.

[39]Sigmund Freud, *Three Contributions to the Theory of Sex*, in *Basic Writings*, p. 612.

[40]John Money, "Developmental Differentiation of Femininity and Masculinity Compared," in Seymour M. Farber and Roger H. L. Wilson (eds.), *Man and Civilization: The Potential of Woman* (New York: McGraw-Hill Book Company, 1963), p. 58.

[41]Herbert S. Kupperman, *Human Endocrinology* (Philadelphia: F. A. Davis Company, 1963), pp. 475, 477.

possible psychosomatic involvement of agency and communion in the development of cancer. At the present time, it is enough only to indicate that anti-androgenic treatment has been used in the management of cancer with some success.

If we put the role of the androgens together with the observation that androgens also have the effect of increasing aggression, particularly sexual aggression,[42] some understanding of the nature of aggression may be arrived at. The condition of heightened sex drive can be viewed as a state of discomfort which requires the manipulation of the "environment" for its removal. Thus, the imperious sex urge which manifests itself much more strongly in the male is related to an aggressive effort to modify the environment to reduce the tension, in the same way as with the other physiological mechanisms. Although the detailed mechanism may be different, the essential pattern of a greater amount of restriction of physiological adjustment internally is the same in sexuality as in temperature and the like in the male.

## SEX DIFFERENCES IN VIABILITY AND LONGEVITY

The data thus far cited and the attendant considerations advanced tend to bring us closer to a specification of the concepts of agency and communion. The data support the presumption that the one is more associated with males and the other with females. Thus, the examination of various differences between males and females should give some indication of the nature of these two features. I have noted that there are sex differences in achievement, in cognitive differentiation and centering of the ego, and in aggression. An important clue to a basic difference is that of the difference between the sexes in homeostatic range, which would suggest that there is more harmony between the body and environment for the female and less necessity for acting upon the environment.

This brings us to considerations of a number of phenomena associated with death. First, since I have decided to study

[42]Kinsey, *op. cit.*, p. 748.

sex differences as a methodological strategy, I simply cannot overlook the facts of sex differences in connection with death. Second, if agency and communion are associated with styles of interacting with the environment, as I am led to believe, then one might look to the data on survival. The relationship between styles of interacting with the environment and survival is one of the most important lessons learned from the researches of Charles Darwin. Third, the thought of Freud in connection with the death instinct suggests itself as being very relevant. I deal with this in greater detail later, but a few observations on this should be made now.

The notion of the death instinct moves survival into the psychological sphere in a rather interesting way. In developing the notion of the death instinct, Freud suggested that it was related to the separation of the ego from the world, that it was manifested in aggression, and that the organ of the death instinct was the musculature. If we now add to this that these are associated with maleness, and that furthermore the death rate for males is strikingly higher than for females, there is the suggestion that the study of these sex differences can enhance our understanding of the death instinct beyond Freud's very obscure writing on this subject.

The greater longevity of the female has long been noted. It has eminent practical significance, in that insurance companies always use different life-expectancy tables for men and women, and that the premiums for men are higher. The death rate for males is higher than that for females at every age level. Prenatal deaths in the United States for the period 1926-29 range from 142.6 to 100 (males to females) at the fourth to the sixth month of gestation to 129.3 to 100 at seven to nine months of gestation; this is an average of 134.5 to 100, compared to the corresponding ratio for live births, which is 105.6 to 100.[43] Studies of early abortions, using the method of studying the nuclear sex-chromatins, have yielded estimates of the

[43]W. I. Russell, "Statistical Study of the Sex Ratio at Birth," *Journal of Hygiene*, XXXVI (1936), 381-401.

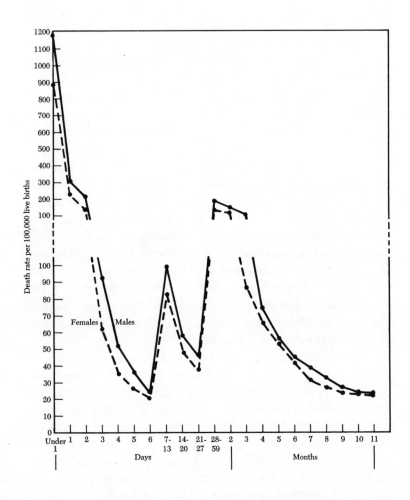

FIGURE 1. Infant mortality rates per 100,000 live births in specified groups for males and females, United States, 1962 (*Vital Statistics of the United States, 1964* [Washington, D.C.: U.S. Department of Health, Education, and Welfare, 1964], II, Pt A, Table 2-2).

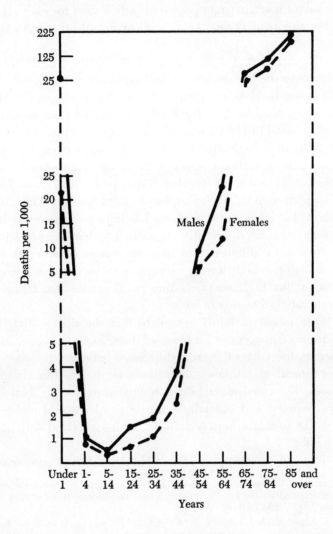

FIGURE 2. Mortality rates per 1000 population for males and females in specified groups, United States, 1962 (*Vital Statistics of the United States, 1964* [Washington, D.C.: U.S. Department of Health, Education, and Welfare, 1964], II, Pt A, Table 1-3).

male to female abortion rate of 160 to 100[44] and 122 to 100.[45] The infant mortality rate is consistently higher for males than for females (see Figure 1), as well as for all other ages (see Figure 2).

The circumstances of life have certainly improved considerably over the last decades, resulting in greater longevity for both sexes. In 1900, the death rate per thousand was 17.8 (for both sexes combined) in the United States. This has declined steadily, until in 1962 it was 7.5. What is of interest, however, is that the drop in death rate has been greater for females than it has been for males. For males, the death rate dropped from 18.6 in 1900 to 9.4; for females, it dropped from 17.0 to 5.8.[46] This is a drop of 9.2 for males, but 11.2 for females. Thus, it is evident that whatever it is which has improved longevity has affected the sexes differently. According to one interpretation, the increasing difference in life expectancy between males and females, which has accompanied an increase in life expectancy for both sexes, is due to a greater resistance to degenerative diseases in women.[47]

One might certainly speculate that the differential life conditions can account for some of these facts. However, it is less easy to explain the great difference between the sexes in the prenatal and infancy conditions as due to life circumstances. The consistency between what appear to be "biologically" caused and "socially" caused deaths would make us think that perhaps there is a single factor associated with both of them.

Data on accidental deaths of children show a similar sex

[44]V. Tricomi, D. Serr, and G. Solish, "The Ratio of Male to Female Embryos as Determined by the Sex Chromatin," *American Journal of Obstetrics and Gynecology*, LXXIX (1960), 504-9.

[45]F. E. Szontàgh, A. Jakobivits, and C. Méhes, "Primary Embryonal Sex Ratio in Normal Pregnancies Determined by the Nuclear Chromatin," *Nature*, CXCII (1961), 476.

[46]*Vital Statistics of the United States, 1962* (Washington, D.C.: U.S. Department of Health, Education and Welfare, 1962) II, Pt A, 1-14.

[47]Frances C. Madigan, "Are Sex Mortality Differentials Biologically Caused?" *Millbank Memorial Fund Quarterly*, XXXV (1957), 202-23.

difference. In the continental United States and in Venezuela, the accident rate for males is higher than for females as shown in Table 1.

TABLE 1

NUMBERS OF ACCIDENTAL DEATHS IN CHILDREN, CONTINENTAL UNITED STATES, 1956, AND VENEZUELA, 1954

|  | *United States* | | *Venezuela* | |
|  | *Males* | *Females* | *Males* | *Females* |
|---|---|---|---|---|
| Children 1-4 years of age | 2057 | 1540 | 135 | 113 |
| Children 5-14 years of age | 3524 | 1585 | 172 | 84 |

Data drawn from J. L. Goddard, "Accident Prevention in Childhood," *Public Health Reports*, LXXIV (1959), 523-34.

Death rates for each of the most common causes with some exceptions are higher for males than for females as shown in Table 2.

TABLE 2

DEATH RATES PER 100,000 MALES AND FEMALES FOR LEADING CAUSES OF DEATH

| *Cause of Death* | *Males* | *Females* |
|---|---|---|
| Diseases of heart | 438.6 | 304.2 |
| Malignant neoplasms | 164.2 | 136.1 |
| Vascular lesions affecting central nervous system | 101.4 | 111.0 |
| Accidents | 72.3 | 32.9 |
| Certain diseases of early infancy* | 41.3 | 28.0 |
| Pneumonia, excepting pneumonia of new born | 34.9 | 26.2 |
| General arteriosclerosis | 18.5 | 21.2 |
| Diabetes mellitus | 14.1 | 19.4 |
| Cirrhosis of liver | 15.7 | 7.9 |
| Congenital malformations | 12.7 | 10.2 |
| Suicide | 16.5 | 5.4 |

Data drawn from *Vital Statistics of the United States, 1964* (Washington, D.C.: U.S. Department of Health, Education, and Welfare, 1964), II, Pt A, 1-9—1-16.
*Includes birth injuries, postnatal asphyxia, atelectasis, infections, and other diseases peculiar to infancy.

The greater frequency of male suicides has been confirmed in almost all of the studies in which the question has been considered. Louis I. Dublin and Bessie Bunzel, on the basis of their analysis of the phenomenon, were brought to the conclusion that suicide is "largely a masculine phenomenon."[48]

The association of high agency and low communion with suicide is the characteristic conclusion of most studies since Durkheim. Durkheim concluded that egoistic suicide is the result of the low degree of integration of society, and explained, for example, the high suicide rate among Protestants by referring to the tendency toward autonomy in Protestant culture.[49] Dublin and Bunzel write, "For nearly every population group studied, it has been found that the married man and woman, living together as part of the family group, are least apt to commit suicide," and that "suicide is much less common among those who have children than among those who do not."[50]

The divorced, widowed, and single characteristically have substantially higher suicide rates than the married. In one study of people rescued from suicide attempts by the police in Vienna, von Andics came to the following conclusions based on close clinical examination of those persons:

1. The sexuality of the overwhelming majority of persons, who attempted to commit suicide, was beneath the average; the overwhelming majority of the women examined were frigid.

2. The few with normal or hypertrophic sexuality, denied any intention of committing suicide, or, as could be proved, they had only been brought to the clinic on suspicion of committing suicide.

3. As far as my material is concerned, subnormal sexuality became an indirect cause of suicide in two ways: either by making the individual incapable of forming lasting attachments, and then isolat-

[48]Louis I. Dublin and Bessie Bunzel, *To Be or Not To Be: A Study of Suicide* (New York: Harrison Smith and Robert Haas, 1933), p. 54.
[49]Emile Durkheim, *Suicide: A Study in Sociology,* trans. John A. Spaulding and George Simpson (Glencoe, Ill.: The Free Press, 1951), pp. 159, 208ff.
[50]*Op. cit.,* pp. 125, 133.

ing him; or by making his attachment to a single partner too strong, and his being unable to get over the loss of this partner.[51]

In the next section, I distinguish between sexuality which is agentic and sexuality which is communal. Later in this essay, remarkably similar data on cancer patients are cited. At this point, however, I should only point out that the sexuality which von Andics is referring to is communal rather than agentic. Von Andics concludes that the more a person "has to collaborate and the more precise such collaboration is (in the most general meaning of the word), the more firmly will the individual be fixed in his surroundings, the less likely is he to come to find his existence worthless, and the more fraught with meaning life will appear to him" (p. 80). Sorokin aptly summarizes our knowledge about the relationship between the social involvement of the individual and suicide as follows:

We know now that the main cause of suicide is psychosocial isolation of the individual, his state of being lonely in the human universe, not loving or caring for anybody and not being loved by anybody. Each time when the love ties of a person are breaking down, especially breaking abruptly, when his attachments to other persons weaken, when he becomes an unattached and disattached human atom in the universe, his chances of suicide are increasing. Each time when one's love and attachment to one's fellow men multiply and grow stronger, the chances for suicide are decreasing.[52]

Sorokin has argued very strongly on the relationship between love and longevity. One of the most interesting bits of evidence is in his analysis of individuals in history to whom sainthood has been ascribed. He makes the assumption that such persons are outstandingly given to a life of love. He finds that the longevity of saints was substantially greater even than that for the United States population in 1920, and thus considerably greater than their contemporaries. This is the case, he

---

[51]Margarethe von Andics, *Suicide and the Meaning of Life* (London: William Hodge and Company, 1947), p. 125.

[52]Pitirim A. Sorokin, *The Ways and Power of Love* (Boston: Beacon Press, 1954), p. 61.

argues, in spite of the fact that a number of them died prematurely as martyrs.[53]

## SEX DIFFERENCES IN SEXUAL DEVIATIONS

Let us consider heterosexual relationships, with marriage, which entail long-term commitment of the sex partners to each other and to children which result from sex relationships, as a norm, defining all other forms of sexuality as deviations. Let us also assume that what is involved in such normative sexual relations is characteristically a greater synthesis of the agency and the communion features. For in such normative relations, there is not only an interest in sexuality per se, but larger involvement of the persons with each other in long-term larger contexts.

It would then appear that what is involved in deviant sex practices is an expression largely of the agentic rather than the communion feature of sexuality. According to Alfred Adler,

. . . every perversion is the expression of an increased psychological distance from the opposite sex. . . . The perversion indicates a more or less deep-seated revolt against the normal sexual role. . . . Perversion emerges regularly from a personality which generally shows traits of excessive oversensitivity, ambition, and defiance. Egocentric impulses, distrust, and the desire to dominate are prevalent; the inclination to "join in the game" is weak. . . . Consequently we also find a strong limitation of social interest.

The perverted individual keeps at a distance from the problem of love, or moves toward it only slowly. Here we also find the exclusion tendency, which is seen most clearly in homosexuality.[54]

Now, if such deviation from the norm is associated with the agentic, and if, as I have indicated, the agentic is more pronounced in the male, we should find a greater prevalence of sexual deviations in the male than in the female. Indeed, this turns out to be the case. Kinsey has shown that the incidence of premarital coitus, extramarital coitus, masturba-

[53]Pitirim A. Sorokin, *Altruistic Love* (Boston: Beacon Press, 1950), pp. 100ff.
[54]Adler, *op. cit.*, p. 424.

tion, homosexual contacts, and animal contacts are all substantially greater in the male than in the female.[55]

One of the observations which Kinsey made about male homosexuals commends itself to our attention. A common notion about homosexuality is that it constitutes an inversion, an adoption of the cross-sex sexual pattern. Such a characterization simply fails in the face of the data which Kinsey collected. Indeed, what he found is that the male homosexual shows an extreme form of the sexual patterns associated with males generally; one of the more important differences between males and females being in connection with the interest in the genitalia. Kinsey wrote:

Homosexual females frequently criticize homosexual males because they are interested in nothing but genitalia; homosexual males, in turn, may criticize homosexual females because "they do nothing" in a homosexual relationship. The idea that homosexuality is a sexual inversion is dispelled when one hears homosexual females criticizing homosexual males for exactly the same reasons which lead many wives to criticize their husbands, and when one hears homosexual males criticize homosexual females for exactly the things which husbands criticize in their wives. In fact, homosexual males, in their intensified interest in male genitalia and genital activity, often exhibit the most extreme examples of a typically male type of conditioning [p. 659].

## SEX DIFFERENCES IN EROTICISM

### 1. Libido and Eros

Freud used two words to discuss sexuality, "libido" and "Eros." There is some lack of clarity in his writings about the reason for the use of these two words. However, if we examine the contexts, when he spoke of libido he was designating the agentic feature of sexuality, and when he spoke of Eros he was designating the communion feature. Thus, in this discussion, I have asserted that the agency feature is more prominent in the male than in the female. Freud explicitly wrote, as I have

[55]Kinsey, *op. cit.*, pp. 173, 330, 437, 474, 509.

already indicated, that libido is masculine: "Indeed, if one could give a more definite content to the terms, 'masculine' and 'feminine,' one might advance the opinion that the libido is regularly and lawfully of a masculine nature, whether in the man or in the woman...."[56]

Masturbation as a deviation from normative sexuality is associated with the agentic feature of sexuality. Here, too, Freud was clear about the masculine association of masturbation:

. . . the autoerotic activity of the erogenous zones is the same in both sexes.... In respect to the autoerotic and masturbatic sexual manifestations, it may be asserted that the sexuality of the little girl has altogether a male character [p. 612].

Marie Bonaparte has asserted that there is less libido in women than in men, explaining it in terms of natural selection, that reproduction for men is more contingent on a goodly supply of libido than for women.[57] Libido is manifested in an internal tension in the individual which leads to a muscular action as a way of reducing this tension, and is, as Freud put it, analogous to hunger.[58] Eros, on the other hand, according to Freud, "by bringing about a more and more far-reaching combination of the particles into which living substance is dispersed, aims at complicating life."[59] It sometimes has "the power to bind the whole of the destructive elements" (p. 80).

## 2. Aggression and Male Sexuality

I have already cited material which indicates that the aggressive component is greater in the personality of males than females. Kinsey's comparison of the physiological state of the organism under different conditions of emotional arousal

[56]Freud, *Three Contributions to the Theory of Sex*, p. 612.

[57]Marie Bonaparte, *Female Sexuality* (New York: International Universities Press, 1953), p. 66.

[58]Freud, *Three Contributions to the Theory of Sex*, p. 553.

[59]Standard Edition, XIX, 40.

led him to conclude that "the closest parallel to the picture of sexual response is found in the known physiology of anger."[60] Halverson has observed that male infants in a condition of frustration and rage develop erections.[61] Biting of the female sex partner appears as a frequent component of sexual behavior in lower animals and in humans.[62] Arousal by sado-masochistic stories is greater in the male than in the female (pp. 676-77), although the response to being bitten is about the same in males and females (p. 678). The association of sexuality and aggression is clear in the many cases of rape, rape-assault, and rape-murder which are commonplace in the records of criminal activity. Although sex offenses constitute the largest category of female crime, the number of instances in which these involve physical assault by the female is very small.

The relationship between masculine sexuality and aggression is seen in the use of "the principal obscene word of the English language."[63] There is great discrepancy between its actual use in conversation and in print. It is the principal "dirty word" of the English language, suggesting its connection with anality and the autonomous tendencies which are associated with the anal stage. It has strong hostile meanings; for example, "to get fucked" means to be injured, and "fuck you" is hardly an expression of endearment. When the word is used literally, it is a transitive verb in which the female is the object. It contrasts sharply in this respect with other intransitive words and expressions such as "have intercourse with," "sleep with," "get laid," "fornicate," and "coitus." It can be used to indicate destruction, as in "the plan got all fucked up." It is used as an adjective to indicate that what it modifies is distasteful or undesirable, as in "the fucking chair." The word

[60]Kinsey, *op. cit.*, p. 705.

[61]H. M. Halverson, "Infant Sucking and Tensional Behavior," *Journal of Genetic Psychology*, LIII (1938), 365-430.

[62]Kinsey, *op. cit.*, pp. 588, 677-78.

[63]Leo Stone, "On the Principal Obscene Word of the English Language," *International Journal of Psychoanalysis*, XXXV (1954), 30-56.

has extensive use in largely male communities such as armies, prisons, and gangs. It is a word which is largely limited to males and used much more infrequently by females. According to Stone, there is a deep unconscious connection between "suck" and "fuck"; the aggression associated with the latter arises from the ambivalent aggression associated with the separation from the mother and the autonomy associated with the anal stage. It would seem that the aggressive component of the word entails a reaction to the dependence of the oral stage of development and is associated with the anal stage of development.

The association of aggression and male sexuality is clearly involved in most of the considerations in Freud's *Totem and Taboo*. This book deals largely with males and only incidentally with females. In it, Freud was evidently mostly concerned with the agency feature of sexuality. He envisaged an early condition of mankind in which "There is only a violent, jealous father who keeps all the females for himself and drives away the growing sons."[64] The father is killed by the sons, and afterward "Each one wanted to have them all to himself like the father . . ." (p. 917). The actual historical factuality of what Freud is talking about is really quite unimportant. The essay can equally well be understood as a discussion of the agentic feature of human sexuality, more conspicuously present in the male than the female, projected upon history. Its psychological validity, which appeared so strongly to Freud, led him to suppose that anything so central to the psyche must, at some earlier time, have been "acted out."

What is important for our understanding is that in this context Freud drew attention to sexuality as intimately associated with "prerogative" (p. 916) in the condition which he projected. In our common parlance, we use the word "possess" to mean sexual relations. Our thought is brought back to our earlier discussion of the Protestant personality and the capitalistic spirit with which Weber dealt. It will be recalled that we

[64]Freud, *Totem and Taboo*, p. 915.

were brought to the view that in both there is a rise of the agentic. Prerogative and possession are both aspects of *property*. To regard women as property is perhaps paradigmatic of property in general, and the rebellion of women against being regarded as property is an expression of agency in the female. Indeed, it can probably be argued that the struggle over the "possession" of women is as significant for understanding the relations between males and females as it is for understanding the conflicts among men.

## 3. *The Role of Visual Stimulation in Male Eroticism*

One of the major sets of findings in Kinsey's investigation of sexuality is the great difference between the sexes in the conditions of sexual arousal. The male is more frequently stimulated by observing the opposite sex, and this has "often led the male to approach the female for physical contact."[65] Males are more frequently aroused by pictures of nude females. Females are much less frequently aroused by pictures, of either males or females. Kinsey made a rather thorough search of the work of female artists and found that the human figure is rarely depicted in an erotic manner. Males are more aroused by observing the genitalia of women than women are by observing male genitalia. Males are more concerned with the female genitalia in sexual relations. Males prefer sex relations in the light more often than females. Males are more given to sexual fantasy than females. Males are more arousable by erotic stories in which images of sexual parts and relations are depicted.

In general, there is considerably greater perceptual differentiation on the part of the male toward those things in the field which are directly related to sexual activity. Much of male eroticism is associated with the eyes, and the visual field is differentiated in such a manner as to direct the musculature to specific sexual activity. According to Freud, the drive to see the specifically sexual parts of the nude is one of the primitive

[65]Kinsey, *op. cit.*, p. 651.

components of the libido.[66] If the drive to see the nude is of the libido, and if this drive is greater in the male than in the female, we have further evidence for the notion of libido being masculine, as Freud has indicated.

## 4. Female Sexuality More Bound with Relationship

Female sexuality, on the other hand, is much more closely bound with larger interpersonal relationships. Kinsey wrote:

Our data indicate that the average female marries to establish a home, to establish a long-time affectional relationship with a single spouse, and to have children whose welfare may become the prime business of her life. Most males would admit that all of these are desirable aspects of marriage, but it is probable that few males would marry if they did not anticipate that they would have an opportunity to have coitus regularly with their wives. This is the one aspect of marriage which few males would forego, although they might be willing to accept a marriage that did not include some of the goals which the average female considers paramount.[67]

In one study of daydreams of men and women, it was found that the most frequent need drive in men was for new experience in the areas of adventure, travel, and sexual intercourse. The most frequent need drive in women was for affiliation in the areas of marriage and the family.[68]

In dealing with the question of stimuli which might be arousing, Kinsey found that women are somewhat more frequently aroused by love scenes in commercial movies than men, although they are less aroused by portrayals of sexual activity in illegal and sublegal movies. The response of women to literary materials involving general emotional situations, affectional relationships, and love, as well as their writing of such materials, however, is higher than that of males.

The data seem to indicate that love and generalized interpersonal involvement are either the main objective or at least the precondition for specific sexual activity in females.

[66]Freud, *Wit and its Relationship to the Unconscious*, in *Basic Writings*, p. 694.

[67]Kinsey, *op. cit.*, p. 684.

[68]C. W. Lacrome, "Sex and Personality Differences in Relation to Fantasy," *Journal of Consulting Psychology*, XXVII (1963), 270-72.

Kinsey wrote that "females ... would prefer a considerable amount of generalized emotional stimulation before there is any specific sexual contact."[69] In one very comprehensive study of sexual behavior and dating, the investigator concluded:

... pleasure among our females is primarily associated with love and among our males with sex.... The limitation of premarital sexual behavior is primarily female determined.... The female limits her behavior with a nonlover primarily because of no desire and lack of interest and with a lover primarily because of moral considerations.... High frequency of dating many companions among the males appears associated primarily with eroticism and among females with popularity.... Female sexual expression is primarily and profoundly related to being in love and to going steady.... Male sexuality is more indirectly and less exclusively associated with romanticism and intimacy relationships.... Females find pleasure in dating without petting lovers and nonlovers alike and in sexual activities with lovers; and males find pleasure in dating lovers and in sexual activities with all females.... females seem more directly and overtly concerned with romanticism and males with eroticism.... [Males] have a consuming interest in the proper methods and techniques for making sexual advances to a female. The core of interest in sex education of girls is pregnancy, childbirth, and child rearing, whereas of boys it is sex techniques, sexual intercourse, and probable erotic reactions of the female.... [Females have a] greater aversion ... to "sex for sex's sake" and the greater desirability of "sex for love's sake".... love comes to the male within a strongly established erotic orientation, whereas the sex interest of females is aroused within a romantic complex....[70]

## 5. Female "Sexiness" and Masculinity

Alfred Adler made the astute observation that the psychology of the prostitute entails a vaulting masculine identification and rejection of the feminine role.[71] In what is generally

---

[69]Kinsey, *op. cit.*, p. 468.

[70]Winston W. Ehrmann, *Premarital Dating Behavior* (New York: Holt, Rinehart and Winston, 1959), pp. 266-77.

[71]Alfred Adler, "The Individual Psychology of Prostitution," in *The Practice and Theory of Individual Psychology* (New York: The Humanities Press, 1951), pp. 335ff.

recognized as "sexiness" or sexual provocativeness in the female, we can identify the agentic feature of sexuality. Not that I would speak against equality of the sexes in the social sphere, but often the clamor for equality comes from the agentic feature of the female personality, and often it entails an exaggeration of the agentic feature of sexuality as well. The masculine posture of some actresses, Marlene Dietrich for example, is readily recognized by audiences as "sexiness." The deep pitch of her voice — empirical study of masculinity in personality has isolated voice pitch as a major component[72] — is masculine and "sexy." For the same reasons, the highly narcissistic woman is also erotically attractive, as was so well pointed out by Freud. For the strong agentic tendency is announced by intense devotion to self-adornment and the like, and by inability to express communion. As Freud wrote, "The importance of this type of woman for the erotic life of mankind is to be rated very high. Such women have the greatest fascination for men . . . because of a combination of interesting psychological factors."[73] The attractiveness of highly narcissistic women consists in the fact that their conspicuous agentic character indicates that the male's agentic feature of sexuality can be satisfied, while still maintaining repression of communion. Alice S. Rossi, in her very interesting article on "Equality Between the Sexes," has somewhat obliquely, but definitively, recognized the masculine feature in female eroticism.

Men and women who participate as equals . . . will complement each other sexually in the same way. . . . This does not mean, however, that equality in nonsexual roles de-eroticizes the sexual one.

[72]Howard Gilkinson, "Masculine Temperament and Secondary Sex Characteristics: A Study of the Relationship between Psychological and Physical Measures of Masculinity," *Genetic Psychology Monographs*, XIX (1937), 105-54. Helen Gurley Brown, whose book (*Sex and the Single Girl* [New York: Pocket Books, 1964]) demonstrates a profound understanding of agency in the female, in the section called "How To Be Sexy" of the chapter equally called "How To Be Sexy," suggests lowering of the timbre of the voice to increase its seductive quality (pp. 72-73).
[73]Standard Edition, XIV, 89.

The enlarged base of shared experience can, if anything, heighten the salience of sex *qua* sex. In Sweden, where men and women approach equality more than perhaps any other western society, visitors are struck by the erotic atmosphere of that society.... the salience of sex may be enhanced precisely in the situation of the diminished significance of sex as a differentiating factor in all other areas of life.... Maslow...found...that the more "dominant" the woman, the greater her enjoyment of sexuality, the greater her ability to give herself freely in love. Women with dominance feelings were free to be completely themselves, and this was crucial for their full expression in sex. They were not feminine in the traditional sense, but enjoyed sexual fulfillment to a much greater degree than the conventionally feminine women he studied.[74]

As will become clear in the ensuing discussion, "sex *qua* sex" refers to the agency feature of sexuality and not to the communion feature.

## 6. Orgasm as an Agentic Aim

At this point it can be said that the aim of agency is the *reduction of tension*, whereas the aim of communion is *union*. The orgasm is clearly a reduction of tension, and I take it as a fundamental human experience associated with the agency feature. However, since orgasm is an experience associated with both the male and the female of the human species, it would seem that it threatens the neatness of the general statistical overview I have been presenting, in which agency is associated with the male and communion with the female. Thus, it behooves us to consider the nature of the orgasm rather carefully.

  *a. The Involvement of the Musculature in Orgasm.* The available data clearly indicate that there is considerable involvement of the musculature in orgasm. Muscles all over the body contract and then relax, with convulsions of varying degrees over the body. In this respect, orgasm in the male and

[74]Rossi, *op. cit.*, p. 648. See Abraham H. Maslow, "Dominance, Personality, and Social Behavior in Women," *Journal of Social Psychology*, X (1939), 3-39; Abraham H. Maslow, "Self Esteem (Dominance-Feeling) and Sexuality in Women," *Journal of Social Psychology*, XVI (1942), 259-94.

the female is the same, except that in the male there is the additional muscular reaction associated with ejaculation.[75] The involvement of the musculature has been observed in the very careful studies of women masturbating to orgasm by William H. Masters at Washington University in St. Louis.[76] If we take seriously Freud's comment that the musculature is the organ of the death instinct (see p. 172) and our identification of what Freud called the death instinct with the agentic, this involvement of the musculature in orgasm is evidence for the association of orgasm with the agentic.

  *b.  Orgasm in the Female Associated with the Stimulation of the Clitoris and Labia Minora.*  The clitoris of the female is the biological homologue of the penis of the male, and the labia minora are homologous to the skin covering of the penis. Kinsey's study strongly points to these as the principal points of stimulation evocative of orgasm in the female. Orgasm during sexual intercourse, according to Kinsey, results largely from their stimulation. Female masturbation is largely limited to the stimulation of the clitoris and the labia minora, and any kind of vaginal penetration is rare.

Kinsey's data also indicate that there is not much difference in the length of time required to produce orgasm when the clitoris and the labia minora are stimulated consistently. The average amount of time to orgasm is less than four minutes under these circumstances, although the time needed to come to orgasm in the female in coitus is about ten or twenty minutes. According to Kinsey, one of the major factors in this difference is that in coitus there may not be consistent stimulation of these parts.[77]

The introspective data which Kinsey collected led him to the conclusion that there is a *type* of satisfaction associated with sexual intercourse and vaginal penetration which is

[75]Kinsey, *op. cit.*, pp. 160-61, 627ff.

[76]William H. Masters, "The Sexual Response Cycle of the Human Female. I. Gross Anatomic Considerations," *Western Journal of Surgery, Obstetrics, and Gynecology*, LXVIII (1960), 57-72.

[77]Kinsey, *op. cit.*, pp. 625-27.

*different in character*—more communal, I would say—than the kind of satisfaction achieved by stimulation of the clitoris and the labia minora, the latter being associated with orgasm.

On the other hand, many females, and perhaps a majority of them, find that when coitus involves deep vaginal penetrations, they secure a type of satisfaction which differs from that provided by the stimulation of the labia or clitoris alone.... it is obvious that the satisfactions obtained from vaginal penetration must depend on some mechanism that lies outside of the vaginal walls themselves [p. 581].

He suggested that there are psychological factors associated with the relationship to the partner involved in the latter type of satisfaction.

This kind of evidence again points to the dual character of the personality, the two features of sexuality actually being to some degree anatomically and physiologically separate: the agency feature associated with the clitoris, labia minora, musculature, and orgasm in the female, and the penis, musculature, and orgasm in the male; and the communion feature associated with the vagina and the interpersonal relationships in the female. I might point out parenthetically that the studies of Masters and his group at Washington University, in which the female masturbates to orgasm in the laboratory while being photographed and measured, have been carried out only with females who could accomplish this feat. These investigations have what I might identify as an agentic "atmosphere," in which only females who are thus agentically inclined can perform. This criticism of these studies has been made very cogently by Leslie Farber, although he does not use our term "agentic."[78]

   *c. Statistical Differences in Occurrence of Orgasm.* One of the important sex differences uncovered by Kinsey's investigations is connected with the frequency of orgasm. The data are clear that the orgasmic experience is much more

[78]Leslie H. Farber, "I'm Sorry, Dear," *Commentary*, XXXVIII, No. 5 (Nov., 1964), 47-54. Reprinted from *Commentary*, by permission; copyright © 1965 by the American Jewish Committee.

common and frequent for men than for women. Whereas all males in his investigation had experienced orgasm by the time of marriage, 36 per cent of the female sample had not.[79] And among married females between the ages of sixteen and twenty, 22 per cent had never experienced orgasm. The average male by the time of marriage had had orgasm on the average of 1500 times; the average female had experienced orgasm 223 times. Even among those women who were experiencing orgasm with any regularity — and many were not — the average numer of orgasms per week was considerably below that for males. It is clear that the orgasm is an experience which is much more characteristic of males than it is of females.

The evidence collected on infrahuman species seems to indicate that orgasm in the female is an extremely rare occurrence. As Kinsey put it, commenting on the difference between human and infrahuman females, "... as far as our knowledge yet goes, the human female is unique among the mammals in her capacity to reach orgasm with some frequency and regularity when she is aroused sexually" (p. 631).

d. *The Sexual Cycle in the Female.* One of the great mysteries of human sexuality has been the finding that the human female is more sexually responsive to orgasm in the pre- and postmenstrual periods rather than midway between the menstrual periods when ovulation occurs. These are also the times of greatest frequency of masturbation.[80] This is rather remarkable in view of the fact that data on lower animals characteristically indicate greater receptivity to sexual advances precisely at the time of ovulation when conception can occur. Kinsey, in considering this question, commented, "Evidently the human female, in the course of evolution, has

[79]Kinsey, *op. cit.*, p. 519.

[80]See *ibid.*, pp. 609-10, where Kinsey reviewed this literature on masturbation and presented confirming evidence from his own data. Female suicide attempts are also higher premenstrually: M. Zacco, *et al.*, "Statistical Data Concerning the Relationship of Suicide to Menstrual Cycle," *Medicina Psicosomatica*, V (1960), 187.

departed from her mammalian ancestors and developed new characteristics which have relocated the period of maximum sexual arousal near the time of menstruation" (p. 610). There is, however, one investigation which serves to clarify this mystery, a study by Therese Benedek.[81] Careful daily clinical notes were kept on women, who were in psychoanalysis, concerning the state of their sexuality, based on psychoanalytic interpretation, much of it being interpreted from dreams. Thus, for example:

June 11. "I feel better today, I seem to be aware of my breathing. I can see you in the window." She thinks of superficial things around the Institute. Then she talks about the supervisor in her office who interferes with her way of handling children. She tells the following dream:

I dreamed about two people. I was accepting my father or my husband without court action, without any decision on the part of the judge.

The analyst asks who the judge is, and the patient replies, "Perhaps the mother, the supervisor." It is obvious that the judge is also the analyst. The dream means, "I wish I could accept my husband and be in love with him without analysis." But it makes reference to the father also. In this dream we are concerned chiefly with the fact that the patient turns emotionally to her husband. The associations continue: "I think of everything. In the waiting room, this doctor. There are so many good-looking doctors here. That is the way I 'transfer' to men." When the analyst asks "How?" the patient answers, "I go from one to another." She tells about men who are interested in her, and how she acts out her sexual interest in them [p. 98].

This is judged by Benedek as "heterosexual tendency." On the basis of the analysis of such judgments, Benedek concludes that heterosexuality is strongest around the time of ovulation. But we need to pause here. If we assume that Benedek's judgments are correct, they are correct about the *unconscious* processes, rather than any conscious sense of sexual arousal or arousability. The analysis of a dream, accord-

---

[81]Therese Benedek, *Psychosexual Functions in Women.* Copyright 1952 The Ronald Press Company.

ing to Freud, tells us about a *repressed* wish. Actually, Benedek is quite aware of the phenomenon of conscious sexuality around the time of menstruation, since she writes "It is a well-known fact that women are more aware of their sexual need during the premenstrual phase, and that the sexual desire may be more compelling than in other phases of the cycle" (p. 152).

If we put these two sets of observations together, that sexual arousal in women is greatest near the menstrual period, and that, *unconsciously,* the height of sexuality occurs around the time of ovulation, we can clarify the mystery. Agency is higher near the menstrual period; communion near ovulation. Benedek believes that the emotional condition of sexuality around the time of menstruation is associated with elimination and the anal stage of development, and with a masculine identification (p. 153), both of which I have identified with the agency feature. The urge for reproduction, which entails the communion feature more strongly, is repressed in the women who have been subjects of these investigations. Thus, what is reflected in these data is the tendency for the communion feature to be repressed and the agency feature to be heightened; and our conceptualization of sexuality in terms of agency and communion clears up the mystery of the difference between the human female and her mammalian ancestors, as Kinsey put it. What exists in the human being is a greater degree of the agency feature which, although greater in men than in women, explains this biological anomaly in women.

*e. The Significance of the Female Orgasm.* Leslie Farber has raised the question of whether orgasm in the female has not been endowed with excessive significance. He suggests that the importance attributed to the female orgasm is not intrinsic to the psychosexual structure of the female, but is rather due to the particular cultural characteristics of those who have devoted themselves to the study of sex and to the particular sociopolitical situation surrounding the role of women in our society, related especially to the problem of the equality of the sexes. Is not the stress upon the female orgasm part of our general effort to make the woman equal to the man, by endowing the orgasm with an equal place in her psychosexual life?

The political clamor for equal rights for woman at the turn of the century could not fail to join with sexology to endow her with an orgasm, equal in every sense to the male orgasm. It was agreed that she was entitled to it just as she was entitled to the vote. Moreover, if she were deprived of such release her perturbation would be as unsettling to her nervous system as similar frustration was thought to be for the man. Equal rights were to be erotically consummated in simultaneous orgasm....

As far as I know, little attention was paid to the female orgasm before the era of sexology. Where did the sexologists find it? Did they discover it or invent it? Or both?... I cannot believe that previous centuries were not up to our modern delights; nor can I believe it was the censorship imposed by religion which suppressed the supreme importance of the female orgasm. My guess... is that the female orgasm was always an occasional, though not essential, part of woman's whole sexual experience. I also suspect that it appeared with regularity or predictability only during masturbation.... Further, her perturbation was unremarkable and certainly bearable when orgasm did not arrive, for our lovers had not yet been enlightened as to the disturbances resulting from the obstruction or distortion of sexual energies. At this stage her orgasm had not yet been abstracted and isolated from the totality of her pleasures, and enshrined as the meaning and measure of her erotic life.[82]

Kinsey, in spite of the fact that he appeared to focus upon the orgasm as somehow quite central to human sexuality for females as well as for males, still came to the following conclusion:

It cannot be emphasized too often that orgasm cannot be taken as the sole criterion for determining the degree of satisfaction which a female may derive from sexual activity. Considerable pleasure may be found in sexual arousal which does not proceed to the point of orgasm, and in the social aspects of a sexual relationship. Whether or not she herself reaches orgasm, many a female finds satisfaction in knowing that her husband or other sexual partner has enjoyed the contact, and in realizing that she has contributed to the male's

[82]*Op. cit.*, pp. 53-54.

pleasure. We have histories of persons who have been married for a great many years, in the course of which the wife never responded to the point of orgasm, but the marriage had been maintained because of the high quality of the other adjustments in the home.

Although we may use orgasm as a measure of the frequency of female activity, and may emphasize the significance of orgasm as a source of physiologic outlet and of social interchange for the female, it must always be understood that we are well aware that this is not the only significant part of a satisfactory sexual relationship. This is much more true for the female than it would be for the male. It is inconceivable that males who were not reaching orgasm would continue their marital coitus for any length of time.[83]

This disclaimer is interesting, for we cannot overlook the fact that it is tucked away in the middle of a book of over eight hundred pages in which female sexuality is conceived of rather singlemindedly in terms of orgasm. There is no doubt that the researches which have been carried out on the nature of sexuality by the Kinsey and the Masters groups contribute valuable information. At the same time, one cannot but regret that investigators have shown some tendency to read the nature of female sexuality largely in terms of the orgasm. The communion feature of sexuality, which is prominent in the female, does not get quite the attention it deserves to put the total picture in perspective. Farber's observations are indeed very significant in attempting to evaluate these researches. Some years before Kinsey published his findings, Theodor Reik made a similar observation, saying that there was a good deal of scientific work on sexual behavior, and investigators "discuss sex fairly fully nowadays, but there is a conspiracy of silence about love. They avoid the subject, they seem to be embarrassed whenever it is mentioned."[84]

*f. The Independence of the Female Orgasm of Adolescence and Menopause.* Adolescence and menopause essentially demark the years in which childbearing is possible in the life of the female. However, there does not appear to be

[83]*Op. cit.*, p. 371.
[84]Theodor Reik, *A Psychologist Looks at Love* (New York: Farrar and Rinehart, 1944), p. 5.

any relationship between these important changes in the life cycle and the occurrence of orgasm. In contrast to the male, in whom there is a sharp upsurge of the frequency of occurrence of orgasm at adolescence, there is no corresponding jump for the female. The incidence and frequency of orgasm rise steadily with age up to about the middle twenties or thirties, with the onset of menstruation having little effect.[85] Incidence and frequency in the female also seem to be quite unrelated to the occurrence of menopause (p. 735), going into the fifties and sixties (p. 542). Kinsey even cites the case of a ninety-year-old female who was still responding regularly to orgasm (p. 542). This is in dramatic contrast to the male, for whom there is a steady decline from adolescence onward.

The utility of the agentic in the female is partly to be understood by remembering that the human female is part of the human species, and that the human species is characterizable in terms of the fact that its life cycle far exceeds the period of time in which it is capable of reproduction. There is, on the one hand, the relatively large lag between infancy and procreative maturity, and, on the other hand, the long period of time which succeeds the years when reproduction is possible.[86] Thus, there are substantial periods of time in the life cycle of the individual which are almost irrelevant to the reproductive process, differentiating man from most other organisms. It may well be that this characteristic is essential in understanding the difference between man and infrahuman species.

g. *Orgasm and Reproduction.* A banal, yet significant, observation is that the orgasm plays a different role in the male and the female with respect to reproduction. In the male, orgasm and ejaculation of semen are hardly separable, and both are intrinsically related to the male role in reproduction, since the orgasm involves the muscular contraction which makes the semen emerge. In the female, however, the orgasm does not appear to have any functional role in reproduction. As

[85]Kinsey, *op. cit.*, p. 125.
[86]Cf. William H. Masters, "Sex Steroid Influence on the Aging Process," *American Journal of Obstetrics and Gynecology*, LXXIV (1957), 733-46.

Helene Deutsch puts it, whatever satisfaction the female receives is a "pleasure prize that is appended to her service to the species."[87] Woman, writes Deutsch, "suffers from an overendowment, so to speak, which leads to complications" (p. 78). The female of the species is possessed of two sets of organs, one principally associated with personal, individualistic, nonreproductive satisfaction—the clitoris and the labia minora—and the other associated with reproduction—the vagina, the uterus, and the ovaries. The clitoris and the labia minora are homologous to the penis, but without its reproductive function. Marie Bonaparte has written, "Nature does not create the girl wholly feminine, but only more or less so, plus an added masculine factor."[88] It would appear that *the female of the human species is more conspicuously genitally androgynic than the male.* The clear presence of the female orgasm would suggest that the androgynicity of the female is considerably more significant than the androgynicity of the male from a biological point of view. Indeed, it may be that the greater longevity and viability of the female, which we have already discussed, may inhere in this greater androgynicity. Her sexuality, which clearly contains both agentic and communal features, brought Kinsey to conclude that the data "do not provide any evidence that the female ages in her sexual capacities."[89] Male sexuality, on the other hand, which is much more clearly agentic, dies out more rapidly, as does the total male, who is more agentic.

I have indicated that I conceive of the orgasm as associated with agency. The data enumerated would strongly indicate that this is the case; and that it is separated in the female from the reproductive function, which is one of the more important expressions of the communion component. Psychoanalysts have stressed the significance of the transfer of eroticism from the clitoris to the vagina in the proper sexual

[87]*Op. cit.*, II, 77.
[88]*Op. cit.*, p. 139.
[89]Kinsey, *op. cit.*, p. 353.

maturation of the female. It has also been pointed out that this transfer is difficult to achieve, and that it can only take place as a result of direct sexual experience in a sustained satisfactory relationship with a man. Marie Bonaparte, for example, writes of the male's "constructive role in female sexuality."[90] What this suggests is that we may understand *the erotization of the vagina in the female as a manifestation of the fusion of the agency and the communion features.* Through the greater agency of the male in contact with the female, in whom the communion feature is greater, the agentic in the female is brought into contact with her communion feature, working to bring about the synthesis represented by the orgasm resulting from vaginal stimulation.

### DIFFERENTIATION BETWEEN AND WITHIN THE SEXES

At the beginning of this chapter, I made the crude but heuristically valuable assumption that I would seek for a clarification of the nature of agency and communion by the consideration of sex differences. However, in discussing the orgasm, which I identified with the agentic, I was faced critically by the necessity of having to qualify this assumption because, in point of fact, although there are significant differences in the facts of male and female orgasm, the orgasm is still nonetheless very much present in the female. I was brought to the view that the female of the human species is more androgynic, and this is most clearly shown by the fact that the female genitalia consist of two sets of organs. It is now wise to back away from the assumption, which was only made heuristically in the first place.

We need to remind ourselves of an important biological fact. In the formation of the multicellular organism, different sets of organs tend to specialize in functions. In the single-celled organism, the one cell performs all of the functions. In

[90]*Op. cit.*, pp. 116ff.

the multicellular organism, some organs exaggerate one or a few of these functions, with the burden of the other functions being carried by other organs. However, the suspension of all functions by a single cell or a single organ of a multicellular organism is rarely complete. Most often, some vestigial forms of all functions remain; and when other organs of a multicellular organism tend to fail in the performance of their functions, there is a tendency for the vestigial functions to come into operation.

This observation is significant in the consideration of sex differences. For in the male and in the female we have instances of differentiation of function, especially with respect to their roles in reproduction. If we think of agency and communion as two major functions associated with all living substance, then, although agency is greater in the male and communion greater in the female, agency and communion nonetheless characterize both.

Agency and communion are functions of living substance which not only must be understood as parallels between the single-celled and multicelled organisms, but are themselves the functions associated with the separation of cells, organs, or individuals from one another and the unions which may be formed among them. The agency feature is what is involved in the process of differentiation, specialization, and separation of function within and between organismic units; whereas communion is what is involved in a variety of relationships among organismic units. Sexual differentiation is thus particularly significant because it is already a reflection of the agentic feature; and if there is less sexual differentiation within the female, as appears to be the case, it is indicative of a lessened operation of the agentic. Agency is associated with division, but it also works to divide the agentic itself, so that, in the case of sex differentiation, it leaves more of the agentic and less of the communal in the male, and less of the agentic and more of the communal in the female.

In the relations between the sexes, we have a fundamental model of the integration of agency and communion. It is largely the agentic in the male and the communal in the female which bring them together. However, in the contact between the sexes over time, there is the cultivation of the integration of agency and communion within the male and the female, corresponding to the integration of agency and communion between them. The ideal marriage which one may conceive of is then one in which, through the integration of agency and communion which takes place between the marriage partners, a corresponding integration takes place within each of the partners. This is one meaning which we can assign to the religious emphasis on the notion of "wholeness." This is the meaning in the Jewish mystical tradition, in which the Biblical comment that "God created man in his own image, in the image of God created he him; male and female created he them" (Genesis 1:27), was taken as central. And this is the meaning of the emphasis on bisexuality in the writings of the psychoanalysts.

# CHAPTER V

## UNMITIGATED AGENCY AND FREUD'S "DEATH INSTINCT"

The previous chapter considered the correspondence of between-individual to within-individual integration of agency and communion. This chapter again considers such a correspondence but with respect to disintegration. The latter possibility was suggested in the earlier discussion of suicide, in which the literature which indicated that failure of social integration and suicide were related was noted.

Freud advanced the notion in *Beyond the Pleasure Principle* that there exists a "death instinct," an instinct within all living organisms to die. His thesis was most boldly put in his oft-quoted statement that "the goal of all life is death."[1] I attempt in this chapter, with important qualifications, to extract from Freud's writings on the death instinct that which appears to have some validity and to have some claim upon our attention. I use the notions of agency and communion and the enrichment which the congruence with Freud's thought may provide to further our understanding. I believe that Freud was both insightful and confused in his writings about the death instinct. I attempt to illuminate the nature of the confusion, and, instead of turning away completely because the writings are confused, attempt to extract from them what I consider to be of value.

---

[1]Sigmund Freud, *Beyond the Pleasure Principle* (New York: Liveright Publishing Corporation, 1950), p. 50.

### THE DEVELOPMENT OF THE NOTION OF THE DEATH INSTINCT

If a great man writes what appears to be nonsense, as Freud's writings on the death instinct have sometimes been regarded even by psychoanalysts, it behooves us to look again to see what might lie underneath the facade. It is particularly important to consider the biographical context of Freud's writing *Beyond the Pleasure Principle,* first published in 1920, and other writings on the death instinct.

Freud was characteristically preoccupied with death, and particularly so at the time when he was formulating the notion of the death instinct. Ernest Jones wrote of Freud,

As far back as we know anything of his life he seems to have been prepossessed by thoughts about death, more so than any other great man I can think of except perhaps Sir Thomas Browne and Montaigne. Even in the early years of our acquaintance he had the disconcerting habit of parting with the words "Goodbye; you may never see me again." There were the repeated attacks of what he called *Todesangst* (dread of death). He hated growing old, even as early as his forties, and as he did so the thoughts of death became increasingly clamorous.[2]

He was preoccupied with the slaughter of World War I. In a letter to Andreas Salome, dated May 25, 1916, he commented, "Spans of life are unpredictable and I would so much like to be able to have read your contribution before it is too late."[3] He had predicted that his life would come to an end in February, 1918. Jones wrote that, in 1916, "Freud must have felt that he had given to the world all that was in his power, so that little remained beyond living out what was left of life — indeed, only the two years that at that time he believed were allotted to him."[4] In a letter to Binswanger, dated April 20, 1918, Freud commented that he was "an aged man who is no longer too certain of the length of his days."[5]

[2]From *The Life and Work of Sigmund Freud,* Vol. III, *The Last Phase 1919-1939,* p. 279, Copyright © by Ernest Jones, 1957, Basic Books, Inc., Publishers, New York.

[3]From *Letters of Sigmund Freud,* ed. Ernst L. Freud, trans. Tania and James Stern, p. 313, Copyright © 1960 by Sigmund Freud Copyrights, Ltd., Basic Books, Inc., Publishers, New York.

[4]*Op. cit.,* p. 39.

[5]Ludwig Binswanger, *Sigmund Freud: Reminiscences of a Friendship,* trans. Norbert Guterman (New York: Grune and Stratton, 1957), p. 64.

I will presently develop the hypothesis that Freud's thinking on the death instinct bears upon a psychosomatic possibility with respect to cancer. I note here only that cancer as a cause of death was on his mind. In a letter to Eitingon, dated December 2, 1919, he wrote about a friend, "Freund's condition is bad, he has a temperature, is kept under morphia, has himself set December 12 as his limit. The situation isn't clear; the sarcoma metastases are probably spreading." Suggestive of an association of cancer and the new theory of the death instinct is the fact that the *very next sentence* is "I am working very slowly at instinct- and mass-psychology."[6]

Freud's daughter Sophie died on January 25, 1920, at the age of twenty-six. He reacted by referring to it as a "narcissistic injury" in letters of January 27 to Pfister and February 4 to Ferenczi (p. 328). I would point out here that Freud used the term "narcissism" in connection with cancer, and that he was thinking of death and its psychological meaning in a most personal way, as was characteristic of him.

In a letter to Binswanger, who evidently also had cancer, apologizing for not having replied earlier to a January 7 letter from him, Freud wrote of two deaths, Freund's and Sophie's, on March 14, 1920:

First I had day by day to watch the gradual failing of a dear friend. . . . You will easily understand why it was particularly to you that I could not write, when I tell you that for a year and a half the thought of what had happened to you filled me with hope for him. He had undergone the same operation as you, but was not spared the recurrence. We buried him on January 22.

He then went on to tell of Sophie's death, which took place a few days later:

Since then a heavy oppression has been weighing on all of us, which also affects my capacity for work. Neither of us has got over the monstrous fact of children dying before their parents.[7]

Later in this chapter, I cite some data indicating the possible association of the loss of loved ones with cancer. It is of

[6]*Letters*, p. 326.
[7]Binswanger, *op. cit.*, p. 68.

interest that Freud has suggested in *Totem and Taboo* that children had a youth-saving effect on parents. "Parents are said to remain young with their children, and this is, in fact, one of the most valuable psychic benefits which parents derive from their children."[8]

Freud wrote of a date almost exactly a year later:

On March 13 of this year [1921] I quite suddenly took a step into real old age. Since then the thought of death has not left me, and sometimes I have the impression that seven of my internal organs are fighting to have the honor of bringing my life to an end. There was no proper occasion for it, except that Oliver said good-by on that day when leaving for Roumania.[9]

In a letter to Binswanger, dated November 3, 1921, he wrote: "It pleased me that despite my advanced age you gave me hope of living to see the first volume of your work; let us hope that the second will not put my stubborn attachment to life to too hard a test."[10]

Freud started writing *Beyond the Pleasure Principle* in March, 1919, about a year after the date he had predicted for his death, and it was published in 1920. *Group Psychology and the Analysis of the Ego*, in which he tried to apply the notion of Eros, the antithetical instinct to the death instinct, to the formation of the larger social group, was published in 1921. In a letter to Romain Rolland, dated March 4, 1923, he said of *Group Psychology and the Analysis of the Ego* that "it shows a way from the analysis of the individual to an under-standing of society."[11] *The Ego and the Id* occupied him between July and the end of 1922. It was very shortly there-after, in February, 1923, that Freud reported he had discov-ered a growth in his jaw and palate, a cancer which he referred to as a "tissue rebellion."[12] Ernest Jones devoted a substantial portion of the third volume of his biography of Freud to

[8]Freud, *Basic Writings,* p. 818.

[9]Jones, *op. cit.,* p. 79.

[10]Binswanger, *op. cit.,* p. 70.

[11]*Letters,* p. 342.

[12]Jones, *op. cit.,* p. 89.

recounting the grim medical details associated with Freud's cancer. Some have criticized Jones on this account. Yet, I believe that he must have been guided by a sense of the significance of this medical history for the appreciation of Freud. I would suggest the hypothesis that *there are connections between Freud's notion of the death instinct and the fact that these works were written at a time when one might presume that the processes associated with the development of cancer may have been active in him.*

A secondary hypothesis — nay, rather, a suspicion — which the data suggest is that these writings may also have been representative of Freud's efforts to manage and counteract these very same forces, that his writings reflect a certain effort at self-analysis and therapy. Simply put, if indeed the locus of the death instinct is in the ego, as Freud suggested, he turned to the understanding of the nature of this ego; and, if cancer is a cellular phenomenon, he sought to understand the nature of the cellular in the best way he knew how, through the analysis of whatever psychological factors may be connected with the cellular level, as he attempted to do in *Beyond the Pleasure Principle.* In February, 1923, when Freud first reported his "tissue rebellion," he was almost sixty-seven years old, and he lived until September, 1939, sixteen and a half years after the diagnosis, to die at eighty-three, a ripe old age under any circumstances. Writing *Beyond the Pleasure Principle* was, for Freud, a genuine turning point in his intellectual career, as he himself indicated.[13] His work after this was largely devoted to the cultural and the social, including *The Future of an Illusion, Civilization and its Discontents,* and *Moses and Monotheism.* What he seemed to be struggling to create in these writings was a social ego identity which exceeded the individual psychology of his earlier writings. In the terms which I have been developing in this essay, the nature of Freud's self-analysis consisted in coming to understand *the association of*

[13]"Postscript to Autobiographical Study," Standard Edition, XX, 71-74.

*death with the agentic and cognizing the communion feature
in the concept of Eros.*

There are indications that Freud's writings on the death
instinct and Eros were very "personal." Ernest Jones, in spite
of his closeness to Freud and his great sympathy for Freud's
writings and ideas, regarded *Beyond the Pleasure Principle*
more as a psychological document to be used for understanding Freud's personality than as a contribution of general
interest. "He had never written anything of the sort in his life
before, and this itself is a matter of the highest interest to any
student of his personality." He was "surrendering the old
control."[14] We might interpret the seeming surrender of the
"old control," as Jones put it, as an effort by Freud to surrender the agentic as a means toward healing, in the way
indicated in Chapter III. Freud said, "Many people will shake
their heads over it" (p. 40), and, wrote Jones, "Freud was right.
Many people, including many analysts, did shake their heads
over the new ideas and are still doing so" (p. 41). According to
Jones,

It is somewhat discursively written, almost as if by free associations, and there are therefore occasional gaps in the reasoning.... 
This mode of writing in itself indicates that *the ideas propounded
must be transmuted from some personal and profound source,* a
consideration which greatly adds to their interest [p. 266. Italics
added.].

In a letter which Freud wrote while he was writing *Beyond
the Pleasure Principle*, he said,

I am writing the new essay on "Beyond the Pleasure Principle,"
and count on your understanding, which has never yet failed me.
Much of what I am saying in it is pretty obscure, and the reader must
make what he can of it. Sometimes one cannot do otherwise [pp. 39-
40].

As I have said, there are some data which suggest that
cancer may be associated with the loss of loved ones. In
*Beyond the Pleasure Principle*, Freud strongly indicates that

[14]*Op. cit.*, p. 41.

his very advancing of the notion of the death instinct had its basis in personal loss. He candidly wrote:

Perhaps we have adopted the belief [in the existence of a death instinct] because there is some comfort in it. If we are to die ourselves, and first to lose in death those who are dearest to us, it is easier to submit to a remorseless law of nature, to the sublime Ἀνάγκη [Necessity], than to a chance which might perhaps have been escaped. It may be, however, that this belief in the internal necessity of dying is only another of those illusions which we have created "um die Schwere des Daseins zu ertragen."[15]

This passage is particularly interesting in that earlier in the book, when he was attempting to show the nature of the death instinct as associated with the development of the ego in the child and the formation of the "repetition compulsion," he wrote, "Loss of love and failure leave behind them a permanent injury to self-assurance in the form of a narcissistic scar," and "love characteristic of the age of childhood is brought to an end" (p. 22). I have already indicated that Freud took the death of loved ones as a "narcissistic injury."

Nor can one avoid seeing a personal reference in the following, which Freud offered in explication of the repetition compulsion, after having read Jones's account of Freud's grief at being abandoned by various of his proteges:

Thus we have come across people all of whose human relationships have the same outcome: such as the benefactor who is abandoned in anger after a time by each of his *protégés*, however much they may otherwise differ from one another, and who thus seems doomed to taste all the bitterness of ingratitude. . . . [p. 24].

INDICATIONS THAT FREUD'S WRITINGS ON THE DEATH
INSTINCT PERTAIN TO CANCER

There are several reasons for suspecting that Freud's writings on the death instinct pertain to cancer.

Freud, as we know from his other writings, was very much given to combining his own life with his scientific contribu-

[15]*Beyond the Pleasure Principle*, p. 59, "To bear the burden of existence."

tions. *The Interpretation of Dreams* is probably the best example of this, in which he created a theory of dreams largely out of a personal analysis of his own dreams. Thus, it would not be at all inconsistent that the considerations which he presented on the death instinct should pertain to the relevant aspects of his experiences at the time. We have already seen that Jones sensed that the ideas on the death instinct were "transmuted from some personal and profound source." If cancer has any psychological features associated with it, then we are in the unusual position of having available to us what we may interpret as the introspective work of the man who was perhaps the greatest psychologist and introspectionist of our age.

Dr. Roy R. Grinker has cited the possibility that a patient may be unconsciously aware of a malignancy before clinical diagnosis. "Our liaison psychiatrists have often found that the nature of a patient's depression and insomnia or the degree of his anxiety enables them to predict that he unconsciously is aware of the presence of a malignant or disintegrating disease often long before the internist is able to make a correct diagnosis."[16] Could we not then suppose that so great an introspectionist, indeed the one from whom these psychiatrists have learned much of their art, might equally have displayed such psychological signs, and furthermore have been somewhat more insightful than these patients? If cancer has any psychological involvement, then we might learn something from the close examination of Freud's writings during the period when we can presume that the factors associated with the development of cancer were operative; and perhaps take some further hints from him from the fact that he lived so long into a "ripe old age" with cancer.

*Beyond the Pleasure Principle* is an explicit attempt to bring the psychoanalytic orientation to bear on the cellular level. Freud wrote: "Accordingly, we might attempt to apply

[16]Roy R. Grinker, "Psychosomatic Aspects of the Cancer Problem," duplicated unpublished manuscript, p. 13.

the libido theory which has been arrived at in psychoanalysis to the mutual relationship of cells."[17] He also explicitly referred to cancer as narcissism: "The *cells of the malignant neoplasms* which destroy the organism should also perhaps be described as *narcissistic* in this same sense. . . ."[18]

[17]*Beyond the Pleasure Principle*, pp. 67-68.

[18]*Ibid.*, p. 68. Italics added. Norman Mailer's *Dead Ends*, which he says is written by a homosexual, is worthy of attention (Reprinted by permission of G. P. Putnam's Sons from *Advertisements for Myself*, by Norman Mailer, pp. 452-57. Copyright © 1959 by Norman Mailer.). It presumably deals with cancer. Mailer, in identifying cancer with narcissism, may have been influenced by this line in Freud. Mailer writes:

> *In the logic of retreat,* said I even louder,
>   *when the body and mind are sick*
>     *(in their cups of*
>       *cowardice and despair and defeat*
>       *and hatred which never breathed*
>         *the air of open rage)*
>   *then we are left only to choose our disease*
>       *for by the sick of logic*
>     *the choice is closed to suffer*
>       *psychosis*
>         *or take one's odds*
>     *that the insanity from which we flee*
>     *will not hunt the boredom of our cells*
>       *into the arms*
>       *of the arch-narcissist*
>     *our lover, the devil,*
>       *whose ego is iron*
>       *and never flags*
>       *in its wild respect*
>       *for cool power.*
>   *Narcissism, I say, yes, narcissism*
>     *is the cause of cancer*
>   *Cancer comes to those who*
>       *do not love their mate*
>       *so much as they are loved*
>       *when they look at themselves*
>         *in the mirror* [pp. 453-54].

Later in the same poem, he writes:

> Our weary Father cannot sleep
>     for fear
>       that our first act
>     upon achieving Him
>     would be
>     to cut
>     His throat.
> So he bribed the devil with cancer
> The queer of the diseases [p. 455].

162

In Freud's relationship to Georg Groddeck, we can find some grounds for suspecting that he may have been aware of and concerned with the relationship between psychological factors and cancer.

In Groddeck's *The Book of the It,* a psychological hypothesis with respect to cancer is clearly formulated:

...it is the unknown It, not the conscious intelligence, which is responsible for various diseases ... or do you find it impossible that a being which has produced from spermatozoon and egg a man with a man's brain and a man's heart can also bring forth cancer....?[19]

...I do not consider it unreasonable to suppose that it'[the It] can even manufacture ... cancer [p. 101].

Freud had certainly read Groddeck's book, having taken the notion of the *It* from it for *The Ego and the Id,* acknowledging his debt to Groddeck for contributions to his thought.[20] In a letter of June 5, 1917, he told Groddeck that he considered him "an analyst of the first order who has grasped the essence of the matter once for all."[21] Not only had Freud read Groddeck's work on organic diseases as psychologically determined, but he had even bickered a bit with him over priority with respect to the notion:

Whether he [Groddeck] gives the "UCS" the name of "Id" as well makes no difference. Let me show you that the notion of the UCS requires *no extension* to cover your experiences with organic diseases. In my essay on the UCS which you mention you will find an inconspicuous note: "An additional important prerogative of the UCS will be mentioned in another context." I will divulge to you what this note refers to: the assertion that the UCS exerts on somatic processes an influence of far greater plastic power than the conscious act ever can [p. 317].

He also wrote, "No doubt the UCS is the right mediator between the physical and mental, perhaps it is the long-sought-for 'missing link'" (p. 318). Groddeck's book was

[19]Georg Groddeck, *The Book of the It* (New York: The New American Library, 1961), p. 31.

[20]Sigmund Freud, *The Ego and the Id* (London: The Hogarth Press, Ltd., 1950), pp. 27-28.

[21]*Letters,* p. 316.

actually not published until 1923, but it is clear that it was available to Freud much earlier. In a letter of March 25, 1923, he congratulated Groddeck on the book being published "at last" and referred to the use to which he put it in *The Ego and the Id*, saying, "I like the little book very much" (p. 342).

I can find no reference in Freud to Groddeck's discussion of cancer specifically, but it is clear that Freud had read Groddeck and was favorable to his notions, even to the point of claiming that he had advanced the psychogenic notion of disease himself before Groddeck. I have already indicated that Freud was thinking about cancer and alluded to it in *Beyond the Pleasure Principle*. The extension I make is that in Freud's writings on the death instinct, it was the phenomenon of cancer which was largely involved in his theoretical speculations.

In *The Ego and the Id*, Freud wrote that the ego, in which the death instinct is located, is "first and foremost a body-ego."[22] In a late paper, he wrote that "for the psychical field, the biological field does in fact play the part of the underlying bedrock."[23] In much of Freud's writings, the biological is taken as such. In *Beyond the Pleasure Principle*, he dealt rather extensively with biological data and theory in connection with the cells, and, as I have indicated, specifically mentioned "malignant neoplasms." He located the death instinct in the ego in personality and within each individual cell. He indicated that he was "driven to conclude that the death instincts are by their nature mute"[24] and that "the death instincts seem to do their work unobtrusively,"[25] which might in some way be allusions to the mute and unobtrusive way in which cancer develops in the early stages. Of all diseases, cancer is most prominent in that it appears to be based on forces "immanent in the organism itself" (p. 51), as Freud referred to the death instinct.

[22]Standard Edition, XIX, 27.
[23]*Ibid.*, XXIII, 252.
[24]*Ibid.*, XIX, 46.
[25]*Beyond the Pleasure Principle*, p. 87.

## FREUD'S MODIFICATION OF THE LIBIDO THEORY

Before writing *Beyond the Pleasure Principle*, Freud had already modified his original libido theory by making the distinction between the sexual instincts and the ego instincts.[26] In *Beyond the Pleasure Principle*, he took the next step of identifying the death instinct[27] with the latter. Yet he was still handicapped by his former libido theory, so that his use of the concept of libido is sometimes entangling and inhibiting of understanding. Thus, instead of abandoning the libido theory completely, he continued to drag it around. He almost literally was not quite sure where to put it. In his earlier treatment, he had considered the ego as the "great reservoir" of libido.[28] In *The Ego and the Id*, he wrote that, with the distinction of ego and id, "we must recognize the id as the great reservoir of libido."[29] The awkwardness of conceptualization was so great that he was forced to produce such a logical atrocity as a "desexualized Eros" (p. 63). The modification of the theory was not thoroughgoing. I believe that much of the unclarity associated with *Beyond the Pleasure Principle* and *The Ego and the Id* inheres in the fact that Freud was struggling to present something which appeared more valid to him, and yet trying to reconcile his newer notions with the older ones.

I have no difficulty in identifying the libido of Freud's earlier treatment with what I have been calling agency. Libido is associated with all of the sexual perversions,[30] with masturbation (pp. 588ff.), with sadism, independence, solitariness, and estrangement (p. 596). Libido is associated with cruelty and looking at the genitalia (p. 596). Libido is associated with acquisition. Libido is associated with mastery (*Bemächtigungstrieb*) (p. 590). Its aim is to get rid of sexual substances,

---

[26]"On Narcissism: An Introduction" (1914), in *Collected Papers* IV, 35.

[27]Freud sometimes used this in the singular and sometimes in the plural.

[28]Freud, *Three Contributions to the Theory of Sex*, p. 611.

[29]Standard Edition, XIX, 30.

[30]*Three Contributions to the Theory of Sex*, pp. 553ff. Cf. the discussion of the perversions.

reducing tension (p. 608). It is associated with the musculature (pp. 598, 600, 662) and with the urgency of sexual desire
(pp. 612-13). It is related to aggression (pp. 612-13). Furthermore, the libido theory which Freud developed appeared
to pertain much more to males than to females, although
he did try to work it in for females. He discussed the fore-
pleasure of sexuality as a perversion (p. 607). We have seen
that there are differences between the sexes in regard to the
importance of the relationship as a precondition for sexual
relations. He wrote quite candidly, "The male sexual development is more consistent and easier to understand . . ." (p. 604).
I would suggest that the male is "easier to understand" *from
the libido theory*, because of the greater agency in the male
than in the female.

A rather interesting change is manifest in Freud's conception of libido. Whereas, in his earlier writing, love is conceived as secondary and in some way *derivative* from libido,
in his later writing, after his formulations of *Beyond the
Pleasure Principle*, he attempted to identify libido in some
*original* sense with love, moving from a definition of libido as
agentic to libido as communal. Thus, whereas earlier libido is
defined as "a quantitative energy directed to an object" (p.
553), he subtly changed libido so that it is not defined as
directed toward an object. Thus, he wrote, in *Group Psychology and the Analysis of the Ego*,

Libido is an expression taken from the theory of the emotions.
We call by that name the energy, regarded as a quantitative magni-
tude . . . , of those instincts which have to do with all that may be
comprised under the word "love." The nucleus of what we mean by
love naturally consists (and this is what is commonly called love, and
what the poets sing of) in sexual love with sexual union as its aim. But
we do not separate from this — what in any case has a share in the
name "love" — on the one hand, self-love, and on the other, love for
parents and children, friendship and love for humanity in general,
and also devotion to concrete objects and to abstract ideas. Our
justification lies in the fact that psycho-analytic research has taught us
that all these tendencies are an expression of the same instinctual

impulses; in relations between the sexes these impulses force their way towards sexual union, but in other circumstances they are diverted from this aim or are prevented from reaching it, though always preserving enough of their original nature to keep their identity recognizable (as in such features as the longing for proximity, and self-sacrifice).[31]

What is evident in this paragraph is a struggle. He had an original notion of libido which was largely agentic. Yet the communion feature of sexuality was pressing itself on his attention. He shifted the meaning of libido to love that "the poets sing of," which is generally love in the communion sense. And then he added that libido is to be recognized in such things as longing for proximity and self-sacrifice, again the communion feature of sexuality.

I might point out parenthetically that, whereas in his earlier thinking sadism and masochism were linked together as simply the expression of ambivalence with an underlying unity, he backed away from this position. Sadism, he wrote, may be regarded as "a pure culture of the death instinct."[32] Masochism he earlier saw as sadism turned around. He wrote that he had been led to believe "that masochism ... must be regarded as sadism that has been turned round upon the subject's own ego."[33] But he was forced to change his view: "The account that was then given of masochism would need to be emended for being too sweeping: there *might* be such a thing as primary masochism — a possibility which I had contested at that time" (p. 75). What Freud is struggling with here can, I believe, be clarified by the distinction between agency and communion. Phenotypic masochism may indeed obscure two different forms of genotypic masochism. First, we may identify the masochism which emerges from the agency feature. These are "the mysterious masochistic trends of the ego" (p. 11), which Freud had in mind as he was expounding the

[31]From *Group Psychology and the Analysis of the Ego* (1921), Volume XVIII of the Standard Edition of *The Complete Psychological Works of Sigmund Freud*, pp. 90-91, by permission of Liveright, Publishers, N.Y., Sigmund Freud Copyrights Ltd., Mr. James Strachey and The Hogarth Press Ltd.

[32]Standard Edition, XIX, 53.

[33]*Beyond the Pleasure Principle*, p. 74.

nature of the death instinct. Second, there are the tendencies associated with identifying with others and exaggeratedly deferring to them, the type of masochism Deutsch has identified in female sexuality, which is much more closely related to the communion feature.[34] Indeed, the so-called masochistic trends in women, trends which appear to be related to the communion feature, may be masochistic only in a very special sense. Such genuine indications of masochism as alcoholism, suicide, and self-flagellation are much more frequent among males than among females. Freud has a footnote to his comment about "primary" masochism, alluding to the writing of a woman, saying "A considerable portion of these speculations have been anticipated by Sabina Spielrein . . . in an instructive and interesting paper which, however, is unfortunately not entirely clear to me."[35] I believe that the "primary" masochism to which Freud was alluding is the masochism which is associated with the communion feature. Indeed, he referred to it as a regression (p. 75), which is exactly the way in which he characterized female sexuality more generally.[36]

In this connection, too, it is interesting to note the way in which Freud dealt with the matter of the death instinct in women. In the psyche, he identified the death instinct as largely in the superego and traced it to the Oedipus complex.[37] Yet, somehow, all of this is not so evident to him in women. In discussing the development of the superego, he commented, "It seems that the male sex has taken the lead in developing all of these moral acquisitions; and that they have then been transmitted to women by cross-inheritance" (p. 50).

In a paper published in 1925, he wrote that in girls "the Oedipus complex . . . is . . . a secondary formation,"[38] and that

[34]*The Psychology of Women*. Feminine masochism, Deutsch says, "lacks the cruelty, destructive drive, suffering, and pain by which masochism manifests itself in perversions and neuroses" (I, 191).

[35]*Beyond the Pleasure Principle*, p. 75.

[36]*Three Contributions to the Theory of Sex*, p. 604.

[37]*The Ego and the Id*, pp. 68ff.

[38]Standard Edition, XIX, 251.

he "cannot escape the notion (though I hesitate to give it expression) that for women the level of what is ethically normal is different from what it is in men" (p. 196). "Their super-ego is never so inexorable" (p. 196), and "they show less sense of justice than men" (p. 197). Freud was clearly dealing with the agentic. Guilt is hardly a feature associated with communion, for, as I have indicated, communion is much more important for female sexuality. It might be pointed out parenthetically that one of the major differences Ehrmann found in his study of sexuality is that whereas men often show a large discrepancy between their sexual code and their sexual behavior, women show a very close correspondence, which would suggest less guilt in the latter.[39]

## THE DEATH INSTINCT AND "DEFUSION"

We are now in a position to understand somewhat better why Freud should have identified the death instinct as being in the ego. *He recognized the force toward death which was associated with the agentic,* which the data cited earlier tend to indicate, as evidenced in the greater propensity for death in males. Understanding that there were reasons for confusion in Freud's thought, let us attempt to extract what may be considered to be positive.

One of the major roles which Freud assigned to the death instinct is that of "defusion." He ascribed to the death instinct a variety of separations both biological and psychological and dealt with these various separations very syncretistically. He cited with favor the view of Plato that there was an original being who was cut in two to make the two sexes. "Shall we follow the hint given to us by the poet-philosopher, and venture upon the hypothesis that living substance at the time of its coming to life was torn apart into small particles, which have ever since endeavoured to reunite through the sexual instincts?" (See pp. 43-44 above.) Out of the ego is differen-

[39]*Op. cit.*

tiated the superego, which becomes a "pure culture of the death instinct." And in the same way that he showed that single-celled organisms are destroyed by their own products, the ego is destroyed: "... the ego is meeting with a fate like that of the protista which are destroyed by the products of decomposition that they themselves have created."[40] Ambivalence and sublimation are conceived of as instances of defusion (pp. 58, 80). There is the "gulf between the actual individual and the conception of the species" (p. 52). He was attracted by Weismann's distinction between the soma and the germ-plasm, the latter being immortal, providing an "unexpected analogy with our own view."[41] He saw the male orgasm as a separation of the semen in which Eros is located.

The ejection of sexual substances in the sexual act corresponds in a sense to the separation of soma and germ-plasm. This accounts for the likeness of the condition that follows complete sexual satisfaction to dying, and for the fact that death coincides with the act of copulation in some of the lower animals. These creatures die in the act of reproduction because, after Eros has been eliminated through the process of satisfaction the death instinct has a free hand for accomplishing its purposes.[42]

The aim of the death instinct is the

... return to the quiescence of the inorganic world. We have all experienced how the greatest pleasure attainable by us, that of the sexual act, is associated with a momentary extinction of a highly intensified excitation.[43]

There are also normal purposes which are achieved by the death instinct. It is associated with self-preservation, even though it leads to death in its own time (p. 51). It is associated with self-assertion and mastery (p. 51). It provides the pleasure of tension reduction for the individual (pp. 3ff., 27ff.), and especially sexual gratification. In "the stage of genital primacy, it takes on, for the purposes of reproduction, the function of

[40]Freud, Standard Edition, XIX, 56-57.
[41]*Beyond the Pleasure Principle*, pp. 60ff.
[42]Standard Edition, XIX, 47.
[43]*Beyond the Pleasure Principle*, p. 86.

overpowering the sexual object to the extent necessary for carrying out the sexual act" (p. 74). It separates the organism from the outside world by creating a dead outer layer which, "By its death . . . has saved all the deeper ones from a similar fate" (p. 32), which outer layer, by the way, protects against stimulation in the identity of the cortex with the ego (p. 28). And, what is perhaps most important psychologically, it is associated with repression, the profound separation of that which is conscious from that which is unconscious.[44]

According to Freud, the death instinct is also associated with illness. Even before he had developed the notion of the death instinct, the communion feature was involved in psychoanalysis, in overcoming repression, transference, and even suspension of the use of the musculature, as when the patient lies on a couch. In his paper on narcissism, in which we can see the beginning of the thought associated with his later development of the death instinct, he wrote: "A strong egoism is a protection against falling ill, but in the last resort we must begin to love in order not to fall ill, and we are bound to fall ill if, in consequence of frustration, we are unable to love."[45] It is the separated unconscious superego, as a "pure culture of the death instinct," which works against the effectiveness of psychoanalysis. There are people who "get worse during the treatment instead of getting better. . . . There is no doubt that there is something in these people that sets itself against their recovery, and its approach is dreaded as though it were a danger."[46] And "there is often no counteracting force of similar strength which the treatment can put in motion against it" (p. 72).

## "SPECIALIZATION" OF THE DEATH INSTINCT

Freud envisaged the possibility that the death instinct can be subject to differentiation and specialization both on the

[44]*The Ego and the Id*, p. 28.
[45]Standard Edition, XIV, 85.
[46]Standard Edition, XIX, 49.

psychological and biological levels. Psychologically, it is lodged in the ego, and more particularly in the superego. It is manifest in such psychological conditions as the repetition compulsion and sadism. When cells unite to form a multicellular organism under the influence of Eros, the death instinct can, so to speak, be concentrated in single organs and directed outward.

It appears that, as a result of the combination of unicellular organisms into multicellular forms of life, the death-instinct of the single cell can successfully be neutralized and *the destructive impulses be diverted towards the external world through the instrumentality of a special organ. This special organ would seem to be the musculature;* and the death-instinct would thus seem to express itself — though probably only in part — as an instinct of destruction directed against the external world and other living organisms [pp. 56-57. Italics added.].

The activity of the dangerous death-instincts within the individual organism is dealt with in various ways; in part they are rendered harmless by being fused with erotic components, in part they are diverted towards the external world in the form of aggression, while for the most part they undoubtedly continue their inner work unhindered [p. 79].

The relationship of the ego, the death instinct which it contains, and the musculature was indicated by Freud as the ego being in control of the musculature: "The functional importance of the ego is manifested in the fact that normally control over the approaches to motility devolves upon it" (p. 30). The relationship of the ego to the outside world is primarily visual, although it also wears "an auditory lobe . . . crooked, as one might say" (p. 29). Verbal images are much more important in internal perception. We might recall at this point the observations that auditory is more important than visual perception in female as contrasted with male sexuality, the greater communicative skill of females, the greater degree of "intuition" in women as described by Deutsch, and Freud's observation that the latent dream thoughts are not visual, as contrasted with the manifest dream. Thus, the ego has its place principally in connection with the

"reality" of the visual world and the control of the musculature acting upon it.

Eros itself, to some degree, also tends to become differentiated and lodged in particular parts of the multicellular organism. But the organism can remain alive if it yields to the major
function of Eros itself, the coalescence with other cells:

> ... the whole path of development to natural death is not trodden
> by *all* the elementary entities which compose the complicated body
> of one of the higher organisms. Some of them, the germ-cells, proba-
> bly retain the original structure of living matter and, after a certain
> time ... separate themselves from the organism as a whole.... These
> germ-cells, therefore, work against the death of the living substance
> and succeed in winning for it what we can only regard as potential
> immortality.... We must regard as in the highest degree significant
> the fact that this function of the germ-cell is reinforced, or only made
> possible, if it coalesces with another cell similar to itself and yet
> differing from it.[47]

As long as the death instinct is thus aided by Eros in
keeping aggression turned outward, there is some possibility
of survival. However, when this diversion through the specialized functions of the ego and the musculature is not possible,
the death instinct is turned against the ego itself:

> It is remarkable that the more a man checks his aggressive tend-
> encies towards the exterior the more severe — that is aggressive — he
> becomes in his ego ideal.... The fact remains, however, as we have
> stated it: the more a man controls his aggressiveness, the more
> intense becomes his ideal's inclination to aggressiveness against his
> ego. It is like a displacement, a turning round upon his own ego.[48]

### THE DEATH INSTINCT AND ASEXUAL REPRODUCTION

I have indicated earlier that the image of Satan is associated with asexual reproduction, as seen, for example, in
Goethe's Homunculus (see p. 69 above). It is thus interesting to note that Freud associated asexual reproduction with

[47]*Beyond the Pleasure Principle,* pp. 52-53.
[48]Standard Edition, XIX, 54.

the death instinct. He discussed Weismann's view that uni-cellular organisms are immortal and that death is only present in multicellular organisms, and some experiments which de-monstrated reproduction by fission alone for 3029 generations by isolating the parts and putting them in fresh water.[49] These data would speak against a death instinct in the single-celled organism. For Freud, the death instinct was conceived of as having come into existence *prior* to the development of Eros and heterosexual reproduction. Thus, whether the data are cogent or not, he seemed to be taken by another series of experiments which demonstrated that single-celled organisms tend to grow weaker, become smaller, lose part of their organi-zation, and die unless they engage in conjugation, "no doubt the fore-runner of the sexual reproduction of higher crea-tures," which saves them from growing old and rejuvenates them (p. 64). Rather than accepting the view of the immortality of the single-celled organisms, which would seem to indicate that they had no death instinct, he tried to argue that there is a tendency toward death within them, at least insofar as they do not display a union with other cells. He backed away from data which would force a contrary position by writing,

The primitive organization of these creatures may conceal from our eyes important conditions which, though in fact present in them too, only become *visible* in higher animals where they are able to find morphological expression. And if we abandon the morphological point of view and adopt the dynamic one, it becomes a matter of complete indifference to us whether natural death can be shown to occur in protozoa or not. The substance which is later recognized as being immortal has not yet become separated in them from the mortal one [p. 66].

What we see here is an effort by Freud to have the death instinct associated with asexual reproduction. He went to the empirical data, cited them at length, and then, when they did not quite bear out the point of view which he wished to express, spoke of them as being of "complete indifference."

I believe that had he been able to find full confirmation of

[49]*Beyond the Pleasure Principle*, pp. 62-63.

a primary death instinct in the single-celled organism, he undoubtedly would have given it considerable weight, for he would have had a confirmation of a relationship between asexual reproduction and the death instinct. But not finding it, he shrugged it off and continued in the same line of thought.

My hypothesis is that what Freud was in some sense trying to point out is a relationship between that which he identified as the death instinct and cancer. For, in the latter, we have a rather clear instance of a kind of asexual reproduction. He handicapped himself with a notion of the death instinct as being more original than Eros — agency more original than communion — and some obligation to find what he was looking for in the single-celled organism. We can, indeed, see in this the same handicap dealt with earlier, the older libido theory which made love derivative from libido. There is no a priori reason for supposing agency to be prior to communion.

Yet the more particular point remains, if we add our interpretation to it. Freud was attempting to formulate the psychological condition which is associated with cancer: *that cancer is associated with the agentic feature.* His insistence on a cellular locus of the death instinct, although his presentation is perhaps superficially lacking in cogency, may become cogent if we consider it to be an allusion to the psychological condition which may be associated with the physical state in which certain cells begin to reproduce asexually within a multicellular organism independent of the organization of the organism as a whole, finally leading to the death of that organism. In addition, he appeared to be making the point that *there is a parallelism between what takes place between the organism and the environment, including other organisms, and what takes place within the organism on the cellular level.* Agency, in its normal functioning, actually serves to bring the total organism into sexual relations. When this normal functioning of the agency feature is broken down, however, it turns upon itself, with the result that there is a corresponding disintegration of the normal organizational structure of the single organism. The "specialization" of the agentic into the ego, and into the musculature, expressing itself as sexual aggressiveness which leads to orgasm, is one of the principal ways in which the death instinct is normally diverted outward. When this outlet is not possible for any reason, the death instinct works to disintegrate the organizational whole of the individual and expresses itself in the asexual reproduction of some of the cells. When the relationship of the organism to other organisms breaks down, the personality becomes narcissistic, and, correspondingly, "The cells of the malignant neoplasms which destroy the organism should also perhaps be described as narcissistic..." (p. 68).

## EROS

As significant as the notion of the death instinct in Freud's modification of his libido theory is his introduction of the notion of Eros.

One of the major functions of Eros is that of having led to the creation of multicellular organisms. Freud conceived of an original condition of single-celled organisms that do not reproduce sexually, but only by fission. The binding of cells into a multicellular organism is conceived of as analogous to sexual relations between organisms. Thus, the yearning of the sexes for each other is the same as the bondage between the cells, expressions of the same instinct, Eros. Conjugation between single-celled organisms is the forerunner of both sexual intercourse *and* the establishment of multicellular organisms. Both are life-producing. Conjugation is rejuvenating to the organism, and sexual relations lead to a kind of immortality in the offspring. As the "coalescence of two germ-cells" (p. 58) is life-producing, so is the bondage of cells life-producing and enhancing. Eros is that which "seeks to force together and hold together the portions of living substance" (p. 84).

Freud wrote:

It is generally considered that the union of a number of cells into a vital association—the multicellular character of organisms—has become a means of prolonging their life. One cell helps to preserve the life of another, and the community of cells can survive even if individual cells have to die [p. 67].

The dynamics whereby this takes place are presumed to be as follows:

... the life instincts or sexual instincts which are active in each cell take the other cells as their object, that they partly neutralize the death instincts (*i.e.* the processes set up by them) in those other cells and thus preserve their life; while the other cells do the same for *them*, and still others sacrifice themselves in the performance of this libidinal function [p. 68].

But the work of Eros does not stop with the individual organism, for Eros attempts "to combine organic substances into ever larger unities" (p. 57). The elaboration of the notion of Eros as that which makes for *social cohesion* was made by Freud in *Group Psychology and the Analysis of the Ego*. Thus, starting with his analysis of the psyche, he simultaneously moved in two directions, the cells and the social group, with Eros as the cohesive force on the three levels, the cellular, the psychological, and the social. He contrasted the social with the narcissistic and cited the organismic conception of the group of Le Bon and Trotter.[50] Le Bon stated:

The psychological group is a provisional being formed of heterogeneous elements, which for a moment are combined, exactly as the cells which constitute a living body form by their reunion a new being which displays characteristics very different from those possessed by each of the cells singly [p. 7].

Of Trotter,[51] Freud wrote, "... we shall be reminded of a valuable remark of Trotter's, to the effect that the tendency toward the formation of groups is biologically a continuation of the multicellular character of all the higher organisms."[52]

[50]*Group Psychology and the Analysis of the Ego*, p. 4.

[51]W. Trotter, *Instincts of the Herd in Peace and War* (London: T. F. Unwin, 1916).

[52]*Group Psychology and the Analysis of the Ego*, p. 25.

Freud's consideration of group psychology at this time leads to a further observation in connection with my view that the growth of cancer may have been significant in his writings at this period. He viewed cancer as a "narcissism" of the cells. If there is a parallelism between the relationship of the cells to the total organism and the total organism to society, then a turn to society at large as the larger organism may have been felt by him as "therapeutic." I have already voiced the suspicion that there may have been a "therapeutic" role connected with Freud's writings. His interest in the transindividual work of Eros, expressed in his growing concern with society at large, may well have been his effort to find a more integrated role for his ego in the larger whole. It was perhaps possible for the death instinct to be "rendered harmless by being fused with erotic components"[53] — by a vigorous entry into the social.

My analysis of Freud's state of mind as he wrote about the death instinct and Eros also suggests an explanation of the meaning of the title *Beyond the Pleasure Principle*. In German this is *Jenseits des Lustprinzips*, which might be more literally translated as "the other side of the pleasure principle." "*Jenseits*" as a noun also means the other world or the life after death, and, according to Jones, Freud jocularly referred to this book as "The Hereafter."[54] The pleasure principle was for Freud one of the essential principles associated with his *individual* psychology. *Jenseits* is the other side of the individual, the place of the individual in the larger whole. Freud was able to conceive of that larger whole as possibly immortal, with the part itself, except for the germ plasm, being mortal. For the relationship of the individual to the larger society, there was another instinct, Eros. I might suggest that the psychological Lamarckianism to which Freud clung was partly an expression of his struggle away from the individual to a transindividual conception.

[53]Standard Edition, XIX, 54.
[54]*Op. cit.*, p. 41.

EMPIRICAL LINES OF EVIDENCE WHICH INDICATE
AN ASSOCIATION OF AGENCY AND CANCER

My analysis of the thought of Freud, together with my
own considerations, suggests that the notions of agency and
communion must be understood as being on a level of gener-
ality which transcends the biological, the psychological, and
the social, yet manifested in each of them. Our common
modes of thought tend to separate the latter three, because
these modes are deeply based in two traditional dualisms,
the mind-body and the mind-world. Allowing these dualisms,
we then seek to find the *interactions.* Certain developments
in modern thought, exemplified in the work of John Dewey
and in the researches in psychosomatic medicine, have led
us to recognize the conceptual mischievousness among these
separations. Yet the state of affairs in our collective intellectual
enterprises is such that, although we are pressed to drop these
artificial distinctions, there is no single comprehensive conceptualization to replace it. Thus, we must blunder along
without the aid of these dualisms and without anything else
to reasonably enlighten us otherwise.

I have extracted a "Freudian" theory of cancer from his
writings on the death instinct and Eros. The quotation marks
around the word "Freudian" are, of course, important, since
Freud's writings are certainly not explicit in this connection.
But, using my term "agency" and the considerations which
Freud has advanced, it would seem that unmitigated agency is
*somehow* associated with cancer.

In the following pages, I review some empirical studies
on cancer which have been conducted largely outside of
Freudian contexts. Each of the studies, in one way or another,
tends to point to the possibility of unmitigated agency being
associated with cancer. This body of research is sparse.
Each of the studies is subject to various criticisms, and none
are completely definitive. Furthermore, each of the studies,
taken by itself, easily allows alternative explanation of the

data. Yet they have a collective impact, at least to me, which I cannot easily shake off, which suggests, albeit only in some global manner, that there may be some validity in what I call the "Freudian" theory of cancer.

One does not eagerly enter into a position of being classified among those who have advanced various quackeries to fill the vacuum of knowledge in connection with cancer. But there is a danger of overmeticulousness as well as undermeticulousness in the effort to advance our understanding. This is that in our pursuit of rigor we may actually become rigid; that we may reject a *possibly* significant approach because it does not immediately submit fully to all of our scientific criteria. What the data I cite constitute is a hint, perhaps not much more. Yet, in something as vital as this, even a hint is valuable.

## 1. Attitudes Toward a Psychosomatic View of Cancer

There is the beginning of the hint of a relationship between agency and cancer in the very attitudes people have toward the disease. There is a fantastically huge literature which seeks a "cause" of cancer. It is important, however, to qualify what I say here. I in no way wish to disparage the research on various aspects of the cancer problem. Certainly, the various discoveries of substances provocative of cancer growth, including the viruses, for example, and the varieties of medical measures associated with the treatment of cancer, are of great value. And yet, one cannot escape the observation that much of this research is premised upon a notion of "otherness" in connection with the "cause" of cancer, that is, the attribution of agency to an outside "agent." I cannot but see in this research, at least to some degree, the mechanism which I outlined in the discussion of the image of Satan, the mechanism of projection of the intrinsically agentic on an outside image.

Freud clearly saw the significance of what is psychologically represented in the image of the Devil, and the possibility that in modern times we would tend to somatize this psychological state. He dealt with this image in detail in a paper, published in the year that he reported the cancerous growth in his mouth, entitled "A Neurosis of Demoniacal Possession in the Seventeenth Century." In this paper he noted the projective quality associated with the Devil and saw how the "otherness" of the Devil becomes the "otherness" of disease.

> The demonological theory of those dark times has won in the end against all the somatic views of the period of 'exact' science. The states of possession correspond to our neuroses, for the explanation of which we once more have recourse to psychical powers. In our eyes, the demons are bad and reprehensible wishes, derivatives of instinctual impulses that have been repudiated and repressed. We merely eliminate the projection of these mental entities into the external world which the middle ages carried out; instead, we regard them as having arisen in the patient's internal life, where they have their abode.[55]

I might again cite the finding by McClelland and Greenberger, in the TAT responses of women with cancer, of the appearance of the illicit lover, Harlequin or the Devil, who takes them to their death.[56]

Flanders Dunbar, one of the leading figures in the advance of our understanding of psychosomatic medicine, cites in a brief treatment of cancer the following lines from W. H. Auden, which metaphorically locate an outside agent:

> Cancer's a funny thing.
> Nobody knows what the cause is,
> Though some pretend they do;
> It's like some hidden assassin
> Waiting to strike at you.[57]

I would suggest that cancer entails the agency feature in man so thoroughly that even those who have come to understand the nature of projection in the formation of physical

---

[55]Standard Edition, XIX, 72.

[56]"The Harlequin Complex", pp. 107ff.

[57]Flanders Dunbar, *Emotions and Bodily Changes: A Survey of Literature on Psychosomatic Interrelationships 1910-1953* (New York: Columbia University Press, 1954), p. 270.

disease must balk somewhat at this point. Dr. George L. Engel, in a presidential address before the American Psychosomatic Society, indicated that even among the members of that society, there was "unconscious resistance" to the study of "psychogenesis or psychological triggering mechanisms" with respect to cancer.[58] In a study of the attitudes of physicians to cancer, Dr. Donald Oken was brought to the conclusion that among physicians,

There is a strong tendency to avoid looking at the subject of cancer and the facts related to it. There is an avoidance of research and teaching, opposition to potential research, resistance to personal experimentation and change, and the projection of strongly held rationalizations into the vacuum of knowledge. To some extent, we do not *want* to know about what we are doing or why, because the subject is so upsetting. Unfortunately, in our denial we go beyond the limits of usefulness. By blocking off access to new knowledge, we cut ourselves off from the acquisition of facts which could be of real help.[59]

It is evident that there is something about cancer, as contrasted with many other diseases, even fatal ones, which creates aversion to beholding it. I suggest that this is because it is a disease which in some very deep sense entails the agentic.

Data collected by Ruth D. Abrams and Jacob E. Finesinger in comprehensive interviews with cancer patients and their relatives also suggest that there is some unconscious association of cancer with the agentic among them. The investigators report that "the most significant and characteristic concept held by our patients was that cancer was a disease of unclean origin.... The idea that cancer is 'a dirty disease,' 'unclean,' 'repellent,' was repeated over and over again."[60] They fre-

---

[58]George L. Engel, "Selection of Clinical Material in Psychosomatic Medicine: The Need for a New Physiology,"*Psychosomatic Medicine*, XVI, No. 5 (1954), 369.

[59]Donald Oken, "What to Tell Cancer Patients: A Study of Medical Attitudes," *Journal of the American Medical Association*, CLXXV (1961), 1127.

[60]Ruth D. Abrams, and Jacob E. Finesinger, "Guilt Reactions in Patients with Cancer," *Cancer*, VI (1953), 478.

quently heard that cancer was associated with venereal disease. Sexual demands made by spouses were frequently suggested as the cause of cancer by relatives. In 56 out of 60 patients, the onset of cancer was regarded as someone's *fault*, either of the patient or of someone associated with the patient. I would suspect also that within the complex attitudes toward cancer patients on the part of physicians, which Oken pointed to, there may be some deference to the agentic of the patient which is unconsciously recognized by the physician.

In spite of this, however, there has been some work in connection with the relationship between personality and cancer, although the resources directed to this are minor in comparison with those which have sought the cause of cancer in outside agency. The work which has been conducted has warranted two reviews of this literature.[61]

## 2. Sexual Maladjustment in Cancer Patients

There is accumulating evidence to indicate that people who develop cancer are also people who are deficient in achieving normal heterosexual relationships. A. Beatrix Cobb observed that in men with cancer of the prostate, there was an unusual "sexual preoccupation leading to multiple marriages."[62] Milton Tarlau and Irwin Smalheiser, studying women with cancer of the breast and cancer of the cervix, concluded that there was "a general disturbance in sexual functioning" in both groups, their attitudes toward sexuality entailing rejection of the feminine role and "uniformly negative feelings toward heterosexual relations."[63] It was found

[61]Lawrence L. LeShan, "Psychological States as Factors in the Development of Malignant Disease: A Critical Review," *Journal of the National Cancer Institute*, XXII (1959), 1-18; George M. Perrin and Irene R. Pierce, "Psychosomatic Aspects of Cancer: A Review," *Psychosomatic Medicine*, XXI (1959), 397-421.

[62]A. Beatrix Cobb, "A Social Psychological Study of the Cancer Patient," unpublished doctoral dissertation. University of Texas, 1953, p. 52.

[63]Milton Tarlau and Irwin Smalheiser, "Personality Patterns in Patients with Malignant Tumors of the Breast and Cervix: An Exploratory Study," *Psychosomatic Medicine*, XIII, No. 2 (1951), 118.

that these women characteristically had mothers who had warned them to stay away from men, and that their reaction to the onset of menstruation "was uniformly one of rejection, ranging from feelings of fear, shame, and disgust to strong hysterical outbursts" (p. 118). The Tarlau and Smalheiser study, which was the first to make this observation, suffered methodologically, especially in the lack of a control group for comparison. The study was replicated by John I. Wheeler and Bettye McD. Caldwell, with the addition of a control group. They confirmed the conclusions of Tarlau and Smalheiser, finding in both breast and cervical cancer patients "greater negative feelings toward sexual relations."[64] Catherine L. Bacon, Richard Renneker, and Max Cutler, in a detailed study of the personalities and personal histories of 40 women with breast cancer, similarly concluded that "sexual inhibition and frustration" were considerably higher than even what "we normally observe in our clinical investigations of neurotic women."[65]

This group has followed up the observation reported in this study with the comprehensive psychoanalysis of five cases of breast cancer. Adding to what they had already reported, they indicate that women with cancer of the breast tend to accept lovers or husbands who are extremely unsatisfactory. These women experience

... frustration of feminine needs through the choice of an inadequate type of lover or husband. The mates of our patients were outstandingly unsatisfying in any of serveral ways: they were cold, sadistic, alcoholic, seclusive, impotent, uninterested, opposed to having children, or monumentally narcissistic.[66]

[64]John I. Wheeler, Jr., and Bettye McDonald Caldwell, "Psychological Evaluation of Women with Cancer of the Breast and of the Cervix," *Psychosomatic Medicine*, XVII, No. 4 (1955), 264.

[65]Catherine L. Bacon, Richard Renneker, and Max Cutler, "A Psychosomatic Survey of Cancer of the Breast," *Psychosomatic Medicine*, XIV, No. 6 (1952), 455.

[66]Richard E. Renneker, *et al.*, "Psychoanalytical Explorations of Emotional Correlates of Cancer of the Breast," *Psychosomatic Medicine*, XXV (1963), 119.

They also observed that in some of the patients, after a disruption of their relations, there is a tendency to "act out," to engage in promiscuous sexual relations, a type of behavior which, on the basis of our earlier discussion of sexuality, can be interpreted as an expression of the agentic feature.

Reznikoff compared a group of women with cancer of the breast with women who had benign tumors and with women who were free of breast pathology, using a questionnaire, the TAT test, and the Sentence Completion Test. The women with cancer of the breast tended to be older when they married. In comparison with the normal and benign tumor subjects, the cancer group tended to describe masculine figures in the TAT cards as "rejecting and unresponsive to women's entreaties for love and attention. Fewer stories expressed basic contentment with interpersonal contacts in this area . . . ,"[67] and "In addition to viewing men as not gratifying their needs for affection and less frequently displaying contentment with their relations in this sphere, the cancer subjects, compared with the normal women, on fewer occasions conceived of men as protective or sympathetic" (p. 102). He also found that cancer patients much more frequently indicated that their marriages were not happy (p. 102). The Reznikoff data are of further interest because, although the cancer group exceeds both the normal group and the benign group on this dimension, the data suggest that the benign group is also alienated from men, although not to the same degree as the cancer group. This would suggest a correlation between the sense of alienation from men on the one hand and a no-growth, benign-growth, malignant-growth dimension on the other. However, "stronger" data would be necessary before this could be maintained.

Outside of the study by Cobb, all of the studies I have been able to find which indicate sexual maladjustment in

[67]Marvin Reznikoff, "Psychological Factors in Breast Cancer: A Preliminary Study of Some Personality Trends in Patients with Cancer of the Breast," *Psychosomatic Medicine*, XVII, No. 2 (1955), 100.

cancer patients are of women. There is a definite need for information concerning sexual adjustment in male cancer patients. Cancer of the sexual sites occurs in about 44 per cent of female cancer patients and in only about 14 per cent of male cancer patients.[68] A subsidiary hypothesis, which would require much closer investigation, is that those organs which are most intimately involved in communion are more likely to be targets for cancer than organs associated with agency. To put it metaphorically, the parts of the body which are the most prominent objects for the agency of the male in heterosexuality become the targets of agency in the development of cancer in the female. It is also interesting to point out that cancer of the musculature, which Freud called the organ of the death instinct, is either rare or nonexistent. If, as I have pointed out, the communion feature is a much more important part of female than male sexuality, and if it should turn out that the sexual maladjustment of the male cancer patient is not as dramatic as that of the female, it would suggest that the inhibition of their sexuality is largely an inhibition of the communion feature, the inhibition of Eros in their personality which would normally have the effect of "neutralizing the death instinct," in the Freudian terminology.

## 3. Inhibition of Maternality

Not only is there an inhibition of sexuality in female cancer patients, but also an inhibition of their maternality. Bacon, Renneker, and Cutler report that only one of their 40 cases indicated a desire for children. Renneker and his associates write:

Most of our patients displayed disturbances of the maternal drive. Children were not cathected through identification.... Conflict over the caring for children disturbed several of our patients.... One wonders whether a sustained, conflictful, psychopathological drive toward pregnancy frustrated by infertility may be part of the

[68]Based on data presented in Herbert L. Lombard, "Statistical Studies in Cancer," in Freddy Homburger (ed.), The Physiopathology of Cancer (2nd ed.; New York: Paul B. Hoeber, 1959), p. 998.

hormonal disturbance in developing cancer of the breast. A psychogenical factor could conceivably be the block against pregnancy which frustrates the life-restitutive urge.... We would postulate that this powerful conflictful intrapsychic constellation may constitute a force which would upset the normal hormonal balance. This, too, is a subject for further research.[69]

Reznikoff found that "the cancer subjects were more ambivalent toward accepting responsibilities associated with raising children and distinctly more fearful and threatened by pregnancy and the birth process."[70]

### 4. Lack of Social Involvement

Cobb, on the basis of her study of 100 male cancer patients, concludes the following about their social adjustment:

As a group they seem to have had some difficulty in making their way into a world of adequate social relationships ... they often regard emotional involvements as dangerous ... they tend to avoid emotional involvements.[71]

Reznikoff found that female cancer patients "apparently ... had developed few interests or diversions outside their homes,"[72] and that "their husbands tended to spend less available leisure time with them than did the mates of the normal women" (p. 102).

### 5. Inhibition of Aggression

The relationship of aggression to agency has been discussed earlier. Freud, in his discussion of the death instinct, conceived of Eros as neutralizing the death instinct of the cells and of the death instinct as being directed outward in the form of aggression. It is thus extremely telling that one should find cancer patients to be people who are remarkably unable to express aggression.

The observation has been made that males with cancer

[69]*Op. cit.*, p. 121.

[70]*Op. cit.*, p. 101.

[71]*Op. cit.*, pp. 254, 257.

[72]*Op. cit.*, p. 100.

of the prostate are superficially very "nice," in the sense of not expressing aggression and being very compliant and superficially cooperative.[73] In 25 out of their 40 cases of breast cancer, Bacon, Renneker, and Cutler observed that there was

> ... excessive pleasantness ... under all conditions and a common inability to deal appropriately with anger. Thirty had no technique for discharging anger directly or in a sublimated fashion. Most of these even denied having ever been angry. These were the ones who maintained a cheerful, pleasant facade through all adversities. Friends were prone to describe them as "the nicest woman we know," "she wouldn't hurt a fly," or "always thinking of others."[74]

This group indicates that in cancer patients "the pattern of caring for the needs of others rather than their own gradually assumed a coloring of superficial cheerfulness and pleasantness."[75] LeShan and Worthington found that 64 per cent of cancer patients compared with 32 per cent of a normal group showed "inhibition of hostility" as inferred from a paper-and-pencil questionnaire.[76]

Not only does the tendency to express aggression outward seem to distinguish persons without cancer from persons with cancer, but there is also some evidence that it is related to the *rate* of growth of cancer among cancer patients. Dr. Philip M. West and his co-workers had casually observed that patients in whom the cancer grew slowly were "too mean to die" and that patients in whom the cancer grew rapidly were "too good to live." "Or ... when contrasting two similar cases of early rectal carcinoma; — one a 'worthless rascal' was apparently cured, the other, 'a prince of a fellow' was dead of generalized metastases in a few months."[77] This group indicates that they

[73]Cobb, *op. cit.*, p. 39.

[74]*Op. cit.*, p. 456.

[75]Renneker, *et al.*, *op. cit.*, p. 119.

[76]Lawrence L. LeShan and Richard E. Worthington, "Some Recurrent Life History Patterns Observed in Patients with Malignant Disease," *Journal of Nervous and Mental Disease*, CXXIV (1956), 461.

[77]Philip M. West, "Origin and Development of the Psychological Approach to the Cancer Problem," in Joseph A. Gengerelli and Frank J. Kirkner, *The*

... were impressed by the polite, apologetic, almost painful acquiescence of the patients with rapidly progressing disease, as contrasted with the more expressive and sometimes bizarre personalities of those who responded brilliantly to therapy with long remissions and long survival.[78]

There is the suggestion in the literature that psychotherapeutic measures, especially those entailing aid in ventilating aggression, may have some effect on the course of the development of the disease. Needless to say, such an approach must be evaluated by research conducted in the most meticulous fashion. One study which opens up this possibility is that by LeShan and Gassman, in which patients with cancer were undergoing psychotherapy. The investigators cite, for example, the following case:

A 34-year-old female, with a markedly anaplastic carcinoma of the breast, had visible metastatic growths in the right shoulder region. These had slowly and steadily increased in size over a three-month period. This woman had never accepted her hostility toward her husband and children, and had guilt feelings over the fact that she sometimes wished she were free of them. After approximately 45 hours of psychotherapy, she was able to accept and ventilate some of her hostility toward her children, and to accept the reassurance of the therapist that these were normal and valid emotions, and that they would not cause her to hurt or desert her family. In the following three days, there was a temporary but definite shrinkage of the visible tumor growths.[79]

## 6. Loss of a Significant Person as a Precipitant of Cancer

The data cited thus far would tend to confirm that part of the "Freudian" theory which suggests that health of the individual is associated with his relationship to the larger social "organism." They have largely pointed to features which are

*Psychological Variables in Human Cancer: A Symposium* (Berkeley: University of California Press, 1954), p. 24.

[78]Eugene M. Blumberg, Philip M. West, and Frank W. Ellis, "A Possible Relationship Between Psychological Factors and Human Cancer," *Psychosomatic Medicine*, XVI, No. 4 (1954), 277.

[79]Lawrence L. LeShan and Martha L. Gassmann, "Some Observations on Psychotherapy with Patients Suffering from Neoplastic Disease," *American Journal of Psychotherapy*, XII (1958), 730.

within the personality which prevent the individual from relating to others. The data also indicate that when such a separation takes place as a result of external factors, the probability of developing cancer also increases.

Although one needs to be extremely cautious in attempting to draw inferences from lower animals to humans, there is one study on C3H mice which might be indicated parenthetically. C3H mice develop spontaneous mammary tumors and have been used extensively in laboratory research bearing on cancer. It was found that mice raised singly in cages developed mammary tumors significantly earlier than mice raised with cagemates.[80] One of the arguments which has sometimes been made against psychosomatic factors in cancer is that lower animals get cancer. This item might perhaps indicate that there may be psychological factors associated with cancer even in lower animals.

There are no doubt relationships between extrinsic and intrinsic alienation. In this section I cite some evidence of data which indicate that a loss of a significant person through death or other reasons is related to cancer. It should be pointed out that there is evidence that such a loss plays its role in other psychosomatic diseases as well.[81]

This observation is perhaps one of the oldest in connection with cancer. Kowal, in reviewing the literature of the eighteenth and nineteenth centuries, has shown that in numerous instances physicians have noted that a condition of despair, generally resulting from the loss of a husband or child, was the precursor of the cancerous condition.[82] One

[80]Howard B. Andervont, "Influence of Environment on Mammary Cancer in Mice," *Journal of the National Cancer Institute*, IV (1944), 579-81. One of my students, Mr. Barry Dworkin, with the help of Dr. Eric Simmons, has been replicating this investigation. At the time of this writing the mice are about 470 days old. At this point 67 per cent of the mice caged alone have displayed tumors. In the group of mice caged together with other C3H mice, only 34 per cent have displayed tumors. This difference is significant at the 2.5 per cent level of confidence.

[81]Hyman L. Muslin and William J. Pieper, "Separation Experience and Cancer of the Breast," *Psychosomatics*, III (1962), 230.

[82]Samuel J. Kowal, "Emotions as a Cause of Cancer: 18th and 19th Century Contributions," *Psychoanalytic Review*, XLII (1955), 217-227.

nineteenth-century physician commented, "The influence of grief appears to me to be, in a general way, the most common cause of cancer."[83] A statistical analysis of cases in the late nineteenth century in the London Cancer Hospital had demonstrated that in a large proportion of the cases "there had been immediately antecendent trouble, often in very poignant form, as the loss of a near relative" (p. 4). An observer in a report in 1931 said that there was reason to believe that "sad emotions" are associated with the precipitation of cancerous growth:

How many times have I heard ... the litany: "Since the death of my child, doctor, I am not the same. I do not recognize myself. I cannot find my equilibrium, and that is certainly the beginning of my illness because before, nothing like this had come to my attention" [p. 6].

An early psychoanalyst, having studied 100 cases of cancer, concluded that "the downfall of the objective attachment" to another person was a precipitant of cancer.[84] The loss of a person close to one in the relatively recent history of cancer patients has been confirmed by Bacon, Renneker, and Cutler, Greene, Greene and Miller, Muslin and Pieper, and Neumann.[85] Le Shan and Worthington found "tension over the loss of a vital relationship" in 75 per cent of cancer patients compared with 14 per cent of a noncancer control group.[86]

In one comprehensive statistical analysis of cancer in women, the data very clearly indicate that the loss of a hus-

[83]LeShan, "Psychological States . . .," p. 3.

[84]Elida Evans, *A Psychological Study of Cancer* (New York: Dodd, Mead and Company, 1926).

[85]Bacon, Renneker, and Cutler, *op. cit.;* William A. Greene, "Psychological Factors and Reticuloendothelial Disease: I. Preliminary Observations on a Group of Males with Lymphomas and Leukemias," *Psychosomatic Medicine* XVI, No. 3 (1954), 220-30; William A. Greene and Gerald Miller, "Psychological Factors and Reticuloendothelial Disease: IV. Observations on a Group of Children- and Adolescents with Leukemia: An Interpretation of Disease Development in Terms of the Mother-Child Unit," *Psychosomatic Medicine*, XX (1958), 124-44; Muslin and Pieper, *op. cit.;* C. Neumann, "Psychische Besonderheiten bei Krebspatientinnen," *Zeitschrift für psychosomatische Medizin*, V (1959), 91-101.

[86]*Op. cit.*, p. 461.

band through death is associated with the occurrence of cancer. The author of this study concludes that the higher rate of cancer among widows, controlling for other variables, "should be traced ... to the reactions of the body incident to the loss of the *pater familias*."[87]

Le Shan and Worthington administered questionnaires to 250 cancer patients, interviewed 71 patients for an average of 2.2 hours and 9 patients for an average of 119.3 hours, and used a control group of 150 cases without cancer. They reconstruct the following pattern, which, they say, would characterize 62 per cent of the cancer cases, but only 10 per cent of the noncancer cases. This is a composite "ideal type" of cancer patient in terms of personality and life experience.

Sometime in the first seven years of life, there was a trauma to the child's developing ability to relate to others. This trauma may have come from a variety of causes – the physical or psychological loss of a parent, the death of a sibling, or others. This trauma was related by the child to one or both of the parents, and a great deal of hostility resulted. However, the hostility could not be consciously accepted by the child for obvious reasons, and it was repressed. A large part of it was turned inward as self-hate and guilt feelings. *In addition, the ability to express emotion in relating to others was severely damaged, and the child experienced unusual difficulty in establishing strong cathexes of either a positive or negative nature.*

The ability to express positive emotions was weakened by the pain of withdrawing love from the parental figure. Negative feelings were hard to express due to the strong, unacceptable hostility also directed in this direction. Guilt feelings over the relationship with the parents tended to produce feelings of unworthiness.

The trauma producing these results was not of an intensity or timing likely to produce obvious neurotic problems or to prepare the person for a psychotic breakdown in the event of later stress. Although it made his later relationships generally superficial and invested in only cautiously, from a surface viewpoint, he managed to adjust to his social environment.

The personality development before the trauma was such that

[87]Sigismund Peller, "Cancer and Its Relations to Pregnancy, ... Delivery, ... to Marital and Social Status: I. Cancer of the Breast and Genital Organs," *Surgery, Gynecology, and Obstetrics,* LXXI (1940), 1-8; "II. Cancer of Organs Other then Reproductive: Total Cancer Mortality," *loc. cit.,* p. 186.

the individual had a need for warm relationships. As he developed and continued to have this need for, but inability to attain easily, warm cathexes, sooner or later a situation arose which offered him an opportunity to relate to others and which provided time for slow and cautious experimentation. This experimentation indicated that this was a "safe" relationship, one that would give him the warmth he needed, and would not mobilize the repressed hostile feelings.

The cathexis was accepted, and the person poured into it all the relationship needs that he had carried over the years since the original trauma. This tie became the focus of his life and all other relationships were essentially peripheral to it. The self-hatred was largely dissipated as the energy that once fed it was now rechanneled. Life-long patterns and basic guilt feelings, however, frequently still made it difficult for the person to express hostile feelings when his own needs were frustrated.

Eventually this cathexis was lost. This may have been due to any one of a number of events. The examples we have most frequently seen include the death of a spouse, or an event which markedly changed the marital roles, such as the chronic illness of a spouse; children growing up and attaining independence, thereby making parental roles obsolete; and job retirement. The self-hate was now rearoused as the blocked relationship energy turned inward through the old channels and was again expressed against the self. The loss of this all-important cathexis made it very difficult for the individual to relate again to others. He unconsciously saw what was happening as a "double desertion." The unconscious belief that to relate meaningfully to anyone brings the pain of desertion was reinforced by the second loss. The child's belief that he was responsible for the rejection was again accepted, and guilt and self-hate were again strongly felt.[88]

## 7. The Relative Success of Anti-Androgenic Measures in the Treatment of Cancer

Our earlier discussions indicated that the androgens were related rather closely to the agentic feature in personality, associated with aggression, the development of the musculature, and the agentic feature of sexuality. In this chapter, I have attempted to indicate that cancer is a disease which is associated with agency. It is thus telling that one of the most

[88]*Op. cit.*, pp. 462-63. Italics added.

significant of the medical measures in connection with cancer should be the so-called anti-androgenic forms of treatment.

There have been varieties of experiments on the treatment of cancer through the use of hormones. Among these has been the actual administration of androgens. However, as one reviewer has put it, "it may be concluded that androgen therapy does not prolong life."[89]

The data do indicate that anti-androgenic treatment is more effective. Huggins and his co-workers at the University of Chicago observed that orchiectomy (surgical removal of the testicles) and the administration of estrogens in dogs resulted in the arrest of the growth of neoplasms of the prostate gland.

These findings in the dog proved to be pertinent to the human. Translated to man with prostatic carcinoma, they turned out to be directly applicable *en bloc* and permitted the introduction of anti-androgenic therapy in clinical practice.... Both orchiectomy and phenolic estrogens ... were effective in controlling cancer of the prostate in certain cases, while, conversely, the administration of testosterone intensified the growth of the neoplasm.[90]

Androgens are found in both males and females. They are produced by the testes, the ovaries, and the adrenal glands, and possibly by other organs in the body.[91] There is evidence that the administration of estrogens can control growth of mammary cancers.[92] In women with cancer of the breast, the removal of the ovaries and the adrenal glands produces a significant drop in sexual desire, sexual activity, and sexual responsiveness to intercourse *simultaneously with* an increase in subjective well-being and arrest of metastatic activity as indicated by roentgenological evidence and clinical criteria.[93]

[89]Alfred Gellhorn, "Clinical Cancer Chemotherapy," in Homburger, *op. cit.*, p. 1047.

[90]Charles Huggins, "Control of Cancers of Man by Endocrinologic Methods: A Review," *Cancer Research*, XVI (1956), 826.

[91]See Kinsey, *op. cit.*, pp. 729ff., for a review of the literature.

[92]Huggins, *op. cit.*, p. 828.

[93]Sheldon E. Waxenberg, Marvin G. Drellich, and Arthur M. Sutherland, "The Role of Hormones in Human Behavior: I. Changes in Female Sexuality

The nature of the detailed mechanisms of the interaction of hormones and personality and the great problems of "cause and effect" in psychosomatic conditions are beyond the scope of this essay. Yet I cannot but be impressed with the fact that "castration" should have been developed as a relatively effective way of controlling cancerous growth. It would appear that certain of the organs of the body are particularly associated with the agentic in human personality and that perhaps the removal of these organs has the effect of reducing the agentic and reducing what may be one of the manifestations of unmitigated agency, the growth of cancerous tissue.

I might comment, parenthetically, on what might be the deeper meaning entailed in Freud's frequent use of the notion of "castration" in his writings. Some of the critics have dealt with this as but another instance of Freud's great tendency to overconcretize what he was saying: that the notion of castration is simply a metaphorical concretization of something else. But such things as the fear of castration, castration complex, and penis envy can now be understood in terms of the way in which the individual manages the agentic feature of his personality. Penis envy, for example, may in part be the actual envy of the penis, but is better interpreted as the envy of the greater agency associated with the male, who has more specialized organs for the expression of the agentic; and the fear of castration is the fear of the removal of the specialized organs for the expression of the agentic.

In closing this chapter, I need to emphasize that it is not being suggested that what these data seem to point to, that internal and external barriers to social and sexual integration are in some way related to the onset of cancer, constitute the only factors associated with it. Such a position would be much

after Adrenalectomy," *Journal of Clinical Endocrinology*, XIX (1959), 193-202; Sheldon E. Waxenberg, John A. Finkbeiner, Marvin G. Drellich, and Arthur M. Sutherland, "The Role of Hormones in Human Behavior: II. Changes in Sexual Behavior in Relation to Vaginal Smears of Breast Cancer Patients after Oophorectomy and Adrenalectomy," *Psychosomatic Medicine*, XXII (1960), 435-42.

too foolish and dogmatic. Yet it would seem, on the basis of these data which I have summarized, that the degree of social and sexual integration of the individual, which we have attempted to comprehend in terms of the notions of agency and communion, are certainly relevant, suggesting that further investigation along these lines may be fruitful.

# CHAPTER VI

# TOWARD A
# PSYCHOTHEOLOGICAL VIEW

In the last two chapters, I have hardly spoken of religion explicitly. I have dealt with sexuality, death, and disease. Yet I have not really left the discussion of religion, for these have been items of religious concern.

In *The Future of an Illusion*, Freud said that the gods that man creates have a

... threefold task: they must exorcise the terrors of nature, they must reconcile one to the cruelty of fate, particularly as shown in death, and they must make amends for the sufferings and privations that the communal life of culture has imposed on man.[1]

In the previous discussion, I have indicated that by the gross separation of the agency and communion features of the psyche, we have been brought to the point where man's dominion over nature has essentially been won; we have succeeded in exorcising the terrors of nature, and found many ways by which to reduce "sufferings and privations," Freud's first and third points. Man himself has largely taken over these functions, which he had in the past ascribed to God.

## COMING TO TERMS WITH DEATH

But it is with respect to the second problem, that of coming to terms with death, that an anthropocentric view appears to be of relatively little value. We are presented with a

[1] *The Future of an Illusion*, p. 27.

paradox. Whereas it is clear that the exaggeration of agency at the expense of communion has worked to exorcise the terrors of nature and to reduce suffering and privation, death is also associated with agency unmitigated by communion.

The material on cancer which I have presented may be read as a kind of modern parable. Cancer appears to be a disease associated with the psychological feature which has been critical in our victory over the material world. This victory has given us greater longevity and has spared us from various causes of death, leaving us to die, at last, from something which is "immanent in the organism itself."

Even if we were to find, on the basis of further research, that the seeming relationship between agency and cancer is spurious, it still remains true that man is mortal. He was indeed a genius who put together the inexorability of logic with the inexorability of death in the famous syllogism of Socrates' mortality. It is a certainty that "I will die." Doubt concerning mortality applies only to the question of *when*, not *whether*, and even the when runs between very narrow limits.

In purely biological terms, there is only a scrap of immortality. This is, as Weismann was aware, and was so cited by Freud, the immortality of the germ plasm. However, there is characteristically little comfort to be derived from this, because the germ plasm, while still a part of the body, tends to be removed from the ego. Even if the ego is foremost a body ego, as Freud said, the germ plasm is a part of the body which is hardly central to it. The semen in the male is characteristically as remote from the ego as urine and feces. In the formation of the ego, such products of the body are the original "other." But here we must note again the factor of sex differences. It may be that in some sense menstruation in the female, which indicates that she is not pregnant, is a "weeping of the uterus." But there is little reason to believe that the male weeps for the semen which has not fertilized an egg cell. It is the "I" that dies, the ego. But that which has not been included within the ego may possibly be immortal. Freud and Jung speculated on

the possibility of a transgenerational existence of the unconscious. Freud wrote that "Our unconscious, then, does not
believe in its own death; it behaves as if it were immortal."[2]
His psychological Lamarckianism must have involved taking
the unconscious at its word, as it were. On the other hand, the
ego, which is consciously aware of death, and which contains
within it the mute death instinct, does die. Immortality of the
germ plasm as a part of the ego is further compromised in
that, in order to live, it must fuse with the germ plasm of
another, an "other" who is, at least at first, alien to the ego.

Up to this point, I have leaned very heavily on the thought
of Freud, although with qualifications. And here I must
qualify again. I do not share his deep pessimism and gloom.
These I attribute to his deficiency in mitigating agency with
communion, although he appreciated the latter in a way which
has been rare. I cannot share his psychological Lamarckianism; his case for the latter is remarkably lacking in cogency.
He was insufficiently aware of the possibility of our urban
industrial society working to reduce the suffering and privation resulting from want of material things. But, most impor-
tantly, in his various writings on religion *he tended to focus on
the filiocentric rather than the patrocentric character of religion.*

In the remainder of this essay, I attempt to elaborate on
the meaning of this sentence. My effort is to follow the injunction of Bultmann and attempt to read out of the Judeo-Christian heritage to which we are heir the significant meanings
which are relevant for us. The considerations of the last
chapter brought us up sharply to the problem of death. Religion in the past has been helpful in coming to terms with
death. Contemporary intellectuality has entailed the rejection
of religion, but it has largely failed to come to terms with
death. The question I pose is whether there is not something
in the religious tradition which can be helpful in coming to

[2]Standard Edition, XIV, 296.

terms with death and which also is compatible with contemporary intellectual canons.

## PATROCENTRISM AND FILIOCENTRISM

Man, in the course of life, passes from a stage in which his dominant role is that of a child to his parents to one in which he is independent of his parents and becomes an adult himself. In his adulthood, he may exist in an independent state or shift into the position of being a parent. There is the stage of early childhood, the intermediate stage in which he is less a son and not yet a father, and the stage of fatherhood. In the first and third stages, the communion feature is a very significant part of his role. In the intermediate stage, he is largely given to the exercise of the agentic. I would suggest that the substance of religion is much more relevant to the first and the third stages than it is to the intermediate stage. I would also suggest that mankind at the present time is largely in the intermediate stage, and that this is reflected in the ideology and in the kind of rejection of religion which is characteristic in the modern world.

One of the fundamental notions of psychoanalysis is that man projects himself in the images he creates, although the nature of projection is such as to endow his projections with phenomenological "otherness." This was, for example, the critical insight which enabled Freud to comprehend the nature of dreams; the dreams a person dreamed are not "other," but are of the person's psyche itself. It is remarkable and interesting that Freud should have failed to avail himself of this fundamental insight in his discussions of religion. He interpreted the notion of God as the projection of the *father*. In all of his interpretations, he took it that this was based on the person's real father projected upon the heavenly father. God was then the father and man the son. *What Freud failed to see was that the projection of fatherhood on God must also be interpreted as mankind projecting its own fatherhood.* In this instance, he failed to realize what he had seen so clearly in other instances, that phenomenological "otherness" must be circumvented to appreciate the meaning of man's images. Freud's analysis of the psychology of sonhood, especially as contained in his various discussions of the Oedipus complex, was eminently profound. Yet he failed to give much recognition to that part of the Oedipus story in which the infant Oedipus is *first* put out to die by his father, Laius. His concern was principally with that which is associated with moving from sonhood into the intermediate stage between sonhood and fatherhood. His attitude toward religion indicates that the integration was incomplete, reflected in his difficulty in coming to terms with death. Thus, there may have been deep relationships in Freud among his *Todesangst,* his views on religion, and, finally, his cancer—although, as I have indicated, his very thought in connection with these things may have had a "therapeutic" significance.

GOD AS FATHER

I take it, then, that the notion of God as father is a projection of a characteristic of man. I shall attempt to read the Bible as a "psychological document" in which important problems of ultimate concern are reflected. My thesis is that the Old Testament expressed what we may consider to be the "motherization" of man, including the conflicts and the crises associated with this process. Alluding back to our earlier discussion of the nature of projection, in which I said that projection occurs partly because the individual would make of that part of himself something "other" than himself, it would then appear that the projection of fatherhood onto God is already indicative of man's difficulties in conceiving of himself as father. And I would also allude back to Bultmann's notion that the separation of man from God is already the beginning of the sinful state. My task is then based on the psychoanalytical injunction to circumvent the "otherness" of projection, to discover the kerygma entailed in the projection of God as father.

One of the pervasive themes that runs through the Bible is that there is *a biological role for the male in conception*. We may presume that there was a time in history prior to Biblical times in which this was not known. It is certainly not "obvious." Sexual intercourse can take place without conception. The interval between conception and either the signs of pregnancy or the birth of a child is considerable. And whether a particular woman has had intercourse or not often remains her "secret." If we consider a two-way table with pregnancy-no pregnancy on one axis and intercourse-no intercourse on the other, observation would show that there are instances of pregnancy and no pregnancy with intercourse; and definitive data in the no intercourse cells are hard to come by. We can presume that there was an early "scientist" who made the discovery of the relationship between sexuality and pregnancy. Furthermore, as I have already indicated, the natural development of the male ego does not usually encompass the ejaculated semen; and we might presume that there may have been a good deal of resistance to the acceptance of the validity of this "scientific discovery." In contrast, there was probably no time in human history in which the biological connectedness of the mother to the child was ever in question, the act of childbearing being too prominent a part of experience. In the same way that more recent scientific discoveries have shocked mankind with their implications, so must there have been a time in history when mankind was similarly shocked by this particular "scientific discovery," and its implications. I take it that the Bible is a document which expresses man's efforts to come to grips with the problems presented by the fact that the male has a biological role in conception.

The Bible expresses man's effort to extend the boundary of his ego to include his "seed." This particular metaphor for semen is interesting in that it not only suggests property and food, but also tends to make the male even more important than the female, as seed is the determining factor of the nature of the plant, with the soil, water, and sun playing only enabling roles. The very conception of semen as "seed" which is deposited in the ground is suggestive that the ego has moved to include the semen.

The major personages of the Old Testament are presented principally in their role as fathers to their children. This is particularly evident in the patriarchs Abraham, Isaac, and Jacob. Even the sonhoods which are represented are transitionary to fatherhood. The very name "Abraham" means father. Jacob has two names, Jacob, largely for his sonhood, and Israel, characteristically used to designate his fatherhood. In these figures, there is evident not only the extension of the ego to their "seed" but to the children themselves. Their principal preoccupations are with their children. As I have indicated, we can interpret the image of the father as presented in the Bible as a kind of "motherization" of the male. These are males who provide for their children. Yet this provision, too, takes place through the agentic. The Biblical patriarchs are affluent; they have flocks and servants and position. It is through their property that they can provide for children; and the economic conditions of their lives are such that by the increase of their children they themselves increase in wealth and power. Thus, we can perhaps speculate that conditions of the patriarchate were such that the motherization of the male served the agentic in him.

Let us consider Abraham. The Biblical account essentially begins when he is seventy-five-years old, with the Lord telling Abram (his name later to be changed to Abraham) to separate himself from his "kindred," that the Lord will make of him a "great nation," which will inherit the land of Canaan (Genesis 12:1-2). In Egypt, where Abram goes to avoid famine, he passes off his wife, who is also the daughter of his father but not of his mother, as his sister; she is taken by Pharoah to be his "wife." Following this, Abram's bounty increases greatly. The Bible makes repeated references to the

Lord's promise with respect to his "seed." The Lord tells him that "out of thine own bowels shall be thine heir" (Genesis 15:4). The Lord enjoins him to circumcise himself, all the males in his household, and all subsequent males on the eighth day after birth. Here is an aged man, without children, relatively rich but tenuously so because he owns no land, concerned with food and famine.

He is a man in whom the boundary of the ego has come to encompass his "bowels" from which the "seed" emerges. He has a deep wish for children, a further extension of this ego boundary. He envisages a God who promises him not only children, but a land for them to live on. This God is one who takes care of children and who abides in time past the time of his own mortality. He is functionally a primitive, personalized insurance policy which provides for one's children after one's death. In Abraham and his fantasy, we see the fusion of agency and communion. The image of God is of one who abidingly looks after children.

Freud, we know, conceived of the circumcision as a symbolic castration. If we can read Freud's notion of castration more generally as the attenuation of agency, then we can see its significance in Abraham. For in order to integrate the agency and communion features within himself, it was necessary for the agentic to be reduced to allow the repression of communion to be overcome. Furthermore, if agency is indeed related to death, and if Abraham were seeking to overcome death, it is essential that agency be mitigated.

The significance of Abraham's *mono*theism may also be noted here. The God which is projected is a motherized father, a father in whom there is an integration between the agency and the communion features of the psyche. To a certain extent, this ideal is depicted in the Biblical notion of God as father. The dread of deviation from a strict monotheism is the dread of the separation of agency from communion and the repression of communion.

## THE INFANTICIDAL IMPULSE

But the integration in the Bible is an uneasy one, reflecting the difficulties of making it. It is manifested in providing abiding care for children, and its failure is manifested in *infanticide*. Freud had made killing the father central in his various discussions of religion. This feature may be important in psychological development. However, I believe that close examination of the Biblical text indicates that, in addition to the Old Testament being much more patrocentric than filiocentric, the killing of children as a psychological impulse is highly significant. If there was some original holocaust of the kind that Freud envisaged, it appears less likely that it was the killing of the father by the son than the killing of the children by the father.[3] The allusions to the killing of children in the Bible are numerous, and the injunction against it is repeated so often as to indicate that this was not only a psychological tendency, but one which was at least sometimes "acted out."[4] If the characteristics attributed to God come from man himself, we may note an infanticidal tendency in the numerous references to God killing people, his children, throughout the Old Testament, as exemplified in the Flood and in his killing of the Sodomites, the Egyptians, and so on. God is tempted to kill all of the Children of Israel but is dissuaded by Moses (Exodus 32:9ff.), who then goes down from the mountain and himself kills about three thousand men (Exodus 32:28).

The story of Abraham's move to sacrifice Isaac is indicative not only of the infanticidal impulse, but also of ambivalence about infanticide. God enjoins Abraham to sacrifice Isaac as a burnt offering. Psychologically, Abraham has projected his infanticidal tendency onto God. When he is about to

[3]After I completed this study, a book came to my attention (E. Wellisch, *Isaac and Oedipus* [London: Routledge and Kegan Paul, 1954]) which expounds on the significance of infanticide and is very relevant in this connection.

[4]Leviticus 18:21; 20:1ff.; Deuteronomy 12:31; 18:10; Judges 11:3-40; I Kings 11:7; II Kings 3:27; 16:3; 17:17; 17:31; 21:6; 23:10; Psalms 106:37-38; Isaiah 57:5; Jeremiah 7:31; 19:3ff.; 32:35; Ezekiel 16:20-21; 20:26; 23:37; 23:39.

slay Isaac, his arm is restrained (Genesis 22:1ff.). The infanticidal impulse in Abraham is also evident in his treatment of Ishmael, whom he banishes to the wilderness with only bread and a bottle of water for himself and his mother (Genesis 21:14). Abraham is told, after demonstrating his readiness to kill Isaac, "because thou hast done this thing, and hast not withheld thy son, thine only son: That in blessing I will bless thee, and in multiplying I will multiply thy seed as the stars of the heaven, and as the sand which is upon the sea shore" (Genesis 22:16-17). This may be interpreted as a reaction to the infanticidal impulse. God of the Bible is deeply ambivalent about this tendency within him. Its "neurotic" character is indicated by his tendency to kill and then make promises not to do it again (Genesis 9:9ff.). The story of Abraham and Isaac is, as has often been pointed out, a harbinger of the crucifixion of Jesus, in which the arm that would kill the son, referred to as "thine only son," is not restrained.[5]

It may be pointed out, parenthetically, that this same ambivalence has been represented by Freud in a "myth" of his own making, his analysis of the statue of Moses by Michelangelo. This strange essay by Freud, which I have discussed elsewhere,[6] projects upon the figure of Moses an impulse to kill the children of Israel, which he restrains:

In his first transport of fury, Moses desired to act, to spring up and take vengeance and forget the Tables; but he has overcome the temptation, and he will now remain seated and still in his frozen wrath and in his pain mingled with contempt.[7]

In this essay, too, it should be pointed out, Freud took it that he was of "the mob upon whom his [Moses'] eye is turned" (p. 213), and appeared to fail to appreciate the way in which he himself was projected upon the figure of Moses, or upon God, with whom he identified Moses.

We can identify two sets of motives for the infanticidal

[5]See, for example, John 3:16: "that he gave his only begotten Son."
[6]*Sigmund Freud and the Jewish Mystical Tradition*, pp. 121-31.
[7]Standard Edition, XIII, 229.

impulse. The first is that the necessities of child care are such as to force the integration of agency and communion, so that the existence of children threatens the agentic and its separatistic tendencies. The second is that, in an early stage of the integration of agency and communion, in which the ego boundary has extended to include the semen of the male, the authenticity of paternity of children becomes very important. Doubt over this authenticity provokes the tendency to kill the child of doubtful paternity.

INFANTICIDE AS A RESISTANCE TO THE INTEGRATION OF
AGENCY AND COMMUNION

In our earlier discussion of the nature of human sexuality, it was indicated that the coming together of male and female entails the integration of the agency and communion features of the human psyche both between and within individuals. The child is a reminder of the fusion of agency and communion, and his existence demands the continuation of the fusion. Killing the child is an expression of resistance to such an integration. Sexual relations without children, or sexual relations and the killing of children, allow the expression of the agentic feature of sexuality without mitigation by the communion feature and maintain its repression.

A major threat to the integration of these two features occurs when individual survival is in jeopardy or when want prevails. Under these conditions, the agency feature asserts itself to the exclusion of the communion feature; the boundary of the ego is drawn inward to become a "body ego" bent on its own survival. Our knowledge of the social conditions of Canaanite culture, which constitutes the background of the development of our religious tradition, is relatively small.[8] But we do know that often poverty prevailed and that children were

[8]Wayne E. Barr, "A Comparison and Contrast of the Canaanite World View and the Old Testament World View," unpublished doctoral dissertation, University of Chicago Divinity School, 1963.

sometimes sold or exposed by their parents. The Canaanites, we learn from the writing of King Rib-Addi of Byblos, were sometimes forced to sell the "wood of their houses, and their sons and daughters in order to procure food for themselves."[9] Both from the Bible and other sources, we know that child sacrifice took place in Canaanite culture. To put it most simply, the child constitutes another mouth to feed and an inhibition of the freedom to go out and find food for one's self; when there is crowding and a shortage of food the impulse to kill and even eat (2 Kings 6:29) the child arises.

Reference to the agentic feature throws some light on the question of why the Biblical writers so often saw idolatry, sexual deviation, and infanticide as essentially one and the same. Idolatry, as the splitting of the image of the divine into parts, was indicative of the splitting of the agency feature from the communion feature. Ezekiel complained, for example, "For when they had slain their children to their idols, then they came the same day into my sanctuary to profane it" (Ezekiel 23:39). We know that there were varieties of deviant sex practices associated with the worship of some of these idols, and we hear Isaiah charging: "Enflaming yourselves with idols under every green tree, slaying the children in the valleys under the clifts of the rocks?" (Isaiah 57:5). The Biblical writers freely used "adultery" and "whoredom" as euphemisms for idolatry. The essential object of criticism of the prophets is agency separated from communion, which they attacked in three of its manifestations, idolatry, sexual deviation, and infanticide, all of which they saw as one.

There are inherent threats to the integration of agency and communion in the very interaction of parents with their children. On the one hand, the child is so evocative of the communion feature that it threatens the repression of communion, leading to a strong compensatory rise of the agentic. This point has been recognized in a very astute paper by Friedman and

[9]*The Interpreter's Dictionary of the Bible* (New York: Abingdon Press, 1962), I, 497.

Jones, in which they indicate that the Oedipus complex is not only to be understood in terms of the reaction of the child to the parent but also of the parent to the child. They point out that capacity for intimacy by the child threatens the stability of the contra-intimacy forces in the adult, leading to the impulse to kill the child.[10] On the other hand, the later development of a strong, unmitigated agentic tendency in the child, such as arises in the anal stage and persists into the later stages, manifested particularly in disobedience, is also provocative of the agentic in the father, because it threatens the father's mastery. The integration of agency and communion in the father is always tenuous. In this integration, he has managed to allow the boundary of his ego to extend to encompass the child; as long as the relationship of the child to the father is such as to serve the latter's ego, his integration can be maintained. However, when the agentic becomes prominent in the child, that extension finds it difficult to maintain itself, and the father is tempted to say, "You are not my son!" The writers of the Bible were particularly aware of this dynamic and projected it upon the image of God, who threatens to kill in response to disobedience. The emphasis on obedience in the religious tradition has its foundation in the necessity of maintaining the integration of agency and communion in the father in order that he not be tempted to lose it, to regress to a condition of unmitigated agency, and kill the child. "Honour thy father and thy mother" is followed by "that thy days may be long" (Exodus 20:12).

The God of Mount Sinai and the people at the foot of the mountain cannot be separated. The people of Israel are suffering from lack of food and water in the desert. We may presume that the children are a threat to the food supply, and that the Israelites are tempted to kill them, as they long for the flesh-pots of Egypt. According to my interpretation, the agentic

[10]Neil Friedman and Richard M. Jones, "On the Mutuality of the Oedipus Complex: Notes on the Hamlet Case," *The American Imago*, XX (1963), 107-31.

in them is aroused, and they make a golden *calf*, symbolic of the child they are tempted to kill. Attributed to God are the words, "let me alone, that my wrath may wax hot against them, and that I may consume them" (Exodus 32:10). Some scholars have even argued that an early form of the Jahwe religion actually entailed the sacrifice of children, and that, around the seventh century B.C., this was dissociated from the religion of the Israelites and attributed exclusively to the other Canaanite cults.[11] But whatever the validity of this, the Bible itself presents adequate information to indicate that infanticide, whether acted out or sufficiently counteracted so that it would not be acted out, was a significant psychological problem.

### THE FIRST-BORN

My interpretation suggests a reason for the special importance of the first-born in the Bible. In our earlier discussion, it was indicated that agency is particularly exaggerated in the first-born (see pp. 59ff.). I would suggest that the reason for this lies in the fact that the first-born is the particular target for the agentic in the father and he tends to react defensively by exaggerating his own agency.

The first-born is the child who critically demands the integration of agency and communion in the father. The birth of the first child is the occasion of the crises and conflicts associated with such an integration. It is therefore of interest that the Bible should manifest great ambivalence toward the first-born particularly.

On the one hand, the first-born is favored. The first-born is entitled to the "birth-right" and "blessing" (Genesis 25:29-34; 27:1ff.). The first-born is to inherit twice as much as the other children and is protected against arbitrary action which would take this away from him (Deuteronomy 21:15-17;

[11]Otto Eissfeldt, *Molk als Opferbegriff im Punischen und Hebräischen und das Ende des Gottes Moloch* (Halle [Saale]: Max Niemeyer Verlag, 1935); W. Robertson Smith, *Lectures on the Religion of the Semites* (New York: D. Appleton and Company, 1889), pp. 352-53.

II Kings 2:9). The right of succession to rule is given to the first-born (II Chronicles 21:3). Pharoah, who yields to nothing else, yields to the slaying of the first-born (Exodus 12:31). The favor of God to the Israelites is shown by his so referring to them: "Israel is my son, even my first-born" (Exodus 4:22). Even firstlings among animals are not to be eaten (Deuteronomy 12:17).

On the other hand, there are several instances in the Bible which indicate that the first-born is not favored. God favors the younger Abel over Cain, which is Cain's reason for killing Abel (Genesis 4:3-5). Abraham favors Isaac over Ishmael. Isaac gives the birthright to the younger Jacob. Jacob curses his first-born (Genesis 49:4). Jacob favors Joseph's younger son (Genesis 48:13-20). Er, Judah's first-born, is killed by God (Genesis 38:7). Jephthah kills his oldest daughter (Judges 11:34ff.). The king of Moab kills his first-born (II Kings 3:27). Hosah makes a younger son the chief instead of the first-born (I Chronicles 26:10). And Jesus is a first-born!

The profound ambivalence is shown by making the first-born belong to God. To give the first-born to God entails removing it from one's self. Thus, the Biblical writers attributed to God such things as: "Sanctify unto me all the first-born, whatsoever openeth the womb among the children of Israel, both of man and of beast: it is mine" (Exodus 13:2). And

Thou shalt not delay to offer the first of thy ripe fruits, and of thy liquors: the firstborn of thy sons shalt thou give unto me. Likewise shalt thou do with thine oxen, and with thy sheep: seven days it shall be with his dam; on the eighth day thou shalt give it me [Exodus 22:29-30].

There is little ambiguity throughout the Bible of what it means to "give" a living thing to God. "Giving" to God is a euphemism for killing, with what appears to be divine permission.

The male, prior to the birth of the first child, has tenuously moved toward the integration of agency and communion in his relations with his wife. The first-born is the critical test of this integration. With respect to the child, he needs to be a motherized father. The communion of the mother, which has been directed toward him, tends to turn in the direction of the child, and he regresses toward his earlier agentic condition. His impulse to say, "You are not my son" is then particularly strong with respect to the first-born.

## DOUBT CONCERNING PATERNITY AND INFANTICIDE

This condition is facilitated by the intrinsic doubt concerning the authenticity of paternity. And this doubt is particularly exaggerated in connection with the first-born, because the woman was not under the male's surveillance before marriage. I have already indicated that it must have been with a certain wrench that the male was brought to extend his ego to include his semen and his children. But if the child is not "his," the necessity for the integration of agency and communion is not incumbent upon him.

Abraham and Joseph, the husband of Mary, can be taken to be the "heroes" of the Old and New Testaments, respectively. Joseph has reason to doubt the paternity of Jesus, but allows himself to be a motherized father to the child anyway and does not kill him or allow him to be killed as an infant. Yet, even if the arm of Joseph is restrained from killing the child, Jesus must be crucified. I discuss this in greater detail presently.

The way in which the Biblical story of Sarah's conception of Isaac is told raises questions concerning the authenticity of the paternity of Isaac and throws some light on Abraham's temptation to kill him. The Biblical text has several "difficulties." These allow for an interpretation of dubious paternity of Isaac, if they do not suggest it. It should be made clear at this point that I am making no effort to attempt to find out what "really happened." It is rather that I am seeking to understand the nature of the Biblical text as a document which renders a state of mind for our understanding.

On two occasions Abraham conceals the fact that Sarah is his wife, allowing her to be married to someone else. This happens once before the visit of the angels, and once afterward. In the first instance, she enters the house of Pharoah. The text has Pharoah saying, "I took her to me for a wife," although the Biblical text is sufficiently ambiguous to make it possible for the King James version to render it as "so I might have taken her to me to wife" (Genesis 12:19). Whether she actually has sexual relations with Pharoah is not so important as is the fact that the Hebrew text would allow one to think so. In the second instance, she is taken into the house of Abimelech, who has a dream which prevents him from having sexual relations with her (Genesis 20:1ff.).

The possibility of Abraham not being the biological father seems to have been enough on the mind of the distinguished commentator Rashi for him to deal with it and deny it. The proof is, according to Rashi, that the text reads, "And these are the generations of Isaac, Abraham's son; Abraham begot Isaac."[12] Why does the Biblical text deviate from its usual pattern here? If these are the "generations of Isaac," why does the Biblical writer go backward to mention Abraham? And why is it necessary to say it twice? Rashi's commentary is:

Since the text wrote "Isaac, the son of Abraham," it became necessary to state, "Abraham begot Isaac"; for the scorners of the generation were saying, "From Abimelech did Sarah conceive, since for many years she tarried with Abraham and did not conceive from him." What did the Holy One Blessed Be He do? He formed the features of Isaac's face similar to Abraham, and there attested everyone, "Abraham begot Isaac." And that is why it is written here, "Isaac was the son of Abraham," for there is testimony that "Abraham begot Isaac" [pp. 235-39].

Needless to say, Rashi and his sources in the *Midrash* had neither photographs nor testimonials. Having to add a facial

[12]*The Pentateuch and Rashi's Commentary*, trans. Abraham ben Isaiah and Benjamin Sharfman (Brooklyn, N.Y.: S. S. & R. Publishing Company, 1949), Vol. I, Genesis 25:19.

similarity between Abraham and Isaac would indicate that doubt was suggested by the text.[13]

Chapter 18 of Genesis, which deals with the visit of the angels, has difficulties. In this chapter it is foretold that Sarah will have a son.

In the sixth verse, Abraham instructs Sarah to bake cakes for the guests, while in the seventh verse, he runs off to get and prepare a calf. But in the eight verse, where the meal is served, a meal of "butter, and milk, and the calf which he had dressed," there is no mention of the cakes. The text here allows a period of time in which Sarah was supposed to have been baking cakes while Abraham was away, and yet there are no cakes!

This chapter begins with three angels. Then the next chapter begins with only two angels, and there is no indication of what happened to the third angel. The ninth verse is "And they said unto him, Where is Sarah thy wife? And he said, Behold, in the tent." According to Biblical scholars, the next six verses, verses 10 through 15, are a substitution by the J2 author for something which had been put there earlier by the J1 author.[14] These six verses are the critical ones in connection with the birth of Isaac, and one can only speculate that perhaps what is now only hinted at in the text might have been more explicit in the earlier version. The tenth verse is as follows: "And he said, I will certainly return unto thee according to the time of life; and, lo, Sarah thy wife shall have a son. And Sarah heard it in the tent door, *v'hoo acharav.*" I have simply transliterated the Hebrew at this point, rather than rendering the usual translation, "which was behind him." Rashi made it that the door was behind the angel, which probably was the basis for the translation in this manner. It

[13]That such doubt may even have been on Paul's mind is suggested by "Neither, because they are the seed of Abraham, are they all children: but, In Isaac shall thy seed be called" (Romans 9:7).

[14]Cuthbert Aikman Simpson, *The Early Traditions of Israel: A Critical Analysis of the Pre-Deuteronomic Narrative of the Hexateuch* (Oxford: Basil Blackwell, 1948), p. 76.

can, however, be translated equally well as "and he behind it," suggesting that the angel was in the tent with Sarah. In one commentary, *Sifte Hakhamin*, it is explicitly suggested that the angel was in the tent and Abraham was outside. Tradition has it that the message was delivered to Sarah secretly. And tradition also has it that Sarah was radiant and that a beam of her beauty struck one of the angels.[15]

Isaac's name, which can mean "one laughs," the laughter of Sarah, and her denial of it, are also suggestive. Sarah laughs at the prediction that she will have a child, presumably at the irony of it. But it would appear that if she were laughing at the irony of it, she could certainly share this with her husband, who himself laughs at it (Genesis 17:17). The fifteenth verse is "Then Sarah denied, saying, I laughed not; for she was afraid. And he said, Nay; but thou didst laugh." Certainly the irony could provoke the laughter. But then why is she afraid? Because she does not want to offend her guests by laughing at their outlandish prediction? The laughter and the denial might also be at Abraham's cuckoldry, with Isaac, "one laughs," the incarnation of the joke.

It is indicated that they will appear again at the time of the birth of the child. Yet they do not reappear in the Old Testament. It is not until several hundred years later that the men, the wise men from the east of the New Testament, can be considered to appear again, at the birth of Jesus, "the son of Abraham," as Jesus is described in Matthew (1:1), for whom the delayed fate of Isaac is in store.

What we may presume is that Abraham is a man who, in spite of tendencies and provocation to infanticide, would restrain his arm from killing. The Biblical text at this point provides some further illumination of the conflict and Abraham's handling of it in his personality. The Bible blends the story of the angels' visitation with the story of the destruction of Sodom. It would appear from the Biblical narrative that they

[15]Louis Ginzberg, *The Legends of the Jews* (Philadelphia: Jewish Publication Society, 1913), I, 244.

stopped off to visit with Abraham on their way to Sodom. Fused here are the two tendencies I have been speaking of, the extension of the ego to include children and the tendency to destroy. The remainder of the chapter contains an interesting dialogue between Abraham and God, God bent on destroying the people of Sodom, and Abraham trying to dissuade him. Within this chapter is an explicit description of Abraham as the "good father." "For I know him, that he will command his children and his household after him, and they shall keep the way of the Lord, to do justice and judgment" (Genesis 18:19).

I have already commented on one of the significances of the circumcision, that it was a symbolic castration, the curtailment of the agentic. We are now in a position to understand the symbolic significance somewhat further in terms of the conflict within Abraham. By circumcising his children, he puts "his" mark upon them. Thus, even if doubt exists in his mind concerning his paternity, he makes them "his" by putting a mark upon them as he has upon himself and seeks to arrange it so that his offspring will carry this mark indefinitely from generation to generation.

But what is equally important is that the act of circumcising the male child takes place on the eighth day, the day when children are to be "given" to God. The circumcision may be interpreted as a symbolic infanticide, whereby, instead of putting the child to death by the knife, only the foreskin is removed. By this ritual, while making the child "his," he symbolically expresses the infanticidal impulse in a partial "acting out." Later in the Bible, we find that Moses has not circumcised his child. His wife Zipporah performs a hurried circumcision. She "cut off the foreskin of her son, and cast it at his feet, and said, Surely a bloody husband art thou to me. So he let him go: then she said, A bloody husband thou art, because of the circumcision" (Exodus 4:25-26). In this text the association of circumcision and infanticide is strongly suggested.

JUDAISM

One cannot hope to plumb the meaning of the Old Testament by any single interpretation. Yet its significance as a document which tells of the crisis involved in becoming a good father to children cannot be overlooked. I have presumed that there must have been some time in history when the biological role of the male in pregnancy was unknown, and that there must have been some historical period in which this particular fact was discovered and integrated into the social structure. Yet this is not only historical, but must be repeated in the life of the individual male. Abraham, presented as the father of nations, is a paradigmatic figure in whom is formed a transgenerational ego identity. His psychological problem is that of finding a way by which the strongly agentic feature in his personality will be mitigated and become integrated with the communion feature.

Moses and the Law which he delivers may be viewed generally as a series of resolutions made by man to firm up the integration of agency and communion which is, as we have already indicated, tenuous. The series of "commandments" in the Old Testament largely constitute a set of injunctions, the aim of which is to mitigate the agentic. Such injunctions as those against murder and theft are clearly against unmitigated agency. I shall enumerate some other of the injunctions of the Old Testament and indicate the way in which they would appear to achieve the result of the mitigation of agency.

## 1. Idolatry

I have already commented on this. The monotheistic aspect represents an effort to maintain the integration. Divisiveness, splitting, and derelationalizing are characteristic of the agentic.

The injunction against idolatry is also an injunction against making any *visual* representation of God. Instead, it substitutes the word and *hearing*. In our earlier discussion, I indicated that vision is much more closely related to the agentic, that the ego, as Freud put it, wears an auditory lobe only crooked. Freud commented on this feature of the Jewish religion: "If this prohibition was accepted, however, it was bound to exercise a profound influence. For it signified subordinating sense perception to an abstract idea; it was a triumph of spirituality over the senses...."[16] One of the fundamental expressions of Judaism is "*Hear,* O Israel, The Lord our God is one Lord." The emphasis on audition is an emphasis on communion. It should also be pointed out that the Biblical expression for deviant sex practices clearly entails the visual, "Thou shalt not uncover the nakedness of...."

When the Biblical writers spoke of sexuality which leads to the conception of children, they generally used the expression "know," which may suggest a greater degree of interpersonal intimacy. And, I might point out parenthetically, Oedipus *blinds* himself, an act that has been interpreted in the psychoanalytic literature as a "castration."

## 2. Laws against Deviant Sex Practices

I have indicated earlier that deviant sex practices are principally associated with the agentic. A major function of injunctions against deviant sex practices is to guarantee that the children are genuinely the father's "seed," and thus to reduce the temptation to infanticide. One of the interesting characteristics attributed to God is jealousy. The association of jealousy and infanticide is very evident in the commandment, "for I the Lord thy God am a jealous God, visiting the iniquity of the fathers upon the children unto the third and fourth generation of them that hate me" (Exodus 20:5). In other instances in which God is referred to as jealous, the Bible characteristically follows the reference with an allusion to children.[17] The Biblical writers found it relatively easy to identify God's jealousy for his people with the jealousy of a

[16]*Moses and Monotheism,* p. 144.

[17]Exodus 34:14, followed by Exodus 34:19; Deuteronomy 4:24, followed by Deuteronomy 4:25; Deuteronomy 5:9 is the same as Exodus 20:5; Deuteronomy 6:15, followed by Deuteronomy 6:20.

husband over the adultery of his wife, so dramatically indicated in the prophets generally and in Hosea so strongly.

## 3. The Sabbath

The Sabbath (as well as the circumcision, which has already been discussed) is the sign of the Covenant with God in which the children are provided for. It is an injunction against the performance of any labor. The significance of the Sabbath consists in the fact that it entails a surrender of the use of the musculature, whose relationship to the agentic has already been discussed.

## 4. The Dietary Laws

One of the significant features of the Law is that it provides for the sacrifice of animals instead of children, as Abraham sacrifices a ram instead of Isaac. Although the Bible does not enjoin against the eating of meat, it and the later rabbinic elaborations severely regulate the whole butchering operation. Some of the characteristics of animals which may be eaten are *not* characteristics of the human, such as chewing cud, cloven hoofs, feathers, fins, and scales. One of the more interesting dietary injunctions is "Thou shalt not seethe a kid in his mother's milk" (Exodus 23:19; 34:26; Deuteronomy 14:21). This can be seen as deference to the sensitivity of the "mother," a projection of the sensitivity to the violation of the communion feature which is involved in killing any offspring.

## 5. Redemption of the First-Born

Although the first-born belongs to God, the Bible directs that substitutes for the first-born should be given. They are to be "redeemed" through the Levites, and by means of money (Exodus 13:15; 34:20; Numbers 3:40ff.; 9:18).

## 6. The Phylacteries

The phylacteries worn by the Jews consist of boxes made of the skin of a *calf*, one placed as "a token upon thine hand" and the other "for frontlets between thine eyes" (Exodus

13:16). Our earlier discussion indicated that the musculature and the eyes are associated with the agentic. The phylactery is put on the arm with leather thongs as though to bind it. Within the phylacteries are four passages from the Old Testament:

 a. Exodus 13:2-10. This contains the commandment "Sanctify unto me all the firstborn, whatsoever openeth the womb among the children of Israel, both of man and of beast; it is mine"; an account of the Passover and an injunction to teach the son of it; and the injunction to wear the phylacteries.

 b. Exodus 13:11-17. This contains another reference to the first-born belonging to God, the slaying of the first-born of Pharoah, an injunction to wear the phylacteries, and an injunction to instruct the son.

 c. Deuteronomy 6:4-9. This contains "Hear, O Israel: The Lord our God is one Lord"; an injunction to "love the Lord thy God with all thine heart, and with all thy soul, and with all thy might"; an injunction to instruct children:

> And these words, which I command thee this day, shall be in thine heart: And thou shalt teach them diligently unto thy children, and shalt talk of them when thou sittest in thine house, and when thou walkest by the way, and when thou liest down, and when thou risest up.

 d. Deuteronomy 6:13-23. This contains injunctions against idolatry and violating the commandments; it indicates that God is jealous; it commands instruction of the son about the Passover.

The story of the Passover is, of course, the story of the slaying and sparing of the first-born. These four passages, and the placing of them on the arm and between the eyes, can be interpreted as the binding of the agentic which would engage in infanticide. What is most significant is that they are combined with the commandment to give instruction to the son. Essentially what is involved is *the diversion of the force which would kill the son to his education.* I believe that this is a major moral imperative of the Old Testament, the integration of agency and communion in the educational enterprise.

## PSYCHOLOGY OF JESUS

My analysis of the Old Testament in terms of the effort to counteract the infanticidal tendencies in man also suggests an interpretation of Christianity. The centrality of the crucifixion of the "only begotten Son" would indicate that the infanticidal impulse plays at least an equal role in Christianity. However, the New Testament contains a significant change from the Old Testament. The "Son" is much more prominent; and we may allow that, whereas the Old Testament entails the projection of man in his role as father, the New Testament also entails the projection of man in his role as son, a change from patrocentrism to filiocentrism, the psychodynamics of which I will discuss presently. It is noteworthy that Jesus was a child and a young man who died before he became a father.[18]

In this section, I venture some speculations on the psychology of Jesus, recognizing that he grew up in a culture in which the thought patterns associated with the Old Testament were dominant. I accept his historicity and the general facts of his life as indicated in the Gospels. I especially assume that he knew the Old Testament well and that its substance was of deep concern to him, as indicated in the Gospels (Luke 2:46-47).

My interpretation of the Old Testament has been that the management of the infanticidal tendencies in man is a major concern. Jesus was under the influence of the Old Testament, but there were a number of factors in his life which would have made the matter of infanticide of immediate rather than merely historical or religious significance. He was born in a country which had an infanticidal king, Herod, who, in 7 B.C., killed his own sons. Herod sought to kill

[18]Thomas Jefferson once suggested that it was regrettable that Jesus died before his ideas could fully mature.

the infant Jesus and killed all the children of Bethlehem two years old and under (Matthew 2). Joseph escaped with Mary and the infant Jesus to Egypt, where they stayed until it was safe to return; and then went to Nazareth, still in fear of returning to Bethlehem. We can presume that Jesus was raised in an atmosphere in which the possibility of infanticide was not only unconscious or merely historical or religious, but very concrete. We might also imagine that an infanticidal impulse may have been very real in Joseph, who not only had reason to doubt that Jesus was his child but was forced on the child's account to flee from his home and live under uncomfortable circumstances.

Children are sensitive to unconscious or even restrained aggression toward them. Perhaps this is what Jesus meant when he said, "I thank thee, O Father, Lord of heaven and earth, because thou hast hid these things from the wise and prudent, and hast revealed them unto babes."[19]

Whatever the psychodynamics associated with its development, and whatever the ethical implications, Jesus' personality was such that he deferred to the aggression of others and even cooperated with them in their expression of aggression toward him. This is tellingly expressed in "whosoever shall smite thee on thy right cheek, turn to him the other also" (Matthew 5:39) and "Love your enemies, bless them that curse you, do good to them that hate you, and pray for them which despitefully use you, and persecute you; That ye may be the children of your Father which is in heaven" (Matthew 5:44-45). Note that this deference to the aggression of others comes together with being the child of the Heavenly Father, suggesting *deference to the aggression of the Father also.*

Jesus' behavior, as reported in the Gospels, strongly suggests that he did all that he could to provoke his own execution. It would appear that this behavior is an example of what Freud referred to as "deferred obedience,"[20] allowing

[19]Matthew 11:25; cf. Luke 10:21.

[20]Standard Edition, XIX, 88.

the expression of what he took to be the wish of the father, a wish which was projected onto the God of the Old Testament. That his suffering and death were of his own choosing is clearly indicated in the Gospels: "No man taketh it from me, but I lay it down of myself."[21]

Throughout the New Testament, Jesus is referred to as both the "Son of God" and the "Son of Man." In addition to other significances of the term, "Son of God" may be interpreted psychologically as compensatory of doubtful paternity. Not having a known father, it is the Heavenly Father who is made the father. In the Gospels, there are about 150 instances in which God is referred to as "Father." "Son of Man," however, is the term that Jesus characteristically used when he spoke of his suffering and death.[22] *It was as the Son of Man, the son of man with the tendency to infanticide, that he suffered and died.*

In spite of the fact that the Christian message spread out to include many people other than Jews, it is important to recognize that the life context and tradition within which Jesus participated were Jewish, and that he was responding to features within that tradition. It was his "frame of reference" rather completely, and we cannot really understand him without taking this into account. His identification with the Jewish "peoplehood" is most tellingly revealed in his initial refusal to heal the daughter of the Canaanite woman, saying, "I am not sent but unto the lost sheep of the house of Israel" (Matthew 15:24). There are some similarities between the life of Jesus and the life of Moses which must have impressed themselves upon the mind of the young Jesus. As Moses was raised in a household nursed by his mother but separated from his father, so was Jesus raised in a household nursed by his mother but separated from his "Father." As Moses was saved from a general holocaust of infant slaughter (Exodus 1-2), so was

[21]John 10:18; cf. John 10:11-17; Mark 10:45; 14:24
[22]Some examples are: Matthew 20:18, 28; 26:45; Mark 8:31; 9:31; 10:33, 45; 14:21, 41; Luke 18:31; 19:10.

Jesus. But there are also some interesting parallels in reverse. Moses fled from Egypt in order not to be killed and then returned. Jesus fled to Egypt for the same reason and then returned. Whereas Moses went into the wilderness for forty days and received the Law, Jesus went into the mountain for forty days and encountered Satan. Psychologically, Moses interiorized control over agency in the form of the Law. Jesus projected the figure of Satan to make him "other" than himself. Psychologically, he projected the agentic. Here, indeed, is a fundamental distinction between the classical Judaism to which Jesus was reacting and Christianity.

The Passover, in my interpretation, had to be the time of Jesus' crucifixion. For it was in connection with the Passover that the infanticidal tendency of God had been made very clear, at which time the first-born of the Israelites had been spared. God had withheld his arm and not killed Jesus in his infancy. But the "deferred obedience" could only take place on the Passover, the holiday of the slaying and the sparing of the first-born. Jesus repeated in his own life the history of the Jews from the time of the Exodus. The religion of Moses, who was himself spared in his infancy, succeeded, at least for a certain length of time, in preventing the acting out of the infanticidal impulse. But by the time of the birth of Jesus, it no longer appeared to be sufficiently effective, as witness especially the holocaust of infant slaughter under Herod in Bethlehem. The rituals, the Sabbath, the circumcision, the phylacteries, the redemption of children by money, the substitution of animals for children, and other manifestations of the Law did not seem to be effective any longer. Jesus' own circumcision would no longer substitute. The total effectiveness of Mosaic Law had been considerably undermined under Herod and Roman law, and the rituals associated with the Mosaic Law were becoming perfunctory and empty. What, according to my interpretation, was their major function, the prevention of infanticide, was no longer being effectively performed. Whereas Moses had given the Law, Jesus now saw himself as coming to "fulfill" the Law: "Think not that I am come to destroy the law, or the prophets: I am not come to destroy, but to fulfill" (Matthew 5:17). Jesus certainly knew enough about the Mosaic Law to know that its fulfillment consisted in the daily regulation of behavior indefinitely. The "fulfillment" of the law meant that the impulse which was associated with it, and so long restrained, would be expressed, and expressed in his being killed.

The father of the child could no longer be trusted to restrain his infanticidal impulse: "And call no man your father upon the earth" (Matthew 23:9); "the father [shall deliver up . . . to death] the child" (Matthew 10:21). And the family was no longer to be considered significant as a device for achieving "everlasting life," as it can be said to have been for Abraham: "And every one that hath forsaken houses, or brethren, or sisters, or father, or mother, or wife, or children, or lands, for my name's sake, shall receive an hundredfold, and shall inherit everlasting life" (Matthew 19:29).

The Hebrew word for covenant or testament is *brith*, the word which is also used for circumcision. The "New Testament of Christ's blood"[23] would replace the circumcision. In the place of a symbolic infanticide, there would be the "real" infanticide of Jesus.

Jesus seems to have been aware of the profound "resistance" in the mind of man to facing the infanticidal impulse, a "resistance" which, interestingly enough, was also commented on by Freud. In a paper entitled "A Child Is Being Beaten" Freud expressed surprise at the frequency with which his patients fantasied the beating of children. He noted that this fantasy was told to him only with hesitation, and that its analysis was met with great resistance. He commented that the shame and guilt connected with this fantasy were even greater than the shame and guilt connected with sexual matters. This fantasy, he wrote, "Very probably . . . [is] still more frequent among those who have not become patients."[24] It would seem that at the Last Supper, the Passover celebra-

[23]Matthew 26:28; Mark 14:24; Luke 22:20; I Corinthians 11:25.
[24]Standard Edition, XVII, 179.

tion, which became the basis for the Pauline Eucharist, Jesus came close to the repressed wish by forcing his disciples to "eat and drink" him, in much the same way that Moses forced the defectors from the Law to consume the Golden Calf (Exodus 32:20), as an ironic demonstration of what they were so deeply involved in. Jesus gave the disciples bread to eat and said, "Take, eat; this is my body," and wine to drink and said, "For this is my blood of the new testament" (Matthew 26:26, 28). In John (6:61), when he enjoins his disciples to eat his body and drink his blood, they "murmured at it," and he said, "Doth this offend you?" sensing that he had come very close to the quick, the repressed infanticidal wish including the eating of the child. Reacting to the confrontation, "From that time many of his disciples went back, and walked no more with him" (John 6:66), as a patient might do when confronted too quickly by the psychoanalyst's interpretation of his unconscious wishes. We might say that Jesus was attempting to do what, according to Freud, the psychoanalyst tries to do, to bring the repressed wish to consciousness.

## CHRISTIANITY

We may interpret the Christianity of Jesus as an "insight" into the nature of a repressed wish. It involved a release from various of the defense mechanisms associated with the maintenance of repression. It took the repressed wish out of the deep unconscious and made it at least partially conscious, providing also a kind of fantasy satisfaction of this repressed wish in the image of the crucifixion of Jesus and the Pauline Eucharist. The "vail" that Paul spoke of in connection with Moses may be interpreted as repression:

And not as Moses, which put a vail over his face, that the children of Israel could not stedfastly look to the end of that which is abolished: But their minds were blinded: for until this day remaineth the same vail untaken away in the reading of the old testament; which vail is done away in Christ. But even unto this day, when Moses is read, the vail is upon their heart. Nevertheless when it shall turn to the Lord, the vail shall be taken away [II Corinthians 3:13-16].

The "newness of life" (Romans 6:4) may be identified with the release from the defenses against the repressed wish which comes with insight. It is the integration of agency and communion made possible by beholding what was denied. Paul no longer found it necessary to follow the Law of Moses. "Christ hath redeemed us from the curse of the law" (Galatians 3:13), he said. The kerygma in Christianity may be identified with the corresponding "good news" of psychoanalysis, a moral imperative to bring to consciousness the deepest repressed wishes, out of which can emerge a "newness of life."

It in no sense entails an imperative to "act out" this repressed wish. On the contrary. When the wish is unconscious, it acts in such a way as to bypass the conscious moral sense. Making it conscious places the person in a position to control it sensibly in the light of more mature perception.

In my interpretation, one of the most significant features of the Christian doctrine is that it tended to lift the infanticidal impulse closer to consciousness. In so doing, it universalized the crucifixion of Jesus. Several features of the crucifixion are relevant to its universalization: (1) The infanticide of Jesus constituted *full* payment, the full ransom. It was not a token of a life, like the redemption money, and not only a wound in the flesh, like the circumcision, but a full killing of the son. (2) The killing of Jesus was to happen once for all time. (3) This one sacrifice would serve for all men: "Christ Jesus; Who gave himself a ransom for all."[25] The crucifixion of Jesus could serve all men fully at all time, so that any further infanticidal acts would have been "covered" by this one; and this one "acting out" would serve instead of any other "acting out."

Yet the challenge to bring a deeply repressed wish to consciousness cannot be without difficulties. Even this one historical acting out is sufficient to create guilt. This guilt has been managed in at least three ways. The first is through the notion that Jesus died voluntarily, that he "gave himself." The second is the resurrection. If Jesus was resurrected, he did not "really" die. For Paul, the resurrection was an essential part

[25]I Timothy 2:5-6; cf. Mark 10:45.

of salvation: "And if Christ be not risen, then is our preaching vain, and your faith is also vain" (I Corinthians 15:14), and "ye are yet in your sins" (I Corinthians 15:17). Jesus "was delivered for our offences, and was raised again for our justification" (Romans 4:25). The resurrection is psychologically demanded by the fact that the crucifixion is an expression of the fulfillment of the infanticidal wish and thus creates guilt, plus the fact that it cannot be fully faced as such. Some, like the theologian Bultmann, are ready to say, "An historical fact which involves a resurrection from the dead is utterly inconceivable" and can speak of "the incredibility of a mythical event like the resuscitation of a corpse."[26] But this is by a theologian who has been able to comprehend the way in which propositions on the nature of God come from man, and who sees the basis of sin in the very cognitive separation entailed in talking of God.[27] A contemporary theological view must be based on a fully honest apprehension of the nature of man, including the recognition of the ubiquity of infanticidal tendencies. What has been "revealed . . . unto babes" needs to be faced by adults. The third way of coming to terms with the guilt involved is through anti-Semitism, in which the infanticidal impulse is attributed exclusively to the Jews. Both the statement "the Jews killed our God" and accusation of the ritual murder of Christian children are projections of the infanticidal impulse onto the Jews, who are the psychological "other" in the anti-Semitic mind.

The Eucharist has been the central sacramental rite of Christianity from its beginning. For Paul, it was the re-presentation of the crucifixion. There is little doubt but that the Mass has been one of the profoundest influences in the culture of Western civilization. In the form of this rite, mankind has been in a position to participate psychologically in this "aweful sacrifice" for many centuries. The adamance of the Roman

---

[26]*Kerygma and Myth*, p. 39.
[27]Bultmann, "What Sense Is There To Speak of God?"

Catholic Church against conceiving of the bread and wine as symbolic can perhaps be understood in this light. For one of the critical features of Christianity is that, instead of having symbolic infanticide, as in Judaism, the death of Jesus was *full* payment, a "real" infanticide. Participation in this "real" infanticide is substituted for the "Law" as a way of restraining infanticide in men. The notion of transubstantiation as expressed in the Definition of Faith of the Fourth Lateran Council of 1214 and reaffirmed in the thirteenth session of the Council of Trent in 1551, or the notion that the communion objects are "transmade" or "transelemented" into Christ's body and blood, as expressed by Gregory of Nyssa, kept the Eucharist from becoming merely symbolic. Very early in the history of Christianity, it was found necessary to have a *priest* celebrate the Eucharist. Ignatius of Antioch, at the beginning of the second century, insisted that only a bishop or one whom he appointed could perform this rite. The priests are the historical successors to the priests of the ancient temple, those consecrated to perform the sacrifice on behalf of the community. If my interpretation has any validity, it gives another reason why the priest is also conceived of as "father," and should not have children of his own.

The Christian tradition which followed Jesus could *not quite* come to cognize fully the message "revealed . . . unto babes," that men have infanticidal impulses, however. It partially elevated the revelation from the unconscious, but at the same time aroused forces of resistance to it. A major psychodynamic mechanism of this resistance is expressed in the development of an ego identity principally on the basis of the "Sonhood" of Jesus, keeping men from fully becoming fathers psychologically. With the development of Christianity, there was an intensification of the "otherness" of God, the Father. Facilitated by the notion of the Son, Jesus, being God incarnate, there was an intensification of man conceiving of himself as a son. By making the priests a separate class, clearly distinguished from other men, the Fatherhood was projected upon them as "other" as well. If God, the Father, was repeatedly envisaged as expressing his infanticidal tendencies, then, by remaining a son, one is spared the dangers, conflicts, and temptations of fatherhood. God, the Father, engaged in infanticide; but man, the son, did not. It is partly through this mechanism that the filiocentric emphasis of religion comes about. Needless to say, the religion of society is not something which is created by children. It is rather the creation of the adult members of the society, principally the men. The need for an adult male to be a son inheres in his reluctance to enter into and bear the conflicts which are associated with civilized fatherhood.

I might comment parenthetically on Freud again. Freud's position on religion, as I have indicated, was essentially filiocentric. His notion that God was the projection of one's own father can be regarded as an example of what Bultmann has referred to as "shallow enlightenment."[28] It is interesting that Freud, who was so well able to uncover unconscious material within himself, still participated in this same mechanism whereby one keeps one's self from entering into and managing the conflicts of fatherhood, indicative of his relative failure to integrate agency and communion. He clung tenaciously to the centrality of the Oedipus complex and his filiocentric interpretation of the Oedipus myth, his version of the Christian identification of himself as son. Indeed, it makes equal, if not better, sense to think of the father as being threatened by the birth of a child and wanting to kill the child as did Oedipus' father, Laius. We might speculate that the Oedipus complex is a secondary process in response to the father's tendencies toward the child.

In the same way that the Christian tradition removes the "vail" by making almost literal the infanticidal tendency, so does it remove the "vail" of the father's sexuality. It does this by suggesting that Jesus was "begotten" of God, and that the

[28]*Kerygma and Myth*, p. 3.

angel Gabriel "came in unto" Mary,[29] a Biblical expression for sexual relations. The New Testament would appear to fill out the characteristics of God by adding biological paternity.

At the same time that it alludes to sexuality in God, however, the New Testament attempts to remove it from man. This is seen in the idealization of Mary, who has a child without sexual intercourse with man, and in the image of Jesus, in whom there does not appear to be the slightest hint of sexual desire. Paul's injunctions concerning marriage are interesting in that he conceived of sexuality almost completely in terms of its agentic feature, and paid little attention to the relationship between sexuality and the having of children. Drawing back from "commandment" about marriage (I Corinthians 7:6), he nevertheless saw the unmarried state as better than the married state. "He that is unmarried careth for the things that belong to the Lord.... But he that is married careth for the things that are of the world" (I Corinthians 7:32-33). Sexual relations in marriage are to keep Satan from tempting one (I Corinthians 7:5), and "it is better to marry than to burn" (I Corinthians 7:9). He was at best tolerant of sexuality. Whereas, in the Old Testament, deviant sex practices were forbidden, and sexuality in marriage was conceived of largely in terms of the having of children and the significance of having children, Paul was against all forms of sexuality and only tolerated it in marriage to prevent "burning." The father as the progenitor and caretaker of children was essentially bypassed. Thus, what we have in Christianity is a splitting of agency from communion, with agency attributed largely to God. The aversion to the agentic is so great that even its role in procreation appears to be given at best a secondary place.

---

[29]Luke 1:28. In the Greek this is καὶ εισελθὼν ... πρὸς αὐτὴν (literally, and entering to her). That this expression may be used to designate sexual intercourse quite literally in the Greek is indicated by the fact that it is the phrase used in the *Septuagint* for the sexual relations between Judah and Tamar, when he took her to be a harlot, καὶ εἰσῆλθεν πρὸς αὐτὴν (Genesis 38:18). I am indebted to Professor Meyer W. Isenberg for help with the Greek on this point.

Psychodynamically, the reaction to the infanticidal impulse is so great that the occasion for the expression of the impulse would be avoided by not having children. The role of the male in procreation is conceived of as sin in the Christian tradition, as Augustine put it in his discussion of his son, "... for I had no part in that boy, but the sin."[30]

That the problem is still very real is indicated by the combination of the encouragement of celibacy, on the one hand, and the aversion to contraception and abortion, on the other hand, on the part of the Roman Catholic Church. For celibacy keeps one from the situation in which one is tempted to commit infanticide; and, in the profound aversion to infanticide, contraception becomes a kind of infanticide as well. Of course, infanticide has other forms. Besides the actual beating and murder of children, we can recognize the infanticidal impulse in child neglect and undereducation, the poverty associated with the too rapid multiplication of people, and total war, which does not separate children from adults. In our times, the absence of contraception is conducive to these other forms of infanticide.

### THE JUDEO-CHRISTIAN TRADITION AS COMING TO TERMS WITH DEATH

The most primitive form of coming to terms with death is in its denial. This is expressed in such notions as a literal resurrection, an afterlife, or some form of salvation in "Heaven," an "other" place or at an "other" time. This type of "solution" needs to be rejected on two sets of grounds. The first is simply that it cannot be maintained on the basis of contemporary intellectual canons. The second ground is actually the more important one: it projects onto the afterlife the individualistic existence, the egotism, the commitment to the agentic, which is at root the "sting" of death, to use Paul's word (I Corinthians 15:55).

[30]*Confessions*, p. 158.

One of the profoundest features of the Christian message is the way in which it would distinguish between actual literal death in the sense of the cessation of the vital functions and the kind of "death" which can prevail throughout life. Christianity recognized the fundamental identity of the two by using the same term for them, taking note of the despair which is associated with the agentic, as well as the difference between them. Christianity saw that the agency which served to keep the individual alive was at the same time related to its death. Thus, we can understand such a paradoxical statement as, "Whosoever shall seek to save his life shall lose it; and whosoever shall lose his life shall preserve it" (Luke 17:33). Agency seeks to preserve life, but in this preservation it can, if unmitigated, bring onto the whole of life the condition of its termination. Paul's invocation, "And deliver them who through fear of death were all their lifetime subject to bondage" (Hebrews 2:15), becomes equally clear. Death, in the literal sense of the termination of the vital functions — Unamuno's cry that he wants an immortality of flesh and blood can certainly not avail[31] — is not to be avoided. It is the intrinsic counterpart of the agentic split of one being from another in being born and growing into a separate being. Being conceived and born is, in this sense, "original sin." And when we recall the relative number of males who die by spontaneous abortions (see pp. 125, 128 above), it seems that even *in utero* the wages of agency are death. But it is to the possibility of mitigating agency in other aspects of existence that the religious tradition directs itself, that the life prior to its termination should not also be a "death."

One of the most prevalent forms of such "death" prevails in certain segments of our intellectual community. William James, who was admired by Freud because of his evident readiness to face the termination of his life (Freud having been with him when he had an angina attack), saw this very

[31]Miguel de Unamuno, *The Tragic Sense of Life, in Men and in Peoples* (London: Macmillan and Company, 1921).

clearly. There is, wrote James, a "sadness [which] lies at the heart of every merely positivistic, agnostic, or naturalistic scheme of philosophy.... Place round them ... the curdling cold and gloom and absence of all permanent meaning which for pure naturalism and the popular science evolutionism of our time are all that is visible ultimately, and the thrill stops short, or turns rather to an anxious trembling."[32] Paradoxical as it may seem, there is a fundamental identity between that religious primitivism which creates for itself an afterlife for the existence of the individual and the kind of positivistic philosophy to which James was referring. Both work to prevent the mitigation of agency by communion in that part of life which precedes its termination. Both essentially deny the reality of death and conceive of the processes before and after death in the same agentic terms.

The essential task of the religious enterprise is to face the actual termination of individual existence, on the one hand, and to create a transindividual ego identification, on the other. The recognition of the inexorable death of the individual need not demand anticipatory deference to it. And we can recognize that in the time before the inexorable death one can avoid that other death by allowing communion to function together with agency.

The religious tradition has worked toward the creation of a transindividual ego identification. There is the extension of the ego to include the children, as in the case of Abraham; the deflection of the infanticidal tendencies toward the education of children, including especially the art of integrating agency and communion. The greatest threat to the integration of agency and communion is the condition of want which mobilizes agency and represses communion. But if, as I suggested in the first chapter of this essay, our total life condition is such that want will be less of a problem in the centuries to come, it is now possible for us to devote ourselves to the care and education of children to an extent which has rarely been

[32]William James, *The Varieties of Religious Experience* (London: Longmans, Green, 1914), pp. 140-41.

possible before in the history of mankind. The musculature, called by Freud the organ of the death instinct, which has been so significant in the creation of material goods, is rapidly being supplanted by machinery. We can turn from single-mindedly "making a living" to the care and education of the young. We are in a position to "suffer little children" (Matthew 19:14; Mark 10:14; Luke 18:16) in ways far more extensive than ever before. The kerygma of the Messianic tradition is that our salvation inheres in those who are yet to be born. This is true both in the Jewish Messianic tradition and in the Christian tradition that looks to the "second coming."

The ecumenical tradition of Christianity and the emphasis on charity of both Judaism and Christianity have attempted to bring communion to bear upon agency throughout the centuries. This attempt has been strained sorely when the interests of one group have conflicted with the interests of another. But this world upon whose threshold we now stand is pledged simultaneously to two major commitments, the commitment of mankind to manage its own affairs and the commitment of human beings the world over to live with each other. On an everyday level, the foreign aid program of the United States, say, is based not only on simple "charity" but on the recognition of the world-wide mutual dependence of people on each other. It is no longer a strain between charity, on the one hand, and self-interest, on the other. We have rather a situation in which there is a coalescence between charity and self-interest, between communion and agency. The crucifixion is a reminder of the fact that there is only one real death, the termination of the vital processes, for each of us. That "Christ died for us" and was resurrected does not mean that we will be spared termination as individuals. What it does mean is that we need not submit to the forces of unmitigated agency while we are yet alive. It is the destiny of all of us that our individual existences will be terminated, and we are "all in this together." But insofar as we are, we can be spared the sense of ultimate despair by not separating ourselves from each other.

One final word is in order about psychoanalysis before we close this discussion. The approach of psychoanalysis is, in some important senses, the proper successor to the more classical forms of the Judeo-Christian tradition. In my earlier essay on Freud, I took the Jewish mystical tradition as the proper background for the appreciation of the nature of the development of psychoanalytic thought. That tradition stressed the communion feature. Freud added such things as the intimate communication that takes place in the psychoanalytic chamber, the transference, the relaxation of the musculature on the couch, the recognition of the significant revelations which take place when the action of the musculature is profoundly surrendered and the eyes closed, as in sleep when dreaming takes place, and a moral imperative to overcome repression, to behold that which has been denied. He was linked to the religious tradition, quite aside from his actual writings on religion, in seeing the profound relationships between mental health and ultimate concern. His key to man's psyche was contained in the recognition that what appears as "other" to man is really himself, although Freud failed sometimes, as I have indicated, to use this key in unlocking the nature of man's religious life. His ideal was that man should properly pass through the various stages of life and always be open to the freshness of experience, not hampered by the weight of defensive, agentic armor that he himself fashioned. But recognizing that man must move through the various stages of life, he also was brought to the recognition of the forces within the individual which lead him to death.

What, then, is a "proper" way to die? It is the agentic within us that brings us to death. That petulant arousal of the body in asexual reproduction which we call cancer is certainly not a desirable termination of the vital functions. Our thought is brought back to the musculature, the organ of the death instinct. There is a model for a proper way of dying in that daily suspension of the agentic we engage in which we call sleep and rest. The proper way of dying is from fatigue after a life of trying to mitigate agency with communion.

# INDEX